International African Library 26
General Editors: J. D. Y. Peel, Colin Murray and Suzette Heald

FROM WAR TO PEACE ON THE
MOZAMBIQUE–MALAWI BORDERLAND

The *International African Library* is a major monograph series from the
International African Institute and complements its quarterly periodical *Africa*,
the premier journal in the field of African studies. Theoretically informed
ethnographies, studies of social relations 'on the ground' which are sensitive to
local cultural forms, have long been central to the Institute's publications
programme. The *IAL* maintains this strength but extends it into new areas of
contemporary concern, both practical and intellectual. It includes works
focused on problems of development, especially on the linkages between the
local and national levels of society; studies along the interface between the
social and environmental sciences; and historical studies, especially those of a
social, cultural or interdisciplinary character.

International African Library

General Editors

J. D. Y. Peel, Colin Murray *and* Suzette Heald

FROM WAR TO PEACE ON THE MOZAMBIQUE–MALAWI BORDERLAND

HARRI ENGLUND

EDINBURGH UNIVERSITY PRESS
for the International African Institute, London

© Harri Englund, 2002

Edinburgh University Press Ltd
22 George Square, Edinburgh

Typeset in Plantin
by Koinonia, Bury, and
printed and bound in Great Britain
by MPG Books Ltd, Bodmin

A CIP record for this book is available
from the British Library

ISBN 0 7486 1577 6 (paperback)

CONTENTS

LIST OF MAPS, TABLES AND FIGURES

PREFACE

The war in postcolonial Mozambique enjoys dubious fame among the political conflicts of the late twentieth century. Up to one million persons died – some directly of warfare and others of war-related disease and famine – one-and-half million fled to neighbouring countries, and some three million were displaced within Mozambique. It was not like the 1994 genocide in Rwanda, a sudden carnage that stunned the world mass media for a few terrible, passing moments. Waged from the late 1970s until 1992, the war in Mozambique had its atrocities spread over several years, often in remote rural areas. Only occasional media coverage publicised the war outside Mozambique, and humanitarian interventions consisted mainly in relief aid to refugees who had crossed international borders. And yet, many of these refugees were able to relate stories which insisted, in haunting detail, that all evil had taken over Mozambique. Renamo rebels, fighting the Frelimo government, often gave a face to this evil.

Consider one common story from northern Mozambique, recounted by refugees in Malawi and Zambia. *Machanga*, as Renamo was locally known, came to a village, looking for loot and food. The guerrillas found a woman, carrying an infant on her back, alone at her house. They ordered her to prepare food. She replied, in anguish, that there was no relish in the house. The guerrillas had become used to having meat at every meal and could not accept the woman's excuses. They seized her baby, killed it with a machete, and roasted it outside the house. According to one version of the story, the mother was forced to taste her baby's flesh. According to another version, she was herself killed when the machete slashed in one terrible stroke both the baby and the mother carrying it.

What is there to be said, by way of analytical ethnography, about people who lived with such evil in their midst? Anthropologists, responding to the moral and intellectual need to confront the atrocities of our times, are debating ways in which ethnographic accounts could be written *against* violence (see e.g. Taussig 1987; Daniel 1996; Nordstrom 1997; Zur 1998; Besteman 1999). Much of this debate concerns the representation of violence. It brings into a critical focus, on the one hand, the sanitising of violence which erases all that is disturbing about violence. On the other hand, it also questions the representation of violence as a bizarre ethnographic fact.

The ethnographic representation of violence, however, is not the main concern of this book. Although violence and terror assume self-evident importance as topics of ethnographic inquiry in some conflicts, the focus on violence may also privilege the dramatic and the extraordinary, thereby committing the old sins of exoticism. In the case of Mozambique, evidence on mutilated war victims, massacres and the forced recruitment of child-soldiers must be put in perspective. This book is a study of villagers who avoided such atrocities. They certainly had more than their fair share of violence, but a profoundly distorted picture of the Mozambican war would emerge if violence were thought to have devastated the country with the same intensity everywhere. The fact that stories about extreme violence had spread widely with flows of refugees did not mean that everyone was obsessed with such stories. Few villagers who appear in this study felt any special urge to recount stories such as the one above, probably because few had personal testimony to deliver. Villagers were outspoken in their criticism of the parties of the war, but their criticism often revolved around the mundane minutiae of strained personal relationships. The complex moral underpinnings of those relationships form the subject-matter of this book.

The subject-matter evokes, in other words, a whole range of issues other than the ethnographic representation of violence. Personal relationships provide a standpoint from which to address other relations of varying scale. The war and displacement which the villagers in the case studies of this book endured were consequences of the processes of state formation, processes which were themselves shaped by the transnational pursuit of political influence and material accumulation (cf. Tilly 1985; Ferguson 1990). Although very different in scope and achievement, two recent anthropological studies of conflict in Africa admirably describe the interplay between the lived experience and large-scale processes. One qualifies the apparently anarchic violence of youths in Sierra Leone by drawing attention to the declining neopatrimonial state (Richards 1996). The other puts the approaching civil war in southern Sudan in the context of existential uncertainties, ranging from relations between old and young, women and men, to the meaning of death and divinity (Hutchinson 1996). In these studies, a 'context' does not make violence seem less disturbing. It introduces, rather, nuance and complexity into ethnography.

This book brings ethnographic analysis to bear upon war and exile in the borderland of Mozambique's Angónia District in Tete Province and Malawi's Dedza District in Central Region. Based on archival research, eighteen months' fieldwork in 1992–3 and revisits in 1996–7, this study examines the paths of particular villages to nationalism, war, displacement, repatriation and post-war uncertainty. The focus is on Dedza–Angónia borderland villagers' relationships; how these relationships variously enabled and constrained villagers in their aspirations during and after the war, and in their pursuit of refuge during the displacement. A major theoretical-cum-moral assault is made on naturalism, which undermines complexity by seeking determinate patterns of social life on the basis of kinship systems, ethnic loyalties, state ideologies, universal refugee experiences, and so on. Throughout the book, a key question is the extent to which internal social forms are to be understood in the light of external interventions – and what indeed could be the best way to imagine the external–internal divide, deceptively obvious as it is in villagers' encounters with revolutionary and counter-revolutionary movements.

Given the importance of fieldwork for the contribution which this book aspires to make, the Dedza–Angónia borderland must be acknowledged as an intellectual setting on a par with the academic institutions where the writing of this book has taken place. Through their arguments and aspirations, conflicts and compassion, villagers in the Dedza–Angónia borderland continuously challenged my preconceptions of what their lives amid crises might be like. Their views and acts deconstructed the categories that were at my disposal – 'victims', 'hosts', 'refugees' – in many complex ways. It is, therefore, with some dismay that I safeguard their privacy by using pseudonyms in the case studies. It is surely awkward to acknowledge the help and inspiration one has received from one's friends and interlocutors by using pseudonyms for them! And yet, perhaps academic treatises are not the places to repay the kinds of debts I have incurred in the Dedza–Angónia borderland. Those debts are to be readjusted by continuing the long conversation I have become engaged in.

In addition to the Dedza–Angónia borderland, the Department of Social Anthropology at the University of Manchester has been another important intellectual setting during the gestation of this book. I am grateful to the Academy of Finland for funding both my study in Manchester and my fieldwork in Malawi and Mozambique. The Leach/Royal Anthropological Institute Fellowship in 1997–8 brought me back to Manchester, and gave me an opportunity to embark on revision and rewriting in a supportive environment. The Nordic Africa Institute co-funded my revisit to Malawi and Mozambique in 1996–7, and kindly enabled me to take advantage of the Fellowship by granting me leave of absence.

Although my intellectual debts to the Manchester School had already begun to accumulate before my first arrival in Manchester in 1991, two anthropologists, in particular, have taught me to work in a critical relation to its substantial ethnographic and analytical legacy. One of them is Richard Werbner, whose faith in my project has been unfailing even during the most trying times. Friendship and intellectual curiosity have always combined in his critical response, extending far beyond the formal obligations of a 'research supervisor'. The other is Bruce Kapferer, whose commitment to anthropology has been a source of inspiration.

Several other friends and colleagues assisted me in my research and in the making of this book. Many made their contributions during various phases, possibly even without realising it. I must mention at least Jocelyn Alexander, Alice Dinerman, John Gledhill, Maia Green, Barbara Harrell-Bond, Penelope Harvey, Tim Ingold, James Leach, David Maxwell, JoAnn McGregor, Heike Schmidt, Matthew Schoffeleers, Anthony Simpson, Marilyn Strathern, Megan Vaughan and K. B. Wilson. Philip Gillon and the editors and anonymous readers of the International African Library series had the unenviable task of distilling a book from my writings. Although their contribution has been profound, all the fallacies and weaknesses remain my own.

The Centre for Social Research at the University of Malawi provided the institutional affiliation during my fieldwork. My discussions with scholars in different departments of that university – such as Wycliffe Chilowa, Karin Hyde, Paul Kishindo, Kings M. Phiri and E. S. Timpunza-Mvula – were important to my understanding of Malawi. Charles Malunga facilitated my research in the National Archives of Malawi. Finally, I owe a special debt of gratitude to Charles Namondwe, my *mchimwene* and confidant.

Map 1 Malawi and its neighbours

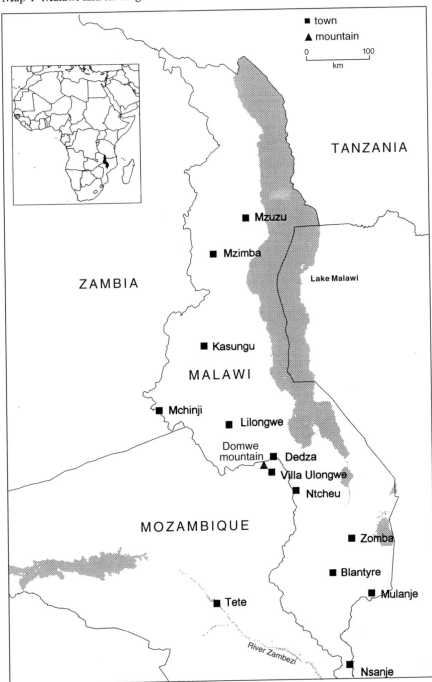

Map 2 The Dedza–Angónia borderland

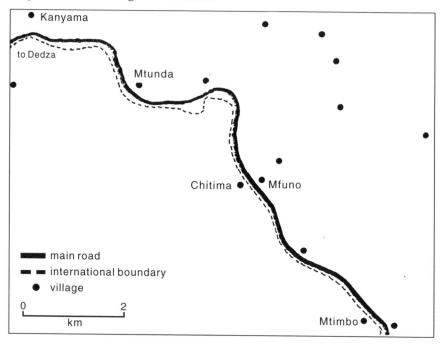

Map 3 The divisions of Chitima village

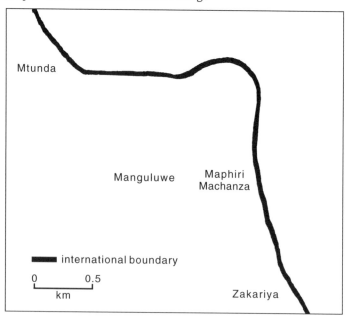

Map 4 Towns and villages of the Dedza–Angónia borderland

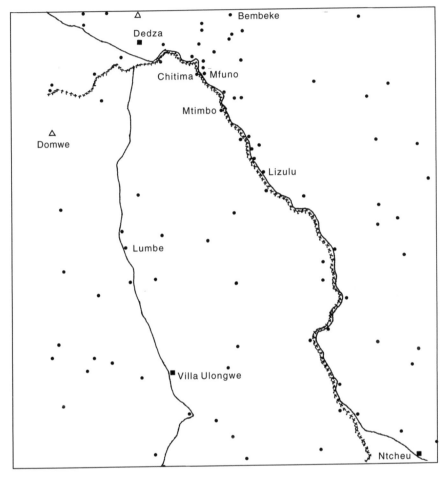

——— main road
xxxxxxx international boundary
■ town
● village
△ mountain

0   10
└─────┘
  km

INTRODUCTION

The peace treaty that ended the prolonged civil war in Mozambique was signed in 1992. On the first anniversary of the signing of the treaty in 1993, a moment of sheer euphoria took place in Villa Ulongwe, the district capital of Angónia in Tete Province. Folk dances were performed, senior district and provincial officials made speeches, and business in the beer-halls of the town boomed as jubilant crowds celebrated until the early hours of the morning.

Peace found its greatest confirmation in the mirthful hullabaloo which defied the darkest hours. Insecurity no longer forced people to retreat indoors at dusk, fearful of the nocturnal attacks by guerrillas and unknown marauders. A whole year had shown that peace could endure in the troubled land, Mozambique. The speeches at the celebration lauded a new Mozambique, a nation united in performing the tasks of reconstruction and reconciliation.

Three men from the remote border village of Chitima participated in the anniversary party in Villa Ulongwe. They were: Rafaelo, the village headman; Luis, Rafaelo's full brother and the village secretary of the ruling Frelimo party; and Alfredo, Luis's henchman and a Frelimo activist. For all three of them, the attainment of peace was also a personal victory. After seven years of exile in Malawi, they had recently witnessed the reconstruction of their village in Mozambique. Its leadership was again firmly in the hands of the three men.

There appeared to be reason for them to celebrate, indulging like sophisticated townsmen in drinking bottled beer instead of the locally brewed opaque brand. Drunk as lords, they were not deterred by the thought of the recent census which they had organised in the village. It was the money they had collected during the census that financed their indulgence. Guilt was to come later, prompted by villagers' criticism of the money wasted on the party and vociferous questioning about whether the border village would ever be integrated into the new Mozambique.

Another snapshot, some seven years earlier in 1986, presented a different picture. Luis and Alfredo were balanced on their knees inside a small enclosure. They were surrounded by half-a-dozen goats. Outside the enclosure stood four guards belonging to the Renamo rebel movement. Their faces were hidden behind pieces of cloth. Their hands clutched AK 47 rifles.

The day had begun with Renamo guerrillas breaking into the houses of the two men at dawn. Although this ominous invasion did not lead to murders, as many had feared, Luis and Alfredo suffered tribulations that were harrowing enough. From dawn to dusk, they were forced to remain on their knees. To make their humiliation complete, the goats were kept in the enclosure, tormenting them with bleating and excrement throughout the whole long day. When Luis and Alfredo were allowed at last to return to their homes, they could hardly walk.

The goats belonged to Rafaelo. When the two men's fate became known, nobody doubted Rafaelo's complicity in their detention by the Renamo guerrillas. His interest in Renamo, the new guerrilla movement, had ceased to be a secret, and his dislike of the Frelimo government was widely regarded as a consequence of his close association with the Portuguese colonial authorities before Mozambique attained independence in 1975. During the colonial period, many nationalists had been harassed as a result of information supplied to the authorities by Rafaelo. When Mozambique became independent, Rafaelo was deposed from his position as headman, and Luis, his younger brother and a pioneer nationalist in the area, assumed the leadership of the village. For Rafaelo and some other villagers, Renamo carried the promise of a new dawn. Their first aim was to suppress Frelimo in the village, and, by humiliating Luis and Alfredo, the new movement flexed its muscles.

This book fleshes out the snapshots. Between the impending war of 1986 and the apparent reconciliation of 1993 many events took place, both in the villagers' own lives and in the wider world. Nor, as indicated above, did the guerrillas enter a pristine community when they reached the border village of Chitima in 1986. Colonial and postcolonial interventions had profoundly affected the historical trajectory of the village. For the war in Chitima village, this book discloses a range of underlying processes which contradict two deceptively plausible perspectives: one on the 'obvious' conflict between Frelimo and 'traditional' leaders, and the other on the 'natural' rivalry between the two brothers. In a similar vein, displacement, repatriation and, in the Epilogue, post-war political pluralism and economic liberalisation appear as complex processes in border villages, to be understood with intimate knowledge of villagers' relationships. For analytical ethnography, therefore, the challenge is to study the interplay between 'external' and 'internal' factors; whether, as Jean-François Bayart has argued in the study of the state in Africa, 'the production of "internal dynamics" is indissoluble from the interference of "outside dynamics"' (1993: 266).

EXTERNAL AGGRESSION, INTERNAL DISCONTENT

No easy consensus seems possible on the causes and nature of the war between Frelimo and Renamo.[1] Waged for most of the years of Mozambique's short history as an independent nation, the war has been subject to various explanatory frameworks, with contradictory perspectives often betraying profound ideological differences. The fundamental dividing line is the question of whether this was a civil war or a national tragedy created by external aggression. In their crudest forms, both perspectives deal with culpability instead of analysing the nuances involved. The civil war thesis blames Frelimo's revolutionary agenda, almost wholly ignoring the hostile international context in which its leadership sought to bring about social and economic transformations (see Hoile 1994). The external aggression thesis, on the other hand, portrays Renamo as a puppet movement designed to 'destabilise' the young socialist state (see Fauvet 1984; Metz 1986; Cammack 1988; Morgan 1990: 605–7; Africa Watch 1992: 17–18, 25–8). Such external enemies included the white minority governments in southern Africa and their right-wing sympathisers in Europe and the United States.

The 'paradigm shift' that took place in the studies of the Mozambican war in the late 1980s discovered some wisdom in both perspectives, which, if taken separately, are now seen as fatally inadequate (cf. Clarence-Smith 1989). No serious student of the Mozambican experience doubts that Renamo emerged and advanced by means of substantial foreign military and material aid. The genuinely contentious issue appears to be what Renamo became in the course of the war, and how that transformation took place. The Frelimo government's unpopular resettlement policies and antagonism to religion and 'traditional' authorities have been increasingly researched by scholars as flawed policies which paved the way for Renamo's support within Mozambique (see Geffray 1990; Hall 1990: 59; Morgan 1990; Young 1990; Vines 1991: 93; Simpson 1993: 323–31).

From the outset of the war, Frelimo and Renamo plunged into a process in which 'external' and 'internal' factors did not divide into neatly separate sets of causes. Any account of the war that leaves out the history of colonialism in Mozambique, and the waging of the Cold War world-wide, must face the charge of distortion. The international context of the conflict, although often recounted in the literature, merits a brief résumé because of the light it sheds on the war as a tragedy that had a history beyond the immediate failures of a new government.

Colonialism and the Cold War also merit attention for what they do *not* explain. Later in this Introduction I review local studies of the war. These studies demonstrate profound variations in the issues and social relationships through which the war was experienced in particular settings. Such local variations show how colonialism and the Cold War, even the activities of the Frelimo government, fall short of providing comprehensive accounts of the war. The challenge remains of how to devise a perspective which makes the appreciation of such variations possible.

The same challenge applies in the study of displacement and repatriation. After reviewing local studies, I situate this book vis-à-vis refugee studies and the anthropology of borderlands. My approach is at variance with attempts to theorise a generalised 'refugee experience' or a 'border culture'. The subjects of this study went into exile as persons enmeshed in relationships, and the processes by which they experienced their displacement were indeterminate because of the myriad relationships which they carried with them. Their relationships were shaped, as both before and after displacement, by historical contingencies. The refugee status and the international border certainly appeared in villagers' arguments, but they were, among many other available notions, means to assess and contest relationships as events unfolded. The aim of this book is not, however, to celebrate indeterminacy at the expense of understanding the emergence of determinate, and yet intermittent, power relations. I discuss these analytical concerns and my method of ethnographic representation towards the end of this Introduction. I end with a synopsis of the chapters that follow.

Colonial peculiarities, nationalist struggles

Unlike the case in Angola, Portugal's other vast colony in southern Africa, no portion of Mozambique remained occupied by the Portuguese for all the five centuries that began in the early 1500s with the first permanent Portuguese settlement and ended with independence in 1975 (Marcum 1969; Newitt 1995). Despite their early involvement in the slave and ivory trades, the Portuguese effectively occupied Mozambique only at the end of the nineteenth century, largely to guard the territory against Britain and Germany. Afterwards, Portuguese colonialism in Mozambique retained a distinctive character. The collection of head tax and the migration of male labour to the South African mines were by no means unique in the region's colonial history. More peculiar was the leasing of large parts of territory to foreign-owned companies. In 1891, for example, one-third of Mozambique was controlled by two companies as virtually private colonies. Outside the plantations producing sugar, tea, sisal and copra, commercial agriculture among smallholders took the form of forced cultivation of certain crops, notably cotton, at fixed prices (Pitcher 1993; Isaacman 1996).

The Salazar government, which took power in Portugal in 1930, had a clearer vision of empire-building than its predecessors and encouraged Portuguese settlement. Whereas in 1930 the white population of Mozambique was 18,000, by 1960 it had risen to 85,000 (Minter 1994: 14). This was the period of the Portuguese 'shopkeeper colonialism' (Hanlon 1984: 188), with settlers managing foreign companies or their own small-scale commercial endeavours in both urban and rural areas. By 1970 Mozambique was one of the most industrialised countries in Africa, but much of its economy and labour force continued to serve its neighbours. The Portuguese settlers themselves hardly feasted on Mozambique's wealth; many were illiterate or poorly educated, and were engaged in menial or semi-skilled tasks as low-level government clerks, taxi drivers and shopkeepers. Black Mozambicans were systematically excluded from having private businesses, and smallholder agriculture was shaped more by coercion than by market incentives.

A case study of a borderland village shows how the shopkeeper colonialism could, in a particular setting, become part of the local social fabric. From the viewpoint of the African elite in Maputo (then Lourenço Marques), however, discriminatory practices were unmistakable. By virtue of education, income and life-style, a small number of Africans were granted an *assimilado* status, becoming Portuguese in the eyes of the colonial masters (Minter 1994: 14). As the numbers of whites in Mozambique increased, it became clear that such a status secured little more than a position as second-class, or even third-class, Portuguese. Whites from Portugal, even when poorly educated, were favoured by colonial authorities and employers over *mestiços* and locally born whites, not to mention Africans.

Until the 1920s, Mozambique witnessed a series of revolts against colonial labour regimes, particularly in the Zambezi valley region (discussed later in this Introduction). A coherent nationalist movement, however, did not emerge until the early 1960s. Apart from short-lived attempts to establish rival nationalist movements in Zambézia, and occasional announcements by exiled Mozambicans in various African capitals, Frelimo encompassed the entire spectrum of liberation forces in Mozambique. Its origin was in the *assimilado* and *mestiço* elite who had been educated by Protestant missionaries from the United States and Switzerland in southern Mozambique, near the capital (see Cruz e Silva 1998). The founding congress took place in Dar es Salaam in 1962. For the fascist government that had assumed power in Portugal in the 1950s, independent Mozambique was not even an option, and the Portuguese security police made it extremely difficult to promote the nationalist cause inside Mozambique (Birmingham 1992: 53–4). In 1964, the year Malawi gained independence from Britain, Frelimo began to pursue independence through armed struggle.

With the aid of bases in Tanzania, and later in Zambia, Frelimo launched attacks in northern Mozambique, achieving 'liberated zones' mainly along Lake Malawi and the Tanzanian border in Niassa and Cabo Delgado Provinces, and in Tete Province. Frelimo's health and education programmes attracted support from the Nordic countries and religious organisations, while the leadership's careful navigation through the Sino–Soviet dispute ensured military aid from both China and the Soviet Union (Minter 1994: 15).

In 1966–9, Frelimo experienced a leadership crisis, not least because of Portuguese efforts to manipulate internal discontent (Minter 1994: 91–2). Although it is patently misleading to represent Frelimo, even during these early years, as a movement of educated southerners (cf. Newitt 1995: 538–41; Hall and Young 1997: 17–18), the top leadership was composed disproportionately of those who had benefited from educational advantages in the south. The southern bias was based on class rather than ethnic identity, with *mestiços* and whites also assuming important positions in Frelimo. Racialism and regionalism became central sources of concern for the Frelimo leadership, and after the assassination of Eduardo Mondlane, its first president, in 1969, a new sense of common purpose was embodied by Samora Machel. The revolutionary agenda of social justice disarmed many critics in moral terms, but certain divisions prevailed in a latent form, reappearing in the post-independence period. Prominent among these was the association of Makonde people in the north with Frelimo, and the virtual absence of Macua-Lomwe-speaking peoples from Nampula and Zambézia from the top leadership. On the other hand, those educated in the Catholic mission in Beira often felt disadvantaged by Protestant-educated southerners (Abrahamsson and Nilsson 1995: 25–6).

Independence in 1975 owed more to a coup in Lisbon in April 1974 than to the liberation war in Mozambique – most areas, including cities, had been unaffected by the war. Frelimo thus came to power somewhat unexpectedly, without an election or a referendum. It had only a rudimentary organisation for national-level coordination, and the shifting governments in Portugal lacked a coherent transition policy (Minter 1994: 94). Rumours and deliberate anti-independence propaganda fostered white exodus in 1974–5. Ninety per cent of the Portuguese fled Mozambique, and with them went much experience in industry, commerce and government (Hanlon 1984: 188–9). Those Portuguese who stayed often found themselves in better positions than would have been possible for them in Portugal, even those with little education securing high posts in the tumultuous state of affairs that prevailed immediately after independence.

Revolution, the Cold War and apartheid

The bias of governments in Western Europe and the United States towards Lisbon during the liberation struggle made a socialist alternative all the more natural for Frelimo's leadership. Already in 1968 the broadly anti-colonial movement adopted Marxist perspectives on its struggle (Ottaway 1988: 213; Young 1988: 167). In 1977, Frelimo declared itself a Marxist-Leninist vanguard party (Isaacman and Isaacman 1983: 121–2; Ottaway 1988: 214–15). According to the Frelimo leadership, Marxism-Leninism, in contrast with earlier experiments with 'African socialism' in some countries, was a revolutionary theory waiting to be applied 'creatively' in the

Mozambican context (Munslow 1983: 155; de Brito 1988; Simpson 1993: 312–16). In practice, however, Frelimo's 'democratic centralism' (Hanlon 1984: 145) followed the oft-trodden paths of 'socialist' transformation. Plantations and factories, even village shops, were eventually nationalised. But even more significant for the subsequent criticism of Frelimo were the communal modes of production and administration, 'communal villages' (*aldeias communais*) in the countryside and 'communal neighbourhoods' (*bairros communais*) in small towns.

Despite Machel's confident declaration that the communal village represented the 'decisive factor for the victory of socialism in our country' (quoted in Hanlon 1984: 138), the actual reach of the project was modest. Communal villages received little funding from the state and had incorporated only about 18 per cent of the rural population by the early 1980s (Hanlon 1984: 122). Moreover, communal villages with functioning co-operatives were in the minority, and, by 1983, 60 per cent of the communal villages were in the former 'liberated zones' (Isaacman and Isaacman 1983: 155). In some areas, such as in Tete Province, communal villages were often a direct continuation of the Portuguese resettlement schemes before independence (Borges Coelho 1993).

The Frelimo leadership was anxious to ensure popular participation in its efforts to build a united nation-state. The turn to vanguardism replaced 'dynamising groups' with more hierarchical party structures of cells, circles, zones and districts, each headed by a secretary (Alexander 1997: 2–3). People's Assemblies were established to give non-activists a more audible voice in the management of districts and provinces. In practice, no policy-making or legislative functions accompanied the elected assemblies (Hanlon 1984: 144). Not only did the party set the policy but its leaders also prepared the lists from which assembly deputies were nominated. Many deputies were, in fact, active in Frelimo or its 'mass organisations' for women and youth. At no level were party and state clearly distinguished; the highest-ranking administrator at the provincial level was also the first secretary of Frelimo and the president of the assembly – the same pattern was replicated at the district level. The directors of state enterprises and farms were also often recruited from the ranks of party leaders.

The age of multipartyism and decentralisation easily gives hindsight to bemoan Frelimo's early practices, but it should not eclipse the widespread hope and enthusiasm that characterised the first few years of independence. Not only was there a stream of *cooperantes*, foreigners sent by solidarity groups in Western Europe and by governments in Eastern Europe and Cuba, to ease the shortage of teachers, doctors and engineers in the country. Even more significantly, a sense of purpose and hope lifted the spirits of most Mozambicans themselves (cf. Minter 1994: 16). The question is, as mentioned, the extent to which Frelimo's project helped the subsequent tragedy to unfold. Clearly, the centralist solutions described above hardly sustained a sense of popular participation. The Frelimo party-state was, in effect, based as much on exclusion as on encompassing party structures. Highly significant contingents of the populace were excluded from the quintessential party membership. The reason was 'obscurantism', thought to be no less an enemy of the revolution than capitalist and feudalist social relations, illiteracy and ignorance (Simpson 1993: 325). Obscurantism included a range of 'traditional' beliefs and practices, from polygamy and the belief in the existence of spirits to the authority of chiefs and village headmen. Its agents were unable to join the party, whilst chiefs and headmen were deposed from their positions of authority.

The Cold War made its impact not only through the havoc caused by the war but also through the conditions that Western governments, particularly the United States, set on their foreign aid. Large parts of Mozambique suffered from drought in 1983, and the final estimate of people starved to death was 100,000 (Minter 1994: 167). The Mozambican government had repeatedly appealed for relief aid, but food aid was actually reduced during the first half of 1983. This was the period when the government engaged in negotiations with South Africa to end its assistance for Renamo and Frelimo's support for the African National Congress. Such an agreement, however, was not the only condition which the United States imposed for Mozambique to receive its aid. It also wanted Mozambique to join the World Bank and the International Monetary Fund. Furthermore, it wanted relief aid to be distributed by the US and other foreign agencies, despite the Mozambican government's own system of relief distribution, at that time virtually free from corruption (Hanlon 1996: 16–17).

Another stoppage in food aid took place in 1986, when Western donors urged Mozambique to accept its first Structural Adjustment package. Ever since, Mozambique has been one of the most foreign aid-dependent countries in the world. In 1990–4 it was the largest aid recipient in sub-Saharan Africa, with a total aid bill of over US$1.1 billion per year. Economic reforms, shaped by the politics of aid, thus preceded reforms in ideology and constitution, but they were enough to make Frelimo acceptable to Western donors (see Hanlon 1991).

The US government's involvement in Mozambique's affairs did not extend to measures against Renamo's material support from groups and individuals in the US (Austin 1994; Minter 1994). A report commissioned by the US government documented Renamo's violent recruitment methods and atrocities (see Gersony 1988). But the government's reaction was merely to denounce Renamo, without pursuing the link between Renamo and its supporters in the US and South Africa. Assistance for Renamo by the South African military had been preceded by support from the Rhodesian government, which, according to the testimony of its intelligence officer (see Flower 1987: 300–2), virtually created Renamo by training and arming its guerrillas. Rhodesia and South Africa had in Frelimo's Mozambique a common enemy, which was providing a safe haven for anti-apartheid liberation movements. After Zimbabwe's independence in 1980, South Africa's economic interests also became apparent. The wars in Angola and Mozambique increased the dependence of such land-locked countries as Zaire, Zambia, Zimbabwe, Malawi, Botswana and Swaziland on South African ports (Minter 1994: 117–20).

As a post-independence resistance movement, however, Renamo did not simply appear from outside Mozambique's boundaries. As mentioned, movements other than Frelimo had fought colonialism, particularly in Zambézia Province, without challenging Frelimo as the largest nationalist movement. One of them was the National Union for the Liberation of Rombézia (UNAR), which appeared in 1968. Its objective was to create an independent territory between the Tanzanian border, the Rovuma river and the Zambezi river (Borges Coelho and Vines 1995: 32). The notion of Rombézia appealed to defectors from other nationalist movements who were looking for new ways to acquire political influence. It appealed, also, to President Kamuzu Banda of Malawi, whose agenda was to incorporate northern Mozambique into his vision of Great Malawi (see Chiume 1975: 167; Phiri 1985: 118–19). The most important supporter was Jorge Jardim, an influential businessman in Beira. With his aid, a new movement, África Livre, began operations in western Zambézia in 1976, launching attacks from Malawi. By 1982, after Jardim's death, Gimo Phiri led the movement to a merger with Renamo (Vines 1991: 53–8; Legrand 1993: 88–91).[2]

África Livre is one example of Renamo successfully appropriating local discontent. During a drought in 1979, small groups of armed men already operated from Rhodesia and brought food and clothes to villages in central Mozambique, an area in which Frelimo had not yet established an effective presence (Hanlon 1984: 229–31). The central Mozambican provinces of Sofala and Manica became the initial settings for sustained Renamo presence. The Gorongosa mountains became the headquarters and Ndau the *lingua franca* of the movement. By 1983, the English-based acronym MNR had been abandoned and a network of semi-permanent bases in Mozambique had been established (Hall 1990: 40; Minter 1994: 41–2). Then began Renamo's expansion, and virtually the whole country became affected by the war.

From a civil war to peace

Allen Isaacman, an eminent historian and Frelimo's early foreign sympathiser, dismissed Renamo as bandits, 'South African backed terrorists' (1988: 12). His verdict was dated as late as August 1987 (1988: 14), and a similar sentiment prevailed among many top government officials at least until the early 1990s. There was certainly evidence to support such a sentiment. The use of coercion in recruiting civilians to act as porters and eventually as guerrillas, and the use of boy soldiers, were publicised in the most shocking details of early refugee accounts (see Gersony 1988; Magaia 1988; Minter 1989; Boothby et al. 1991). Academic analyses followed, pinpointing ritualised violence and terror as means both to initiate civilians into the movement and to demonstrate the movement's superior command of spirits and medical substances (see Nordstrom 1992; Wilson 1992a). These observations, together with the fact that Renamo's political agenda remained vague throughout the war (Geffray 1990: 41; Hall 1990: 59; Finnegan 1992: 74–5; Alden and Simpson 1993: 124), could only underline destruction and terror as the movement's essence. Indeed, such was its meticulous destruction of health and education services that it appeared to 'symbolically banish the state' (Wilson 1992a: 540; cf. Hanlon 1991: 38–41; Vines 1991: 90).

In actual fact, however, Renamo could appear in very different guises in different parts of the country and at different points in time. Extreme violence was by no means the general rule throughout Mozambique (Minter 1994: 182). An early report identified three different types of Renamo operations: the first in regard to taxation, the second in regard to control, and the third in regard to destruction (Gersony 1988: 10–20). Although somewhat rigid, this division has the merit of disclosing a pattern beyond destruction and terror.

Renamo committed its worst atrocities, such as burning alive busloads of civilians in road ambushes, in Frelimo's southern strongholds (Hall 1990: 53). In parts of central and northern Mozambique, Renamo enjoyed some popular support and reinstated chiefs, healers and other agents of 'obscurantism' in their positions of authority (Geffray 1990; Wilson 1992a).[3] The 1994 general elections, marking the end of the war, had an outcome which seemed to confirm this regional pattern of support. Renamo won most of the votes in many provinces throughout central and northern Mozambique, and the national results gave 38 per cent of the votes to Renamo and 44 per cent to Frelimo (Agência de informação de Moçambique 1994a, 1994b). A group of bandits could hardly have posed such a challenge in general elections. As will be discussed further in the Epilogue, however, the election results should not be interpreted as simple indicators of popular support.

The 1994 elections were a culmination of a long and arduous peace process. The Nkomati Accord, signed between the Mozambican and South African governments in 1984, did not manage to stop South African military support for Renamo for at least two years (Minter 1994: 46–7). In 1986, Renamo launched, with the support of South African commandos, offensives from Malawi against the provinces of Tete, Zambézia and Sofala. The Malawian government, in turn, did little to wipe out covert bases for Renamo and its supporters from its territory, although it did send troops to join Mozambicans and Zimbabweans in protecting the economically vital Beira corridor (cf. Hedges 1989).

After 1986, Frelimo began, under the new Mozambican president Joaquim Chissano, to implement wide-ranging political reforms. The Fourth Party Congress in 1983 had already heard critical speeches on centralism and communal villages, and the Fifth Congress in 1989 finally abandoned Marxism-Leninism (Simpson 1993). A new constitution, dismantling the close association between party and state, was established in December 1990. Peace talks, hosted by the Roman Catholic Church and the Italian government, began in Rome in July 1990, but were repeatedly hampered by Renamo's hesitation (Minter 1994: 54). A cease-fire agreement, with provisions for demobilisation, a new national army and elections, was signed in October 1992. The cease-fire proved to be successful, suggesting both Renamo leaders' control over their dispersed troops and general war-weariness.

Whatever its causes and its complex patterns, the war drew Mozambique ever deeper into a morass of debt and dependency. In addition to the one million dead there was the havoc wreaked on basic facilities. Sixty per cent of 5,886 first-level primary schools were closed or destroyed (Hanlon 1996: 15); over 400 teachers were killed or wounded (Minter 1994: 193); 191 rural health posts were destroyed and another 687 were looted or forced to close by the end of 1988. The destruction encompassed 46 per cent of the primary health network – between independence and 1985 the number of health posts had increased from 326 to 1,195.

Confronted with such statistics, one cannot avoid trying to allocate responsibility. In what is perhaps the subtlest general assessment of the Angolan and Mozambican wars to date, William Minter (1994) asks the difficult question of whether these wars would have been possible without the Cold War and South African interventions. For Angola, his answer is a tentative affirmative. Nationalist rivalries were too strong in 1974–6 to have been solved by a purely non-violent resolution. Yet the conflict would probably have been shorter and more decisive without external intervention. For Mozambique, Minter's answer is a definite negative. Ethnic and regional tensions in Mozambique were too weak to sustain a war; rural grievances both fed upon and were fed by the war, albeit not everywhere and not always.

Minter's judgement ascribes responsibility for the war. But the allocation of such responsibility was given a different content among those who were never told of enemies in foreign countries and yet were left to endure the war and the displacement it created. Their war became entwined with particular relationships. The knowledge that this book seeks to impart is knowledge about these relationships and how they were constituted within a transnational configuration of power.

LOCAL STUDIES OF THE WAR

Villagers' war in the Dedza–Angónia borderland bore all its traces of colonial interventions, nationalist struggles and postcolonial tensions. Antagonisms and allegiances within families owed much to these great historical forces beyond villagers' control. And yet, any attempt to understand the particular shape that their relationships took, and the particular shape the war itself took, must acknowledge some discrepancy between the particular history of villagers' relationships and the general history of transnational powers.

Take, for example, the two brothers Luis and Rafaelo, who came to be the most visible local custodians of Frelimo and Renamo, respectively. Translocal forces animated a local antagonism which historically preceded them. But the conditions of this antagonism were forged in colonial times, before Luis and Rafaelo occupied the stage of village politics. The two brothers' antagonism was not inevitable, nor was it a sheer historical accident.

I have already indicated that the war had considerable local and regional variations. This observation alone is enough to question perspectives which give analytical priority to either 'internal' or 'external' factors. A brief comparison between other local studies of the war throws complexity into starker relief and raises the need for an approach which brings the 'internal' and the 'external' into an integrated focus. The comparison shows, for example, that the antagonism between Frelimo and the agents of 'obscurantism' did not need to be insurmountable in particular settings. The comparison shows, also, how the war often brought unanticipated turmoil despite popular interest in Renamo. Throughout Mozambique, villagers' relationships have been embedded in circumstances external to their world. Rather than being an account of history, the study of war and exile thus becomes an analysis of the *processes* by which particular relationships shaped, and were shaped by, these historical predicaments.

While acknowledging the interplay between external and internal factors in the war, some studies none the less reveal theoretical shortcomings which must be avoided in analysing these processes. As mentioned, most scholars no longer dispute that Renamo became, at least in some regions, a veritable social movement beyond its origins as an externally imposed military force. The question is how that transformation occurred; what was the local collaborators' agenda? Here Frelimo's modernist zeal, in its Marxist-Leninist guises, to effect a rural revolution often assumes unduly self-evident explanatory weight. Mark Chingono provides a telling summary statement:

> By resuscitating and defending peasant outlooks of the world, which had been suppressed by Frelimo, Renamo was articulating peasant ideologies. This largely explains its success in the countryside. To

some Mozambican peasants, who had emerged from one form of
social servitude only to fall into another, it appears the central conflict
was between tradition and modernity: the 'peasant war' was fought to
restore tradition, with Frelimo confronting while Renamo defended it.
(1996: 55; see also Saad-Filho 1997)

One difficulty with such a generalisation concerns the capacity of
Frelimo's state actually to implement in practice the changes promised in
its rhetoric (cf. Hall and Young 1997: 185–7). Local studies of the war
provide various examples of unorthodox adjustments of Frelimo's objectives – consequences, at least in part, of Maputo's inability to control the
provinces. Another, more theoretical, difficulty raises the question of how
scholars separate 'peasantry' from the state and other 'external' forces
analytically (cf. Hill 1986; Kearney 1996). Alex Vines, for example, felt
that Renamo's failure to correct Frelimo's mistakes had 'contributed to the
peasantry being ambivalent towards both the government and Renamo'
(1991: 94). William Finnegan, in turn, reported that the message was
clear wherever he went in war-torn Mozambique: 'All the peasants really
want is to be left alone' (1992: 80). A familiar dualism proves its resilience
– peasants may occasionally come into contact with the outside world but
they may also reject that world *en bloc*, as if the 'contact' had not blurred
the boundaries of their social worlds (cf. O'Laughlin 1996, 2000; Cramer
and Pontara 1998). With no theoretical advances made in the analytic
perspective, the 'internal' and the 'external' remain irrevocably separated
from one another.

The scholarly debate on the war of liberation in Zimbabwe appears to
have overcome these basic shortcomings. Early, somewhat triumphant
studies suggested a close correspondence between the agendas of guerrillas
and the rural populace. Such unity of purpose could assume cosmological
proportions, and guerrillas' efforts to reclaim the land appeared to gain
impetus from their association with spirit mediums (Lan 1985). A more
mundane reading of that unity stressed the liberation war as a class struggle
(Ranger 1985). Although these studies did not place a guerrilla movement
and the rural populace in radically different spheres, their homogenising
notions of culture and class have been found wanting in subsequent
research. The challenge began most notably with Norma Kriger's (1992)
account of 'struggles within the struggle', which disclosed considerable
variation in the aspirations of local collaborators. The war became an
opportunity to settle old scores which had little to do with the overall
objective of national liberation. Youth could use the sometimes coercive
methods of guerrillas to undermine rural gerontocracy, while some women
found in the movement a relief from domestic violence. Kriger's study,
analysing conflicts mainly in terms of age and gender, has inspired subtler
perspectives which give more weight to local variations and the complexities

of everyday life (see Moore 1995; Bhebe and Ranger 1995; Maxwell 1999: 119–47).

My brief review of local studies of the Mozambican war discloses variations which make an easy regional pattern suspect. I have chosen studies from very different parts of Mozambique: Christian Geffray's study of Nampula Province in northern Mozambique; Otto Roesch's study of Gaza Province in the south; K. B. Wilson's study of Zambézia Province in the north; and Jocelyn Alexander's study of Manica Province in the centre. Taken together, these studies yield somewhat contradictory insights into the impact of precolonial, colonial and postcolonial histories; ethnicity and regionalism; state capacity in local settings; the relations between Frelimo secretaries and 'traditional' authorities; and the significance of class and wealth differences. This book's aim, however, is not to celebrate variation and diversity at the expense of an approach which would make comparison possible. While comparison and generalisations remain analytical objectives, it is important to know which issues should *not* give rise to generalisations. After that, the case studies from the Dedza–Angónia borderland can assist in formulating a generalising approach of another kind.

War against the state in Nampula

Of the studies discussed here, Geffray's (1990) work has been most widely publicised and has already received sophisticated critiques (see especially O'Laughlin 1992; Dinerman 1994). These critiques have noted a basic discrepancy between Geffray's earlier and later studies about the war in Nampula Province. An early study hypothesised that there were three social groups in Nampula that were particularly prone to support Renamo: chiefs and lineage elders who had been deposed by Frelimo; those who almost suffered a famine after forced resettlement into communal villages; and young men who had remained within the constraints of rural life (see Geffray and Pedersen 1988). In his later work, Geffray (1990: 36–41) regards these hypotheses as being insufficient on two counts especially. On the one hand, these motives were individualistic – they ignored the possibility that Renamo represented an opportunity for entire rural communities, violated by Frelimo's insensitivity, to disentangle themselves from the state. On the other hand, the early hypothesis concentrated too exclusively on the immediate past of Frelimo's interventions. The actual pattern by which rural support for Renamo emerged derived from a more distant, even precolonial past.

Geffray thus came to emphasise an insulted collective identity rather than divergent interests in his analysis of rural discontent and Renamo's expansion (cf. Dinerman 1994: 579–83). Although such an analysis appears to homogenise a local population in ways that were criticised above, Geffray's account of the communal village project in Nampula merits further discussion. He does not mince words about the fallacies of Frelimo's original project. Frelimo operated, according to Geffray, with the ideology of the 'blank page' (1990: 28). In this ideology, peasants had to be 'organised' into communal villages to ensure growth in production and to combat general backwardness. It was as if peasants had so far existed as individuals, with no social bonds to tie them together, a view fostered by the apparent dispersal of homesteads. The communal village was, in effect, not a means of rural development but an instrument of the state's penetration into the countryside (Geffray 1990: 34–5). That production co-operatives did not often produce anything, and that the houses built in communal villages remained unoccupied when peasants returned to their old homesteads, did not cause great concern in Maputo. The aim of achieving an appearance of *administering* the countryside was paramount.

In Nampula, forced resettlement into communal villages reached its peak between 1980 and 1984. As Minter (1994: 207) observes, Geffray glosses over the fact that these resettlements occurred on the eve of approaching Renamo operations; Renamo began them in earnest in Nampula Province in March 1984. Representatives of the state may thus have had practical and military reasons, rather than a modernising mission, when they imposed communal villages on the area. Geffray's account of contrasting allegiances between different chiefdoms is more enlightening. He describes the Erati and Macuane of Erati District, whose social practices were closely related and who had witnessed similar interventions by Frelimo's state (Geffray 1990: 88–92). It was, however, mainly the Macuane chiefs who led their followers into Renamo's orbit. The Erati, by contrast, usually preferred to stay on the government's side.

The roots of this polarisation, according to Geffray, lay deep in pre-colonial and colonial history. The two chiefdoms had very different political organisations before the colonial encounter – the Macuane encompassed dispersed segmentary societies, whereas the Erati had a centralised authority structure. As was often the case during colonial history, communities with a centralised political organisation stood a better chance of benefiting from the colonial encounter than did their more dispersed neighbours. The first formally educated and employed persons in the district were Erati, with the Macuane facing marginalisation. This pattern was reinforced by the post-colonial state, which had, probably unwittingly, Erati presence at all levels of the local administrative hierarchy. Communal villages were also established on Erati land, which caused the greatest disruption among the Macuane, who were forced to leave their own ancestral land. Marginalised and harassed by both colonial and postcolonial states, the Macuane welcomed Renamo as an opportunity to wage 'war against the state' (*guerre contre l'Etat*; Geffray 1990: 90).

Geffray's ability to historicise collective responses to Renamo's expansion compensates for his tendency to romanticise the quest of marginalised rural populations to restore their identity and traditions. Moreover, he shows how Renamo's agenda was ultimately incompatible with local supporters' aspirations. Without a clear political and administrative vision, Renamo was unable to take the rural populace beyond the war and suffering. Geffray also documents how Renamo captured people by force; it was 'an army of captives' (*une armée de captifs*; 1990: 106).

Gaza: Frelimo strongholds and ethnic prejudice

Geffray's study implies that even the unpopular communal villages could appear differently to different communities. Roesch (1992a), writing especially on Xai-Xai District in Gaza Province, notes that Renamo attempted to destroy communal villages in its assaults on Frelimo's projects. Roesch argues, however, that communal villages evoked much less resentment in Gaza Province than was apparently the case in Nampula. Before the economic and political crisis began to take its toll in the 1980s, Frelimo enjoyed 'a massive base of popular support' (1992a: 466) in Gaza and other parts of southern Mozambique. Gaza, with its favourable conditions for agriculture around the flood plain of the Limpopo river, became one focus for the communal villages project. In fact, only Cabo Delgado Province, a northern Frelimo stronghold during the liberation struggle, had higher rates of the establishment of these villages in Mozambique.

In Gaza, about 120 communal villages, inhabited by one-third of the province's rural population, had been created by 1980. Roesch records that many families would have preferred their traditional dispersed settlements but took part in resettlement 'out of a sense of duty and obligation towards Frelimo' (1992a: 466). Communal villages posed a greater economic threat in the hinterlands of Gaza, where dry sandy soils seemed to require extensive cultivation and dispersed settlements (see also Hermele 1988; Roesch 1988). Renamo was denied a ready constituency in this area by the fact that the majority of communal villages were established among intensive cultivators on the alluvial lands around the Limpopo river. Even after the government, in 1983, stopped promoting communal villages actively, and allowed people to return to their ancestral homes, only a minority abandoned the communal villages (Roesch 1992a: 468). These villages had become an established form of rural settlement in Gaza.

Roesch (1992a: 467) stresses the history of labour migration as a further factor that mitigated the adverse effects of communal villages on subsistence. In contrast to the case in Nampula, where the rural populace appeared to earn their livelihoods more exclusively from agriculture, the wage earnings of male labour migrants had long been an essential part of rural household economies in Gaza. Roesch also describes Renamo as an alien movement on ethnic grounds, in addition to the ideological support for Frelimo and the nature of the local economy. The rural populace of Gaza

came to view Renamo as an 'Ndau political project' (1992a: 469) from
Manica and Sofala Provinces in central Mozambique. They were fearful of
the evil spirits which were integral to Ndau warfare. This ethnic stereotype,
in the context of Ndau as the official language of all Renamo bases, served to
alienate people in Gaza from Renamo, quite apart from more direct political
and economic reasons. The only social group from which Renamo drew
active support was, Roesch (1992a: 477–8) writes, young men who felt
marginalised by the deepening economic crisis.

Complexity and conflict in Zambézia

If more evidence is required to unpick the complex patchwork of the war,
Zambézia Province is the obvious area to which to turn. Historically, the
wider Zambezi Valley region has produced myriads of armed groups and
revolts. From 1550 to 1850, before the veritable 'scramble' for Africa,
Portugal maintained a shallow presence mainly through the *prazo* system of
crown estates, which required the settlers to pay taxes to Lisbon (see
Axelson 1960; Isaacman 1972; Newitt 1973; Vail and White 1980; Ishemo
1995). The collapse of the Portuguese presence in *prazos* was precipitated
by settlers' involvement in the slave trade to satisfy the growing demand in
Brazil in the early nineteenth century. In addition to exporting Africans
from their estates, settlers began to export their *achikunda* armies, who,
despite their African origins and slave status, had been the military arm of
the *prazos* (Isaacman 1976: 5–7). Their harassment resulted in bitter revolts
as, in alliance with local chiefs, they attacked estates and disrupted trade.

Guns and powder became accessible to Zambézians through their own
involvement in the slave and ivory trades, and through the Portuguese policy
of co-optation. The Zambezi Valley, described as 'the horror of Portugal'
(Pélissier 1984: 517), witnessed in 1917 an anti-colonial revolt on an
unprecedented scale, after ever-increasing demand for forced labour by the
Portuguese had been exacerbated by conscription to fight against German
colonial forces (Isaacman 1976: 156–85; Pélissier 1984: 649–78). With the
aid of mercenaries and the British, the Portuguese finally crushed the revolt.
Nevertheless, the fact of it having been fought by various Zambézian
peoples under Barue leadership demonstrated not only heightened anti-
colonial consciousness but also a culmination of a 'tradition of resistance'
(cf. Isaacman 1976).

In the light of this tumultuous history, neither Frelimo nor Renamo was
able to count on an easy victory in Zambézia Province. During the liberation
struggle, as already described, Zambézia was unusual in the extent to which
it hosted Frelimo's rival nationalist forces. Frelimo maintained a front in
Zambézia only for a very brief period at the beginning of its armed struggle,
and, according to President Machel, about 2,000 Zambézian guerrillas
defected from Frelimo during the struggle (Abrahamsson and Nilsson

1995: 25). In the mid-1980s the province was the setting for significant military gains by Renamo. But the communal villages project was least successful there, only 2 per cent of the population being resettled in communal villages in 1982 (Minter 1994: 271). The war was also moulded by various third forces, from armed robbers and populist militias to a significant, albeit short-lived, local peace movement.

This movement, known as Naprama, emerged in early 1990 in the border area between Zambézia and Nampula (for more detailed accounts, see Wilson 1992a: 560–81; Legrand 1993: 99–104; Nordstrom 1997: 57–62). A movement that eludes simple ethnic identification, it successfully drove Renamo away from vast areas and apparently enabled hundreds of thousands of internally displaced persons to return to their villages. Its adherents were led by Manuel António, a man in his late twenties who claimed to be possessed by various spirits, including that of Jesus Christ. António provided vaccination, made from a secret plant, against bullets, and prohibited, among other things, the use of fire-arms. Armed with spears, arrows and knives, Naprama adherents typically went to a battle singing special songs and carrying drums and rattles. Naprama's superior powers appear to have impressed both Renamo and Frelimo soldiers, but António's killing by Renamo in December 1991 changed the situation rapidly. Splinter groups, taking up fire-arms, differed little from Renamo in their pursuit of material wealth.

Wilson (1992a, 1992b), on the basis of his evidence from Zambézia, offers more observations to the debate about the Frelimo–Renamo conflict. His research draws attention to the local commercial elite as a target of Renamo's assaults (e.g. Wilson 1992a: 538–9). In the context of popular resentment against this elite, Renamo's practice of sometimes 'celebrating' its attacks by redistributing food among local populations generated occasional support. The commercial elite had largely retained its privileged position from colonialism in independent Mozambique. Hence, for example, in Milange, a border town and commercial centre for Zambézia's multi-ethnic mercantile elite, the business community accepted that it had an obligation to support the government military (Wilson with Nunes 1994: 211). Indicating the futility of describing Frelimo as 'socialist' and Renamo as 'capitalist' in a local context, very few members of the community fled from government-held areas and joined Renamo (Wilson with Nunes 1994: 185; cf. Roesch 1992b: 28). One reason for this was their locally rooted status as *patrões*, based on patronage and intimate knowledge of the local setting.

Wilson (1992b: 6–8) also stresses the war as a process in which military strength and popular allegiances could undergo various transformations. In the Posto Derre area in Zambézia's Morrumbala District, for example, Renamo's arrival in 1982 meant occasional looting and the virtual collapse of health and educational services. Between 1984 and 1986 local conditions became more permanently dominated by war, when Renamo guerrillas, mostly Ndau-speakers calling themselves *Machanga*,[4] actively sought to expand Renamo-held territory but were unable to wipe out Frelimo completely. Security was patchy: some chiefdoms had enjoyed relatively stable conditions under Renamo, others under Frelimo, but there was also considerable internal displacement as local populations attempted to manage the war's impact. In 1986–90 a period of complete Renamo occupation followed, during which many of the troops had Zambézian origins and a civilian-based administration was encouraged. Although schools and clinics functioned with great difficulty under the poor conditions, and consumer goods were in short supply, violence was limited, and most people returned to their homes to enjoy good harvests. Frelimo forces returned in late 1990, and Renamo became, once again, unpredictable in its violence, and largely abandoned civilian-based administrations. Independent banditry also emerged, while increasing numbers of locals sought refuge in Frelimo areas.

The methodological lesson to be drawn from Wilson's analysis is that any generalisation must acknowledge the processual and localised nature of the war; claims about military strength and popular support must be situated in time and place. Equally important is Wilson's (1992b: 5) observation on the variable relationships between chiefs, Frelimo secretaries and Renamo. In the Posto Derre area, examples included a veteran Frelimo activist who was appointed without elections as a secretary, but lacked popular support, and subsequently joined Renamo. Another example is a secretary whom locals chose from a popular chief's family and whose conduct persuaded the whole local elite to resist Renamo's advancement. Thus even the approaches of the 'modernist' Frelimo and 'traditionalist' Renamo to local authorities could appear in so many guises. Wilson's profound observations receive more empirical support from Alexander's (1994, 1997) study of Manica Province in central Mozambique.

'Tradition' and compromise in Manica

Although Frelimo's more tolerant attitude towards chiefs, village headmen and other agents of former 'obscurantism' is usually thought to have begun with Chissano's presidency in 1986, Alexander documents earlier localised departures from the official ideology. The weakness of Frelimo's state explains much. Provincial, let alone central, Frelimo leaders often had little knowledge of who represented the party in rural areas (Alexander 1997: 5). District authorities could even divert from the party line and still win commendation from their superiors. The District Administrator in Manica's Sussundenga District, for example, maintained close working relations with chiefs and incorporated them or their children into Frelimo committees during his tenure in 1980–8. As a consequence, the heavily besieged district resisted Renamo incursions, and the administrator was awarded the Second Degree Medal for Valour and Patriotism in 1985. He was later appointed the Provincial First Secretary of Frelimo. Another example is a chief who was also a Frelimo village secretary (Alexander 1994: 44). In Sussundenga, disputes over rain-making ceremonies revealed particularly clearly the limits of Frelimo officials' willingness to enforce new rules (Alexander 1994: 42–3). Only a few years after independence, in 1979, the local administration sent opaque beer and chickens to a deposed chief with a request that he should organise a rain ceremony. The reason for their action was a drought which threatened Frelimo's state farm.

Alexander's observations also raise serious questions about Renamo's attitude to 'traditional' authorities. In what sense did Renamo 'restore' these authorities? Alexander (1997: 8–11) contrasts two Renamo-controlled areas in Sussundenga and Macossa Districts. In the former, Renamo arrived before Frelimo had achieved an effective presence, and the war was generally blamed on Frelimo. Renamo had a civilian hierarchy, it recruited educated locals to work as teachers and raided Zimbabwe across the border for learning materials. In Macossa, the home of the historic Barue rebellion, Renamo's demands for forced labour and tribute brought to mind a long history of coercion. Many civilians, including chiefs, fled, and those chiefs who stayed and were installed to execute Renamo's orders performed colonial, rather than precolonial, duties.

More generally, Alexander (1997: 18–19) shows how, in the immediate post-war period, both Frelimo and Renamo held views that envisaged chiefs and headmen as enforcers of state intervention rather than as representatives of 'communities'. Chiefs themselves, in both Frelimo and Renamo areas, expected a revival of colonial duties of tax collection and labour mobilisation, in tandem with the regaining of colonial privileges such as uniforms and salaries. Above all, in many cases it was not clear which 'community' a chief would represent, rival candidates competing for the throne, and the war bringing unprecedented social cleavages in its wake.

To sum up this review of local studies of the war, it may be true at the level of conflicting ideologies that Frelimo sought to bring about rural revolution, while Renamo aimed at a neo-traditionalist revival. Much hinges, however, on the scale of the investigation, because local studies undermine efforts at generalisations. A Frelimo secretary and a chief could co-operate, or indeed be one person; Renamo could encourage civilian administration; in some areas Renamo was seen as an ethnic movement, in others ethnic identities played little role in local conflicts. Some local studies, such as one of the situational use of political affiliations during and after the war (see McGregor 1998: 56), enrich the academic and popular debate with further observations. The weakness of the state and the local and regional histories are obvious conditions for these variations. If local studies, however, are to be more than contributions to a bewildering diversity of historical particularism, the definition of the core issues must be worked out theoretically. This book, as pointed out previously, investigates how and why personal relationships assumed their qualities under translocal forces. Before discussing further relevant theoretical and methodological issues, I introduce the other great predicament that this book addresses – displacement.

REFUGEES AND BORDERLANDS

The observations which journalist Hilary Anderson (1992) made in the Malawi–Mozambique borderland echoed perceptions that were common among aid workers, government officials and academics during the refugee crisis. Most refugees from Mozambique, Anderson noted, had never been unduly troubled by 'the artificial borders' (1992: 135) dividing Malawi and Mozambique, 'mixing as easily with Malawians of their tribe as with the Mozambicans of their tribe' (1992: 136). The tribe, in other words, was the locus of a more primordial, more entrenched, affiliation than the nation-state.

When I first arrived in the Dedza–Angónia borderland, my own expectations were not entirely dissimilar to these observations. I already knew, through the literature and from discussions with people who were experts about the crises in Malawi and Mozambique, that the international border had long been open, that most refugees and hosts shared a common language and ethnic identity, and that most refugees had settled in pre-existing Malawian villages. Nevertheless, to my surprise, some villagers, both refugees and hosts, insisted that they belonged to a particular nation-state, and the concept 'refugee' (*lefuchi*, or *anthu othawa nkhondo* – people who have escaped from war) was in common use. These notions coexisted, however, with vehement denials of the border's impact on social relationships, making local understandings of the crisis more complex than the image of tribesmen transgressing artificial borders would suggest.

For all its inaccuracies, this image counters another stereotype, one that is far more common, while being equally distorting. Here refugees are the very embodiments of loss and uprootedness. According to Liisa Malkki's critique of the stereotype, refugees 'stop being specific persons and become pure victims in general' (1997: 224). In the framework of international institutions, the category of the victim, complementing the early United Nations definition of the refugee as an activist or a target, is a recent addition to the definition of refugee (Zolberg et al. 1989: 30). The refugee as a victim has emerged in the context of postcolonial wars which make the conditions of life impossible to sustain, irrespective of who, if anyone, constitutes the persecuted target population. For the 'international community' overseeing the management of humanitarian crises, the use of more restrictive policies by many governments in response to immigrants and seekers of asylum has again shown the importance of definitions (see e.g. Ferris 1993; Loescher 1993; Ishay 1995). An 'economic migrant' may be refused entry with fewer misgivings than a 'political refugee', but contemporary population movements seldom conform to only one pole of the economic–political and voluntary–involuntary dichotomies. For some, the strategy for overcoming such complexities is to deny the existence of any obligations towards strangers from foreign lands; for others, seeking funding and sympathy for humanitarian causes, the counter-strategy is to inflate the status of refugees as victims in need of help.

The classic institution of managing refugees as victims is the refugee camp. Established towards the end of World War II, since then it has been widely used in postcolonial settings. Beyond its obvious function as an efficient method of distributing aid to those who have been defined as being in need of such aid, the refugee camp, through its control of movement and the documentation about its population, is also a device of power (Malkki 1995a: 498; Voutira and Harrell-Bond 1995: 209–10). Patently, to be defined as a 'refugee' does not strip a person of all capacity to manipulate the situation – as a bureaucratic label, the 'refugee' status may be useful in engaging with the state and welfare agencies (Marx 1990: 201; Zetter 1991). But the fact that the vast majority of displaced persons in contemporary Africa have actively sought to avoid refugee camps and settlement programmes, and have preferred self-settlement sometimes to the point of starvation, speaks volumes for such persons' urge to free themselves from victims' helplessness (cf. Harrell-Bond 1986; Kibreab 1989). In Zambia, for example, 86 per cent of the Angolan refugees in the North-Western and Western Provinces were self-settled in 1988 (Williams 1993: 138). This was a remarkable figure in a country where the government required all refugees to be settled under 'schemes' and where it had actively searched for those who had tried to avoid these schemes (Hansen 1979, 1982). Such an approach, opposed to local integration, was part of a wider trend in African refugee assistance during the 1980s (Bulcha 1988: 23).

While often highly critical of attempts to represent refugees as victims, much of 'refugee studies' has focused on issues of aid and policy and thereby rendered wider intellectual and political questions virtually unthinkable (for a critique of 'refugee studies', see Malkki 1995a). This book seeks to pursue some of those neglected connections by investigating human relatedness in the historical predicament of displacement. It must be noted at the outset that the objective is not to theorise a generalised 'refugee experience'. A recent sophisticated attempt by Valentine Daniel and John Knudsen to elaborate on 'the cultural dimension of the refugee problem' (1995: 6) shows how the familiar imagery of loss and uprootedness may live on in such generalising analytic strategies. They examine the problems of meaning and trust in the refugee experience, and argue that such an experience is 'profoundly cultural' (Daniel and Knudsen 1995: 2). Culture, they insist in line with current anthropological discourse, is 'fundamentally dialogic ... a process ... forever emergent' (Daniel and Knudsen 1995: 2–3). Even though this laudable position prevents them from representing refugees and hosts as prisoners of disparate and unchanging world-views, the 'refugee experience' itself appears to arise from constant conditions. Central to these conditions are potential clashes of meaning, and Daniel and Knudsen frequently use such expressions as 'restore' and 'recover' (e.g. 1995: 5) when they discuss subsequent challenges to trust and the cultural process. If something must be lost before it can be restored or recovered, they thus make yet another contribution to the imagery that views loss – or, at least, the threat of loss – as the essence of the refugee experience.

The case studies in this book show how refugees in the Dedza–Angónia borderland went into exile as persons already enmeshed in relationships. The impact of these relationships did not abate, despite the acute dispersal of a person's relatives. Analysis beginning from a generalised 'refugee experience' would ignore variation, as is also argued in Malkki's (1995b) study of two sets of Hutu refugees from Burundi in Tanzania. One set consisted of camp refugees, the other of town refugees. The refugee camp, isolated from Tanzanians and other nationalities, reinforced the refugees' moral and political understanding of their history and present condition. Malkki shows how these Hutu refugees believed in an alliance, at times in an outright equivalence, between 'the Tutsi' and 'the Tanzanians' – categories which received meaning within a compelling 'mythico-history' of ethnic violence. By contrast, the town refugees, mixing with Tanzanians and other nationalities, often denied that they were refugees, and emphasised, instead, other available identities which the urban context provided. Their life-style was an affront to the camp refugees, threatening the purity of 'a people' in exile. In the camp, being a refugee was heroised; in the town, it was negated.

Despite some inherent methodological problems in this simple juxta-position,[5] Malkki's overall argument is cogent. It draws attention to the variable conditions under which refugees live during their exile. Instead of defining a generalised 'refugee experience' within the parameters of, for example, loss and uprootedness, serious studies of displacement leave those parameters undefined and open to investigation. Admittedly, this proposi-tion may be seen to arise from the specific conditions of the Dedza–Angónia borderland, where the spatial proximity of 'home' to 'exile' undermines uprootedness. This book shows, however, how the trajectories of personal relationships, relief aid and historical contingencies intermingled to produce highly variable experiences of displacement under seemingly homogeneous conditions.

These variations in the impact of displacement lead to questioning the effect of the international border in Dedza–Angónia on the borderland villagers' lives. The above quotation from Anderson conveys, in effect, a double stereotype – refugees from Mozambique 'at home' in Malawi and the artificiality of African international borders, which are ignored by the borderland populations. The second stereotype has some basis in the fact that most African borders are not completely guarded or fenced and can easily be crossed (Griffiths 1996: 68). Moreover, African borders are, for half their length, straight lines, arcs of circles or related to roads. These facts cannot, however, determine how the presence of a border becomes en-meshed in the relationships of a borderland population. This book is a contribution to an 'anthropology of borderlands' in which, on the one hand, the metaphorical sense of borderlands challenges entrenched disciplinary perspectives while, on the other, a more literal sense examines the history and actual administration of borderlands (see Alvarez 1995; cf. Asiwaju 1985; Kopytoff 1987; Donnan and Wilson 1994; Miles 1994; Nugent and Asiwaju 1996; Wilson and Donnan 1998).

If the notion of a generalised 'refugee experience' is likely to hinder the study of displacement, a similar danger plagues attempts to define a 'border culture' or a 'border identity'. For example, Donna Flynn (1997a), in her study of the Bénin–Nigeria borderland, argues that the inhabitants of this binational territory form a social group with a distinct identity. Kinship and title to land, rather than ethnicity or nationality, facilitate membership in this group but are not necessary conditions. Membership is determined, Flynn writes, above all by the length of continuous residence in the area. Flynn's observations may be justified, but a difficulty does arise in the very last pages of her account, where she introduces nationality, ethnicity and kinship as factors which 'complicate border solidarity' (Flynn 1997a: 326). The primacy of the border identity appears as an artefact of the ethno-grapher's textual strategy, which all but erases the question of how this identity is linked to other available identities in a framework of power relations. My own approach subscribes to these reflections on the anthro-pology of borderlands by Robert Alvarez: 'As with notions of culture writ large, the notion of a border culture either glosses over or essentialises traits and behaviour, often obliterating the actual problems and conditions in the variation of human behaviour' (1995: 450).

Bluntly put, the analytic preoccupation with identity tends to confuse appearances with the social forces which shape persons' identity prefer-ences. If 'identity is always mobile and processual' (Malkki 1992: 37), identity itself should hardly remain the ultimate subject of analysis. After the dangers of essentialising identities as primordial affiliations have been acknowledged, the studies of refugees and borderlands face the converse danger of exaggerating fluidity. People are often attracted by particular identities, and their capacity to change identities is a function of power relations (Ortner 1998). The case studies in this book show how some villagers' identities were contested, their status as 'refugees' imposed on them, and the border as a barrier asserted. All these things were done by other villagers. The *em*placement of apparently *dis*placed persons was a process that went beyond the identity preferences of any one person, raising questions about power and value which demand solid social theorising.

SOCIAL CAPITAL AND COMPLEXITY

Villagers' participation in the war and their experiences of exile pose similar problems for ethnographic analysis – how did trust, norms and social networks operate to provide political support and refuge during such crises? The problem of trust and norms, long central to social theory, has recently been revived in the framework of 'social capital' (for an introduction, see Harriss and de Renzio 1997). Despite its considerable imprecision and problematic assumptions, the discourse on social capital merits attention for the unusual way in which it has been able to bring social theorists and policy-makers together. Its focus on social organisation in economic development, democratisation and 'good governance' has begun to appeal, among others, to the World Bank (e.g. 1997). As such, the effort to expose and revise, with ethnographic analysis, the pitfalls of the discourse may also enable a wide audience to see villagers' predicaments from a new perspective.

One immediate source of imprecision in the current discourse is the shift, rarely addressed in the literature, by which social capital has come to be understood as a property of entire political communities rather than as a resource accruing to individuals (Putzel 1997: 951). In his pioneering work to systematise the use of the concept, James Coleman (1988, 1990) argued that social capital inheres in relations between persons, and, like other forms of capital, is productive by facilitating the attainment of ends that would not be attainable in its absence. Norms and trust, in Coleman's scheme, facilitate action and make social capital an unintended consequence, a by-product, of other activities.

Robert Putnam (1993), whose work paved the way for 'social capital' to enter the development discourse, extended Coleman's conceptual scheme from interpersonal relations to the realm of government. By comparing the performance of regional governments in southern and northern Italy, Putnam was able to argue that the norms and networks of 'civic engagement', through associational life, newspaper readership and political participation, had contributed to more democratic local governments and greater socio-economic development in the north than in the south. Coleman's perspective on the dynamic of interpersonal relations in kinship and friendship shifted to 'secondary associations' (Putnam 1993: 175), and, by the same token, highlighted collective rather than individual action. With little regard to the history of the idea, it has become easy to view social capital as a 'community-level variable' (cf. Widner with Mundt 1998: 2).

Of the problems which subsequent criticisms have identified in Putnam's work, circularity is perhaps the most fatal (cf. Harriss and de Renzio 1997: 924). For Putnam, social capital appears to facilitate co-operation and 'civic engagement', which, in fact, already presuppose social capital. One way out of this impasse in analysis is to contemplate the historical conditions which give rise to 'unsocial' capital (see Levi 1996; Putzel 1997). The capacity to engage in collective action, these critics point out, is by no means a guarantee of trust and co-operation, as ethnic enclaves and political violence attest. In addition to this fairly well-established criticism, it is important to address a more profound problem in the discourse on social capital, a problem shared by Coleman and Putnam.

This concerns the origins of the concept as a metaphor borrowed from economics. Faithful to the metaphor, Coleman describes norms, trust and other social-structural features as 'a capital asset for the individual' (1990: 302). Some critics of Putnam, accepting his notion that 'trust is an essential component of social capital' (1993: 170), have, in turn, sought a more precise definition of trust in the language of game theory and rational choice. For example, the actor is regarded as a 'player' who makes 'optimal choices' based on 'calculation' (Levi 1996: 48). Action, in other words, is instrumental, and social capital is but an aspect of the apparently universal equation between means and ends.

At least since Marshall Sahlins' (1976) important criticism, anthropology has exposed the utilitarian undertones in instrumentalist perspectives as ethnocentric, based on a notion of persons as individuals. At the same time, it is precisely their resonance with entrenched Western dispositions which makes instrumentalist perspectives reappear in social theory.[6] The appeal of instrumentalism lies in the commonsensical view, shared by rational-actor and norm-based models, that the social world consists of entities which exist apart from the relations between them (Emirbayer 1997). In this regard, there is little difference between Coleman's interest in individual action and Putnam's in collective action. Whether they are individuals or political communities, actors engage in instrumental action by means of the 'capital assets' that norms and trust provide. Lost in such perspectives is the possibility that social relationships, precisely through such compelling moral sentiments as trust, *constitute* actors and make the separation between entities and relations indefensible.

Two closely related analytical tasks have to be undertaken, therefore, if the discourse on social capital is to provide a viable perspective into the processes of war and exile in the Dedza–Angónia borderland. On the one hand, rather than presupposing a universal logic of instrumental action, more attention must be devoted to the variable content of social action than has hitherto been the case in the discourse on social capital (cf. Putzel 1997: 941–2). On the other hand, one way of addressing this question is by accepting that actors in the social world are neither 'individuals' nor 'communities' but *relations* of varying scale, from personal relationships to transnational relations of power.

This book introduces the notion of *the patrimonial logic of social capital* to fulfil these analytical tasks when the focus is on personal relationships. Although patrimonialism is conventionally defined as an extension of household relations to a wider social and political field (cf. Eisenberg 1998), the notion of patrimonial logic is not an answer to Coleman's interest in norm-based action. The sociological quest for codifying 'norms' carries the danger of not only emphasising entities at the expense of relations but also situating social life outside the vagaries of history, with 'social capital' becoming synonymous with a static 'culture' (cf. Bayart 1999). Two further propositions clarify the contrast with the norm-based models of social action. First, rather than defining norms for action, 'patrimonialism' is best understood as a *quality* of relationships in which mutual dependence is an existential, and not merely material, fact. Trust, always emergent in relation to risk (Gambetta 1988), is a more dynamic concept than 'norms' to describe the content of social capital. This book shows how the dynamic of trust revolves more around the production of distinction than around a simple accumulation of followers and dependants.

Second, the dynamic of trust operates under specific historical conditions. In this regard, it is a profound error to view, despite the widespread rhetorical use of patrimonial idioms, the basis of postcolonial African polities in 'precolonial' norms and practices (see Chabal and Daloz 1999). There are, rather, several logics at play, and one crucial task is to understand the processes by which the patrimonial logic of social capital may be transformed under the conditions of war and exile. The relations between borderland villages, postcolonial states and a guerrilla movement sometimes bear witness to *neo*patrimonialism, which, in Christopher Clapham's words, 'can be readily adapted to an instrumental form, in which straightforward considerations of personal benefit and the exchange of favours come to replace the reciprocal obligations which characterise patrimonialism in its original or traditional form' (1985: 49–50).

The notion of the patrimonial logic of social capital also entails a particular view of personhood. Far from being mutually independent individuals, persons are both constituted and constrained by their relationships, an observation that resonates with much African ethnography. From the crafting of the self in various ritual contexts (Riesman 1986) to 'wealth in people' as a source of knowledge and political power (Guyer 1993; Guyer and Belinga 1995), the person appears as a composite which evolves during the course of a life-cycle (Englund 1999). Together with the 'individual' the 'community' disappears from the analytical vocabulary. As has been theorised above all in Melanesian anthropology (see e.g. Strathern 1988), it makes little sense to contemplate a person's belonging to a 'community', or even a 'society', when the self itself is a composite of relationships. By the same token, the conflicts that those relationships entail render the idea of an idyllic 'communal' life highly implausible.

The embeddedness of social capital in variable historical conditions and in phenomena of varying scale, from personal relationships to regional and transnational forces, provides an example of the complexity in social life (cf. Eve et al. 1997). Instead of displaying purely chaotic features, however, the complexity of social life is moulded by determinacies which arise from particular power relations. Even though the war and exile in the Dedza–Angónia borderland assumed specific forms, villagers were also caught up in processes which were firmly beyond their control. However intermittently, new power relations profoundly altered the patrimonial logic of social capital. The problem of power relations rephrases, in effect, the question of external and internal dynamics which has haunted much scholarly debate on the war in Mozambique. The problem will be elaborated in the course of this book, particularly in Chapter 7.

THE EXTENDED-CASE METHOD

When the objective of a study is to highlight the impact of war and exile on personal relationships, the analytical focus is inevitably on certain *dramatis personae*. As contended above, a person's agency indicates relational person-hood, not 'individuality', whose existence antedates a relational matrix. Accordingly, the analytical focus shifts between a number of persons in order to disclose the pull of social relationships. This method of ethnographic representation is known as the extended-case method, developed by social anthropologists associated with the former Rhodes-Livingstone Institute in present-day Zambia and, later, with the Manchester School (see Gluckman 1940; van Velsen 1967; Werbner 1984; van Donge 1985; Burawoy 1998).

During the 1950s and 1960s, the method was widely applied in studies of village politics, witchcraft accusations, religion and modernisation, urban neighbourhoods and work-places (see e.g. Mitchell 1956; Turner 1957; Epstein 1958; van Velsen 1964; Marwick 1965; Long 1968; Kapferer 1972). For the social anthropology of the time, the methodological impli-cations, in Hugh Macmillan's expression, were 'revolutionary' (1995: 42). A. R. Radcliffe-Brown, a key figure during the formative years of British social anthropology, derided 'the actual relations of Tom, Dick and Harry' (1952: 192), treating them at best as raw material that filled fieldnotes. A proper social anthropological analysis, according to Radcliffe-Brown, aimed at the abstraction of general principles from the apparent ephemera of everyday life. The extended-case method, highlighting the conflicts and aspirations of particular, named persons, challenged this bird's-eye view of social life. 'The actual relations of Tom, Dick and Harry' could themselves generate processes that circumvented or modified general principles – processes that were not, however, utterly devoid of logic.

The analytical preoccupations of early social anthropologists using the extended-case method have remarkable similarities with current theoretical issues. For example, studies of migrants in the 'transnational' world have been inspired by the extended cases of migrants to the Zambian Copperbelt (see Basch et al. 1994: 30–1). More broadly, the method of following persons to the various sites and conflicts of their lives is now seen as an early attempt to question the bounded 'place' of ethnographic inquiry (see Marcus 1998: 94–5). Contemporary scholars have also found similarities with post-structuralism, with the insight that meaning is unstable, and that, as Michel Foucault (1972: 200) among others has tried to show, people within the same discursive practice can hold contrary opinions and make contradictory choices (see Bourdieu 1977: 202; Long 1992). Another 'post' which the social anthropologists using the extended-case method seemed to anticipate is postcolonialism, its 'multiple social spaces' and 'plurality of normative realms' (Gould 1997: 245).

Such endorsement often involves forgetting that the social anthropologists themselves did not share a uniform theory as to how the negotiation of meaning and norms took place. At one end lurked the shortcoming of many transactionalist models which represented social life as an idealised marketplace – unconstrained individuals interacting as equals (see e.g. Blau 1964; Barth 1966; Asad 1972; Paine 1974; Kapferer 1976). As Pierre Bourdieu (1977: 26) has noted, J. van Velsen's (1964) study came particularly close to representing social manipulation in utilitarian and individualistic terms. On the other hand, Victor Turner's (1957) study of emerging aspirations and their ultimate failure in village politics paid more attention to social relationships as both constraints and sources of interests.[7]

The extended-case method is often seen to produce situational analysis, but in this book analysis is, rather, *processual*. Although dramatic events often provide insights for analysis, events are not discrete 'situations' – they are followed by more events which can reverse the effects of earlier ones. The process, indeterminate and yet not without effects which indicate power relations, fits uneasily into the four phases – breach, crisis, redressive action, and reintegration or recognition of schism – of Turner's 'social dramas' (1957: 91–2). In the layout of the chapters, although some narrative form is inevitable to ease reading, cases and their analysis are entwined. Analysis does not come after a case, because a case does not fall into a pattern, or constitute a process, by itself. Irreducible to specific events, moreover, the cases in this book are simultaneously historical and personal trajectories – in Chapters 2 and 6, for example, how a village plunged into and faced the aftermath of a war; in Chapters 3, 4 and 5, how particular persons and families endured the predicament of displacement.

The classic application of the extended-case method has been criticised for its negligible attention to the narrative forms of people's own accounts (see Rosaldo 1989: 140–2). Whatever air of authenticity it creates, however, the direct reproduction of informants' 'voices' (in, for example, Kriger 1992; Nordstrom 1997) is no less informed by the analyst's selection and intervention than is the definition of an 'event' in the seamless flow of social life. Richard Werbner's (1991) study of life-historical narratives, moreover, has shown the continuing importance of keeping ineffable social forces in the analytic grasp. Both the said and the unsaid must belong to the purview of social analysis. As Carolyn Nordstrom has reminded us, narrative does not provide an unmediated access to the experience that is being narrated, and especially when the subject is the sensitive issue of war and exile, 'something is always wrong with the facts one is given' (1997: 43).

One alternative would be to argue that there can be no processual anthropology of political violence, only endless juxtapositions of narratives about political violence. That is not the contention in this book. An anthropological understanding of the processes by which particular villages were caught up in war and exile emerges in the course of fieldwork and analysis. Villagers' idioms and narratives are salient, but the need to bring internal and external factors into an integrated focus precisely dictates the effort to reach beyond villagers' own understandings of their predicaments. Fieldwork discloses events and arguments which challenge accepted academic and popular narratives, while other sources make regional and transnational histories accessible.

I-WITNESS OR A FLY ON THE WALL?

The ethnographer's own role in the unfolding events of extended cases also requires reflection. Turner (1957: 138–42), for example, described in one of his social dramas how his cook and 'general henchman' Kasonda came to be accused of witchcraft by his fellow villagers and how the money he had received from Turner could be used to create cleavages and alliances. Moreover, by merely attempting to become closely aware of persons' lives and relationships, the ethnographer is likely to have an impact on the local setting. In a politically volatile fieldwork situation, such as in the Dedza–Angónia borderland, this possibility would seem to be especially potent. However, naïve as it sounds, my own person is virtually invisible in the case studies of this book, because I made a conscious effort to avoid association with any one side of villagers' disputes. I did not employ cooks or henchmen, only a research assistant for the first six months to help me to navigate the initial difficulties with the Chichewa language. A school-leaver and my age-mate, he was introduced to me by a teacher at a local mission, and he commuted the six kilometres between his village in Malawi and the borderland on bicycle, having had no previous linkages to the villages of my study.

The Malawian family who rented a room to me during my fieldwork both in 1992–3 and in 1996–7 lived in a village adjoining the site of my most intensive research. Like my research assistant, they were not personally linked to the subjects of my case studies.

My initial contacts at the local mission and with Malawian chiefs influenced my decision not to seek accommodation in the actual border village where most refugees lived when I began my fieldwork. The high concentration of refugees in one village, I was told, had resulted in many problems, from frequent physical violence to witchcraft, with rowdy beer parties and the widespread consumption of marijuana making it impossible for me to have personal security there. My subsequent fieldwork in the village proved that these views reflected the prejudices of those Malawians who had little contact with refugees. While my Malawian host family never made it necessary to seek new accommodation, I was also careful to convey that the 'refugee crisis' was not the sole reason for my being in the area. Both pragmatic and academic considerations underlay my strategy. When I commenced fieldwork in February 1992, Malawi still appeared to be under the iron rule of its Life President, Kamuzu Banda. It did not seem advisable to emphasise my interest in refugees in a country where authorities were highly sensitive to criticism about anything. I always described my project as a study of 'culture' (*chikhalidwe*; 'way of living') and the Chichewa language. This description was truthful because it also reflected my conviction that I had to know my interlocutors as *persons* rather than as 'refugees' or 'hosts'.

No authority in Malawi or Mozambique ever attempted to intervene in my work, and, to my surprise, no one even asked to see the research clearance which the Office of the President and Cabinet in Malawi had issued to me. As I grew more confident in relationships with the locals, I had begun, like the villagers themselves, to cross the international border at will by the time of repatriation. Among villagers, my status as a 'schoolboy' (*mwana wa sukulu*) came to replace their early assumption that I was somehow linked to the provision of aid in the area. Many of them remarked that my willingness to stay in a village and to learn the language and a wide range of local knowledge distinguished me from those who were seen to bring aid. All villagers accepted that my project made it necessary to encounter as many persons and 'sides' (*mbali*) as possible. For myself, these encounters arose from the obvious methodological need to obtain as many different perspectives as possible, not in order to sustain the illusion of having covered a 'whole society' (cf. Thornton 1988) but to attend to the contrasting and partial perspectives of different protagonists. This approach often required listening and watching rather than the active asking of questions.

In this book, I do not indulge in the 'I-witnessing' of an apparently self-reflexive anthropologist (cf. Geertz 1988: 73–101). At the same time, I was hardly a fly on the wall when I learned about the dilemmas and conflicts which came to be the substance of my case studies. My own person, however, plays no visible role in the case studies for the simple reason that I cannot claim any significant impact on those dilemmas and conflicts, many of which had taken place, or had begun to emerge, before I entered the scene. To be sure, I became closer to some people than to others, but each new interlocutor also widened the scope of my social relationships. For example, my first acquaintance among the *dramatis personae* of the case studies was Nasoweka, one of the wives of Luis, the Frelimo secretary. Our first encounter was by chance. Encouraged by the facility with which she seemed to appreciate my fieldwork, I could soon include her brothers Sandikonda and Hawadi in my circle of closest friends, followed by Luis and several others who appear in the case studies. While everyone became accustomed to using the 'clan-name' Phiri, which I had received in a Malawian village at a very early stage of fieldwork, some also applied other names to me. For Rafaelo the village headman, I was *bwana* (boss; master); for Luis the Frelimo secretary, *boy*. Neither of them used such epithets without good-humoured irony, but the epithets themselves indicated how I, far from upsetting villagers' existing distinctions, came to be situated in them.

In retrospect, it has been the period *after* the fieldwork in 1992–3 which has made me more obviously an actor in the social relationships of Dedza–Angónia borderland villagers. Two circumstances account for this development. First, my absence has raised the question of who those are with whom I have kept in contact. Second, the years after the first fieldwork have brought, as discussed in the Epilogue, much economic hardship to the area, making an outsider like myself even more into a resource. Yet the relationships I have been able to establish with my host family and their village have limited the danger of my associations with any of the protagonists in my case studies becoming too close. My own reliance on such complementary, and yet distinct, sets of relationships has given me, as a matter of fact, insight into the logic of social capital among Dedza–Angónia borderland villagers.

A PRÉCIS

The analysis of external and internal dynamics requires, first of all, an appreciation of the variable histories that impinged upon villagers' experiences of the war. Chapter 1 offers an account of early Ngoni migrations, colonial boundary-making, Christian missions, labour migration and nationalism as historical forces that provided an indispensable context for the emergence of Chitima village, the border village with whose experiences of the war this book is primarily concerned. This chapter also describes refugees' relief aid and Dedza–Angónia borderland villagers' current livelihoods. In order to anticipate the wide range of kin-relationships which will appear significant in the extended-case studies, the chapter ends with an account of cognatic kinship, by which villagers are able to trace relationships through both their mothers and fathers.

Chapter 2 presents an extended-case study of the war in Chitima village. The narrative of village history examines the processes by which, within an unstable historical context, a certain family rose to political prominence and ultimately came to be divided; a cleavage that was reinforced, though not created, by contrasting allegiances to Frelimo and Renamo. Despite its aim of creating a nation without divisions, Frelimo never came to occupy the entire political field in the village. Although the area was spared some of Frelimo's most unpopular interventions, the exclusion of the village headman from local governance after independence inadvertently produced a significant contrast in the social relationships which constituted the Frelimo party-state in the village. The chapter bears witness to villagers' active participation in apparently non-local forces, no less than to the frequent surprises and discontent that have accompanied such participation. Taken together, both villagers' engagement and its unanticipated consequences show how the external–internal divide is not to be equated with specific institutions or forces. It indicates, rather, historically variable power relations.

Chapter 3 begins the extended-case studies of displacement with a focus on Lumbe villagers in the Malawian border village of Mfuno. They belonged to the minority of refugees in Mfuno village thought to have come 'from afar' (kutali). They had fled as one family group and were received by John, their relative who had married in Mfuno in the mid-1970s. The narrative of their diverse experiences of displacement revolves around the complex ways in which space and place could coincide or be kept separate during their exile. The space of valued relationships could coincide with the place where these Lumbe villagers spent their exile, or those relationships could be spatially dispersed, much effort going into travelling between different settlements. All this underlines the need to regard refugees as persons who carry histories of relationships with them, a view that counters the image of a refugee as an 'uprooted' victim. However, displacement itself continued to mould those relationships, and some Lumbe exiles sought little expansion in their pre-flight configuration of relationships, whilst others became entangled in new relationships. John himself provides a case of emerging new interests on the eve of repatriation. The years he spent with his displaced relatives contributed to his wish to return to Lumbe as a commercial farmer. I explore in detail how John was unable to fulfil this aim, not because of envious villagers' resentful attitude to commercial farming but because of his management of relationships during the Lumbe villagers' exile.

John's case highlights villagers' ideas about moral personhood in their arguments during displacement and repatriation. As in the other case studies, at issue are the processes by which trust and legitimate authority are generated in social life under variable historical conditions. Chapter 4 carries this theme further by considering the impact of social age and, above all, gender on villagers' experiences of displacement. Humanitarian aid is often built up on ideas of dependencies and obligations between men, women and children which are not necessarily congruent with the refugees' own relationships. This chapter presents the contrasting case studies of three women who all were associated with one of the most influential men in the Dedza–Angónia borderland, the Frelimo secretary of Chitima village. The chapter shows the insignificant role he played in the three women's attempts to settle on the other side of the border during displacement. Enmeshed in different sets of relationships, the women had pre-existing ties to Malawi, some of which made their flight an effective return, while others made them become 'refugees'. The chapter highlights the exchange of material and symbolic assistance between households as characteristic of women's management of trust and authority. It also shows how, in certain cases, men imposed the international border as a constraint on women's relationships during repatriation.

Although the 1986–93 displacement was a dramatic period in the Dedza–Angónia borderland, it was endured by people who had long become accustomed to migration. Moreover, many other migrants who were not 'refugees' continued to affect social life in the borderland. Chapter 5 focuses on two very different migrants who arrived in Mfuno village during displace-ment. One returned to his area of origin after thirty years of absence, the other followed his wife to the area as a young husband whose area of origin was in a different district in Malawi. Both cases give, however, insight into the political economy of Malawi after the end of large-scale labour migra-tion to South African mines in the mid-1970s. One of the migrants had long worked on tobacco estates in central and northern Malawi, the other had spent a brief period in the capital before his marriage. Both had found these options for internal migration unprofitable and arrived in the Dedza–Angónia borderland with considerable commercial aspirations. The chapter continues to probe the moral conditions of economic and political success by examining why one of them was castigated while the other was more successful in establishing himself. The chapter also draws attention to the significance of relationships which do not fall within the scope of kinship, such as those established through religious congregations.

The peace treaty between Frelimo and Renamo heralded the end of displacement in the Dedza–Angónia borderland, and, well before the beginning of formal repatriation programmes, most refugees had already returned to Mozambique. Chapter 6 examines the immediate aftermath of the repatriation of Chitima villagers. When the government introduced the village headman and the Frelimo secretary as equally legitimate authorities, a new era in villagers' antagonisms began. Villagers' expectations of 'development' after the war brought local leaders under critical inspection, and, when no external assistance other than inadequate food aid was forthcoming, old rivals in village politics found themselves subject to similar demands by increasingly frustrated villagers. Chapter 6 describes the joint efforts by the village headman and the Frelimo secretary to lobby in Villa Ulongwe, the district capital. However, no less than before and during the war, the local configurations of authority were predicated on specific notions of trust and morality, not simply on new state policies. It thus becomes necessary to pay close attention to the specific articulation of villagers' discontent – who took the lead in voicing the criticism against the headman and the secretary, and what was the context of relationships in which this challenge emerged. My analysis discloses paradoxes of repatriation, how the 'homecoming', under dire material conditions, led towards veritable discontent with the government and its local representatives.

My criticism of the external–internal divide has already implied that such discontent with the central government requires an explanation. Villagers' active engagement with translocal forces, abundantly demonstrated in the case studies, bears no witness to the claims of some analysts that juxtapose the 'peasantry' with a wider political and economic world. Villagers' *disengagement* also needs to be regarded as worthy of processual analysis, and Chapter 7, by way of drawing conclusions from the case studies, discusses notions which carry such an analysis further. Key distinctions must be made within the notion of power, whereby the 'external' becomes the historically variable means by which some villagers alienate themselves from personal relationships as constraints of power. War and exile in the Dedza–Angónia borderland highlight these dynamics of value and power, and the external–internal relations, not as distinct 'systems', but as means to elucidate historical variations.

The book ends with an Epilogue, written after my revisits to the area, after over three years had passed since the events described in Chapter 6. The Epilogue raises an uncomfortable question about changing power relations – to what extent are post-war developments actually transforming the nature of the external–internal divide? No longer a dynamic tension between contrasting power relations, the divide would seem to give way to increasing marginalisation. Chitima villagers' refusal to pay taxes and their resort to some illegal or semi-legal measures contributed to their perception of the government as an alien, hostile entity. Many local Frelimo officials took decreasing pride in their party positions, while the local party elite, unable to bring 'development', were seen to remain content with private benefits. Marginalisation did not preclude a certain autonomy, however, and the deeply moral arguments that the previous case studies highlighted continued in local politics and family life. Marginalisation inevitably raised the question of what the predicaments of war and displacement were *for*. Human beings under dehumanising conditions can be compassionate and active rather than mere victims. But no moral or intellectual purpose would be served, if Dedza–Angónia borderland villagers were simply heroised. The world in which they live continues to produce conditions for unabated atrocities. In the post-war discontent, in the realisation that past tribulations are not compensated by present prosperity, lie the seeds of more atrocities to come.

1

BORDERS DRAWN, BORDERS CROSSED

Mwalawankhondo, the stone of the war. A border village recalls in its name a history of turmoil. Here the war was not the prolonged postcolonial conflict between Frelimo and Renamo, nor the late colonial armed struggle for liberation in Mozambique. The village claims a place in Ngoni history during the early colonial period. It was here, on this hill overlooking the plateau betweeen the mountains of Dedza and Domwe, that two factions, clustered around two classificatory brothers, engaged in their final battle. Gomani's faction overpowered Kachindamoto's, and the Maseko Ngoni, hitherto one polity, came to be divided between two great chiefs.

Recalling the blood on the hill, the spears and the gunpowder, villagers narrate their own history as the descendants of heroic warriors who conquered peoples they encountered on their long march from South Africa and settled, and divided, in this landscape of mountains and hills in the north. The narrative conveys admiration for a way of life now long gone, for a past when men lived on a diet of beer and beef, when large herds of cattle roamed the land, when the mere mention of the Ngoni provoked awe among neighbouring peoples – when, in short, it was good to be an Ngoni. The narrative, when it becomes an ethnic charter, ignores the customs and beliefs which the forefathers adopted from the Chichewa-speaking peoples whom they apparently conquered. Nor does it acknowledge colonial influence, such as the impact of the British on the split between Gomani and Kachindamoto.

The borderland of Dedza and Angónia Districts, in effect, cuts across many histories. It was known as the Central Angoni Highlands during the late colonial period, a landscape of high altitudes, which signified, for the villagers of the area, another aspect of the Ngoni military way of life. The Ngoni, they recall, settled on or near hills to have a clear view of the landscape. As a measure against ever-present hostilities, this wide view kept them alert to the approach of strangers, as did compact villages, a pattern of settlement which has prevailed until the present day.

A decade after the battle between Gomani and Kachindamoto in 1894, these highlands attracted the White Fathers, a Roman Catholic missionary order, for a very different reason. They sought refuge from the scorching heat of Chief Kachindamoto's territory towards the shores of Lake Malawi,

their first station in Dedza District. The highlands offered a sanctuary of a
mundane kind where cool breezes, for all but two or three months in a year,
relieved the missionaries from their fatigue and contributed to their recovery
from illness. The mission which soon replaced the sanatorium received the
name of Bembeke, now a symbol for one of the most entrenched popular
Catholicisms in the region.

The imposing cathedral of Bembeke contrasts with other physical signs
of travel and contact in the landscape. Along the international border, the
observant passer-by can still discern the ruins of grinding mills and stores
which Portuguese entrepreneurs maintained for two decades before the
independence of Mozambique in 1975. Some of the ruins have remained
abandoned since the exodus of these Portuguese on the eve of independence; other stores were managed by the state until they became the key
targets of Renamo guerrillas' looting and destruction in the late 1980s.

A decade later, a small group of stores, owned by Malawians, forms a
cluster at the turn-off to the Bembeke mission, and a market takes place on
the site twice a week. Apart from the bustling market-place, the landscape
betrays undeniable impoverishment during the most recent decades. In
villages, the grey sea of four-corner thatched houses made of soil surrounds
islands of larger houses, iron-roofed and often painted. They were built with
labour migrants' money; most of these migrants worked in the South African
gold mines until the Malawian government stopped labour migration in the
mid-1970s. It is these houses, once essential to ostentation, that now give
the most tangible evidence of impoverishment. Their iron roofs partly corroded
and their paint broken, the present condition of the houses bespeaks a lack
of profitable employment.

This would be a landscape of lost opportunities, of isolation, if one paradoxical feature did not cut across it like a scar. The main Malawian highway
runs along the international border. It links Lilongwe to Blantyre, Malawi's
capital and the country's commercial centre; a branch road runs from
Dedza to Villa Ulongwe, Angónia's district capital, and it is possible to
continue the journey from there by road to Tete and beyond. After Renamo
reached the borderland in the late 1980s, Mozambican vehicles largely
disappeared from the highway. The abundance of cars, buses and trucks
bearing Malawian number-plates accords with borderland villagers' closer
ties to Malawian markets and services, a situation that has continued after
the peace treaty and the repatriation.

For villagers in the Dedza–Angónia borderland, the highway is an
integral part of their lives; it brings traders and middlemen from towns to
purchase local produce, it provides a route to relatives and acquaintances in
other villages and districts, and, tragically, its traffic sometimes kills children.
Given the fact that the relatively short distances in Malawi encourage road
traffic, the highway brings a whole world within reach. Although tourists

seldom stop their vehicles in the area, borderland villagers eagerly return their intense gaze. Malawian cabinet ministers and senior government officials speed along the highway, the flag of Malawi flying on the fronts of their black Mercedes-Benz limousines. So near and yet so far, they leave the borderland villagers arguing about the identities of the persons inside these cars, the symbols of so much power and wealth.

For some seven years in 1986–93, the highway was a window through which outsiders could peep at Malawi's refugee crisis. An eerie sight showed one side of the highway completely deserted, taken over by bush, and the other congested with human habitations and activities. The highway was the divide between the lands of war and peace, a divide where the international border apparently made all the difference. Refugees had settled in Malawian border villages and greeted the traffic on the highway with offers to sell cooking oil, maize flour, beans – items of their relief aid. By the 1990s, the careful eye could see patches of maize on the Mozambican side of the border, and since 1993, both sides have again established villages, although travellers on the highway continue to see more open space in Mozambique.

For villagers in the Dedza–Angónia borderland, the postcolonial war left little that was memorable. Here the mention of the war, unlike the battle in Mwalawankhondo, brings to mind more villains than heroes. Nor is exile remembered as a period of heroic suffering. An open square in a Malawian border village where relief aid was distributed is covered with grass and new houses, graciously sending into oblivion a period of shameful dependence on aid, a consequence of a conflict that went very wrong.

This chapter explores what the landscape evokes. The early migrations provide a perspective on the actual heterogeneity of the Ngoni polities at the outset of the colonial period. The demarcation of boundaries during colonialism shaped further border villages, not necessarily as an imposition but as a new political reality which became integral in the dynamics of the villagers' own relationships. This observation on the complex entwining of external and internal dynamics, best elaborated through extended-case studies in the chapters that follow, is also substantiated by a discussion of the impact which Christian missions, labour migration, the colonial and postcolonial wars and, after the war, 'democracy' and economic liberalisation have had on villages in the Dedza–Angónia borderland. The discussion here is brief, a backdrop to the case studies rather than a comprehensive historical analysis in its own right. The chapter ends with an overview of livelihoods, social organisation and refugee crisis in the villages of Mfuno and Chitima, the settings of most of the case studies.

THE MAKING OF THE BORDERLAND
The Ngoni migrations

The present-day area of Natal and Swaziland in 1810–30 may seem to be remote from the postcolonial predicaments in the Dedza–Angónia borderland. That area and that period, known as *mfecane* ('the crushing'; see Walker 1935: 210), were the scene for the rise of Shaka, the despotic Zulu leader whose battles led to the formation of new political entities, or are alleged to have done so. *Mfecane* and its consequences – such as the various Nguni polities in South–Central Africa, the Gaza kingdom established by Nxaba in southern Mozambique and that of the Ndebele on the Zimbabwe plateau (Beach 1984: 52–9; Newitt 1995: 256–64) – are at the core of scholarly controversy. Much of the debate revolves around the question whether 'internal' dynamics were independent of 'external' interventions (see Hamilton 1995).

An early view stressed the pressure which increasing population exerted on scant ecological resources (Gluckman 1960; Omer-Cooper 1966: 24–7; Guy 1980; Peires 1993). The studies of widespread droughts in the region in the early nineteenth century nuanced this view (see Newitt 1988; Eldredge 1992: 30–4). But they also discussed *mfecane* in isolation from the gradual expansion of white colonies. The scholarly controversy arose from the view that the Cape Colony and the slave trade run from the Portuguese port of Delagoa Bay shaped events in the interior (Cobbing 1988), and that the 'Nguni' peoples who emerged were ideological constructs of white settlers (Wright 1986, 1989). This dissident view, in other words, explained the utility of *mfecane* as an *ideological* weapon. Long before scholarly debates took place about the subject, *mfecane*, according to the critics, was used as an excuse to colonise peoples who were seen as inherently belligerent.

With little new evidence to support these claims of the critics, the *mfecane* debate would seem to be closed in favour of earlier views (Davenport 1996).[1] The methodological issues are, nevertheless, intriguing. One studies the role of Africans in shaping their own destinies, and the question of how African history can be more than a narrative of external interventions (cf. Hamilton 1998). Another issue is directly relevant to Ngoni history. The *mfecane* critics accused earlier views not only of keeping entwined histories separate, such as the histories of white settlements and African politics, but also of lumping together *separate* histories (see Wright 1995). The north-bound Ngoni migrations, according to the *mfecane* critics, were seen as direct consequences of Shaka Zulu's emergence. *Mfecane* did not, however, explain the subsequent rise of different Ngoni factions and the continuing importance of warfare. The Portuguese slave trade in southern and central Mozambique during the 1820s and 1830s, the *mfecane* critics asserted, provided the necessary context to understand Ngoni migrations towards present-day Malawi, Tanzania and Zambia.

As long as the European penetration is seen as a context, rather than as the ultimate cause of the complexities of African history, the early Ngoni invasions suggest a pattern of social value which demands of its historian more than awareness of *mfecane* and the international slave trade. The Ngoni, who either killed or captured the populations they encountered, developed an administrative organisation aptly labelled by J. A. Barnes the 'snowball state' (1954: 29). Captives were distributed among their warrior captors, and, while the segments of residential units had agnatic cores, such segments were heterogeneous in composition; they did not consist of agnates alone (Barnes 1954: 10–11). For polygamous and successful warriors, heterogeneous segments – 'houses' (Kuper 1993) – provided the necessary precondition for political prominence.

Prominence derived from the ability to incorporate subjects under one's personal tutelage. This observation is incompatible with a notion of 'Ngoni' as a uniform ethnic group. It is an obvious point but an important one to make, as shown by the major flaw in Margaret Read's (1936, 1938, 1956) studies, which took the historical accounts of the Ngoni elite for granted (cf. Brantley 1997). Against that, Leroy Vail (1972, 1978, 1981) refused to view 'Ngoni' as a taxonomic unit and stressed, instead, the inevitable heterogeneity of the actual populations. The Maravi peoples encountered in central Malawi, for example, may have come to the area as early as the fourteenth century (Schoffeleers 1972: 97). A section of these peoples has subsequently come to be labelled 'Chewa', and the Ngoni in the area were 'Chewaised' in their language and in many aspects of their social organisation (Langworthy 1975: 18). The 'Ngoni' identity marked, for the autochthonous population, a shift in political allegiances, not a profound social revolution.

The logic of social value, achieved in clusters that formed around successful leaders, sheds some light on the continuance of warfare and spatial dispersal. Although an odd suggestion sees the Ngoni groups of Zwangendaba and Maseko crossing the Zambezi river together in 1835 (see Hatchell 1935), several historical accounts have it that the two groups, fleeing turmoil in the south, had already parted company before crossing the river (NCD 1/3/1: 26; Johnson 1922: 102; Read 1936; Winterbottom 1950: 16; Barnes 1954: 17–18; Philip 1975: 6–10; Newitt 1995: 263). More probably 1835 was the year of Zwangendaba's crossing, whereas the Maseko Ngoni only came into being as a distinct polity a few years later, when their crossing of the river marked a separation from Mzilikazi in Matabeleland (Phiri 1982: 98). After the crossing, Zwangendaba's followers divided into factions and established Ngoni enclaves in the present-day Chipata District of eastern Zambia, Mzimba District of northern Malawi and the Rovuma valley in southern Tanzania. The Maseko Ngoni, after having been defeated by a faction of Zwangendaba's group in southern Tanzania, moved down the east shore of Lake Malawi to settle in the

highlands of Dedza, Ntcheu and Angónia in about 1870. In Dedza–
Angónia borderland villagers' accounts of history, Domwe mountain in
Angónia figures as the ultimate 'our place' (*kwathu*).

The international slave trade was scarcely compatible with the logic of
Ngoni expansion. Although some Maseko Ngoni allegedly took part in the
international trade as suppliers (Langworthy 1975: 22), in some areas the
Ngoni elite prohibited slave trade with outsiders (Vail 1981: 240). In any
case, hostilities among the Maseko Ngoni erupted towards the end of the
nineteenth century when the British were actively trying to 'pacify' peoples
who practised slave raiding. Chief Chikusi was particularly astute in his
reading of the emerging political situation. His plea for help, in 1891 when
the Nyasaland Protectorate was established, was virtually the first Ngoni
matter considered by the new administration in Blantyre (NCD 1/3/1: 33).
Violence continued, however. Gomani, Chikusi's son, enlisted the aid of the
Yao people, themselves deeply involved in the slave trade, to drive his
classificatory brother Kachindamoto towards the south-west shore of Lake
Malawi in 1894 (Linden 1972: 243–4). Apparently only the British presence
saved Kachindamoto from total annihilation.

In 1896, Gomani's execution by the British marked the demise of the
military way of life (Linden 1972: 245). In 1933, responding to the needs of
indirect rule, the colonial administration recognised the Paramount Chief
of the Maseko Ngoni in Gomani's name (Timpunza-Mvula 1987: 59–61).
Gomani, who now has his headquarters in Lizulu in Ntcheu District, is the
Paramount Chief for all Ngoni in Dedza and Ntcheu. By contrast,
Kachindamoto is merely a Traditional Authority who rules from the area of
Mua towards the south-west shore of Lake Malawi.[2] As mentioned, however,
Ngoni history makes a 'pure' ethnic identity a dubious proposition. In both
Mua and the Dedza–Angónia borderland, the Maseko Ngoni have settled
among the Chewa. The effect is most obvious in villagers' language and in
some aspects of social organisation, such as the 'matrilineal' features
discussed below, but more dispute surrounds some men's membership in
the Chewa secret society *gule wamkulu*.[3] Even here, Christian identities often
override ethnic affiliations in the arguments about a 'pagan' institution, and
in many villages, such as those described in the case studies, *gule wamkulu*
plays no recognised role.

Colonial boundary-making

The initial Anglo-Portuguese contest over boundaries centred on the Shire
Highlands in southern Malawi, where Scottish churches had been estab-
lished in the 1870s, after the failure of the Universities Mission to Central
Africa in 1861–3 (Smith 1975; White 1987: 74–6; Newitt 1995: 280–2).
The Scottish missionaries demanded action against the Portuguese intru-
sion into the area (Chitsamba 1971: 27–8). The first Anglo-Portuguese

Convention, agreed upon in 1890 but never ratified, conceded the present-day Tete Province to Britain. This area was lost to Portugal in the Anglo-Portuguese Treaty, ratified in 1891, whereas the Shire Highlands and the present-day Nsanje District fell within the British territory (Chitsamba 1971: 30). The Malawi–Mozambique border was fixed until 1954, when, after an intensive on-site survey, another treaty was signed (Chitsamba 1971: 34). This period of the early 1950s, marking a new importance for the frontier in the Dedza–Angónia borderland and its local settlements, belonged to the era of centralised colonial administration on the Mozambican side of the border.[4]

The direct impact of *prazo* land concessions on the Angónia frontier was modest. After being sub-leased by one Raphael Bivar in 1907–11, *prazo* Angónia was leased by the Sena Sugar Estates (Borges Coelho 1993: 110; Newitt 1995: 423). Instead of investing in Angónia, the company turned the area into a huge labour reserve and moved its men to the plantations in the lower Zambezi. Upon coming to power in Portugal in 1930, the Salazar government ended the leases of the *prazo* companies and banned forced labour (Newitt 1995: 448–51).[5] Tete Province, under a single administrative regime for the first time, received the colonial inspectorate on regular visits to supervise the local officials (Newitt 1995: 511). Tete remained, however, the colony's economic backwater. State and private investment, which first took place in the Province during the 1950s, occurred at a modest level and in relatively few areas (Borges Coelho 1993: 139–40). Angónia, prominent among these areas, attracted Portuguese entrepreneurs as commercial farmers and shopkeepers.

The Portuguese entrepreneurs who began to settle in the Dedza–Angónia borderland during the 1950s soon exported the products of Angónia's fertile land to the whole of Mozambique, particularly to Tete town (Borges Coelho 1993: 148). Commercial agriculture remained a relatively small-scale enterprise, drawing its labour force mainly from the local villages. This contrasted with plantations in Zambézia Province, a contrast which can also be seen in labour conditions. The present-day southern Malawian districts of Nsanje and Mulanje received thousands of immigrants fleeing harsh labour conditions in Mozambique from the late nineteenth century onwards (Boeder 1984; White 1987: 87–8; S1/2767/23[6]).

In the Dedza–Angónia borderland, foreign investors were usually as much traders as farmers. Amicable relations with the local populace were in their interests, because these contributed to the villagers' willingness to sell produce through the investors' enterprises and not through those of their rivals. Moreover, the vicinity of the border, and the events in Zambézia, reminded the local Portuguese of the ever-present possibility of villagers fleeing their treatment. The next chapter describes how the exodus of these Portuguese entrepreneurs in 1975 is still recalled with dismay in the Dedza–

Angónia borderland. Indeed, such was the moral acceptance of the local Portuguese that the support for the nationalist cause was not expressed from an unqualified anti-white standpoint.

Largely because of the scant foreign presence in northern Tete, the Dedza–Angónia frontier remained relatively uneventful. The problems of taxation, rather than local unrest, accounted for the increasing Portuguese attention to the Dedza–Angónia borderland in the late 1940s. It was not merely a matter of collecting taxes, a problem common to colonial administrators on the two sides of the frontier in both central and southern Malawi (NS 1/4/1;[7] 8.11.5R 14155[8]). Equally important was the fact that the everyday activities of borderland villagers often spread indiscriminately across both territories. In many cases along the frontier south-east of Dedza town and in Ntcheu District, villagers had gardens in the Portuguese territory and houses in the British.

In Ntcheu District, from the 1930s onwards, the British administration paid the Portuguese administration taxes for the gardens cultivated by British subjects in the Portuguese territory (NCN 1/12/2). With the late 1940s, however, came a considerably tougher attitude on the part of the Portuguese. In tandem with their demarcation work, the Portuguese authorities delivered an ultimatum in October 1949 that the 1949–50 season was to be the last for such 'double citizenship' (NCD 2/1/6). Villagers were offered the choice of either abandoning their gardens in the Portuguese territory or moving there altogether. The seriousness of the ultimatum became apparent in 1950; the Portuguese *administrador* posted armed police along the Dedza frontier. The threat was that any British subject found hoeing in the Portuguese territory would be deported for eight years. As a result, several families became divided by the border. However, the frontier was guarded only in 1950. For the most part, the history of the frontier is that of an open divide, guarded most effectively by the allegiances and antagonisms of the Dedza–Angónia borderland villagers themselves.

The 'open divide' is not, in other words, merely a nuisance imposed by the colonial and postcolonial states. It is best understood as an aspect of reality actively manipulated by the villagers themselves. Both the assertion and the negation of the border contribute to ongoing arguments about valued relationships. Paramount Chief Gomani II demonstrated this eloquently in 1947 when he was becoming increasingly disturbed by the arbitrary demarcation work of the Portuguese dividing his territory. In a letter to the British government, instead of opposing the colonial boundary-making altogether, Gomani made clear on which side of the border his people lived:

> As for me, my chief is King George VI. Therefore all my country should belong to me under my king. You Europeans say the Portuguese claim ownership of this part, because they follow the straight

line between beacons ... I do not want any straight line boundaries, but I want the whole of my country. Please settle these matters speedily and hear the complaints of your people. (PCC 1/6/1[9])

Villagers in the Dedza–Angónia borderland can also explicitly negate the significance of the international border. Boundaries are not, therefore, any more fixed than the situations in which they are defined. Two qualifications, however, must be made at this juncture. First, the capacity to impose the consequences of boundaries on others indicates, of course, differences in power. Second, the internalisation of distinctions and boundaries imposed by, for example, the state does not mean that its agendas are commensurate with the local agendas. In the Dedza–Angónia borderland, this has become particularly clear during the rise of nationalism and during the war between Frelimo and Renamo.

Missions, labour migration and war

Three Christian churches dominate the religious scene in the Dedza–Angónia borderland: the Roman Catholic, Presbyterian and African Churches, by far the largest being the Catholic Church. In Malawi, Protestant missionaries from Scotland established strongholds in the south and the north in the late nineteenth century (see McCracken 1977), whereas the Dutch Reformed Church's mission from South Africa, the present-day Church of Central African Presbyterian (CCAP), concentrated on the Central Region. Although a large proportion of the population in Ntcheu District, including Paramount Chief Gomani II (Timpunza-Mvula 1987: 61), subsequently became Presbyterians, in the Dedza–Angónia borderland only one village has a Presbyterian congregation. The African Church, the largest independent church in the area, was founded, according to one account (see Chakanza 1980), in Ntcheu District in 1932. It has members scattered in several villages and is distinguished from the mainstream churches mainly by its tolerance of polygamy and beer-drinking.

Expelled from East Africa in 1759, Jesuit missionaries re-established their Mozambique mission during the 1880s in Angónia, among other areas (Newitt 1995: 434–5). For villagers in the Dedza–Angónia borderland, however, the missionary work on the Malawian side of the border has been more effective. In Mua, Kachindamoto's territory towards the south-west shore of Lake Malawi, the White Fathers established a mission in 1902 (Linden with Linden 1974), and, in 1905, constructed a sanatorium at Bembeke, some six kilometres from the present-day Dedza–Angónia border-land (Vezeau 1982: 1–4). In 1910, Bembeke became an independent mission, following the opening of the first mission school in 1907. The first baptisms there were performed in 1911. Earlier, the White Fathers had given gifts of salt to local village headmen, who, twenty-three in all, went to the District Commissioner in Dedza to demand the establishment of the mission in the area (Vezeau 1982: 10). The village of the headman who, apparently as a result of a row over salt, failed to join the others on this visit became the Presbyterian enclave in the borderland. Even though officially only the Catholics on the Malawian side of the border belong to the Bembeke parish, it has long been an unrivalled Catholic centre for villagers from both sides of the border. The Bembeke parish now boasts a cathedral with two resident priests, both Malawians, though not from the local villages.

The turn of the century witnessed a rapid increase in labour migration from the Dedza–Angónia borderland. Migration to Zimbabwe through clandestine routes had already begun by 1900, and an active recruitment campaign by the Witwatersrand Native Labour Association (WNLA) took place in Angónia in 1910 (Borges Coelho 1993: 106–8). The recruitment by WNLA, or *wenela* as it is still called in the borderland, temporarily came to a halt in the area in 1913, when the South African government decided to ban the recruitment of 'tropical' Africans in the northern districts of Mozambique (Newitt 1995: 494, 504–5). Clandestine migration continued, however, and in many cases northern Mozambicans and Malawians posed as southerners so as to be employed in South Africa (Newitt 1995: 506–7). A series of agreements between WNLA and the colonial authorities in Malawi in 1932–9 resumed the official recruitment in the area (Crush et al. 1991: 37). Southern Malawians were driven to labour migration by the hated *thangata* system of forced labour (see Kandawire 1979). In other areas, the initial push factor to migrate derived, in the main, from high taxes in both Malawi and Mozambique (Borges Coelho 1993: 111).

For the whole of the Dedza–Angónia borderland on both sides, Dedza became the major international centre for labour recruitment and for the processing and payment of remittances sent from South Africa. By 1938, the increasing burden was the subject of complaints by the Dedza District Commissioner (NCD 2/1/4). Indeed, virtually every Dedza–Angónia borderland man born before the 1960s has at some point worked in South Africa, Zimbabwe or Zambia. The census of Angónia in 1947, for example, assumed that 7,000 able-bodied men out of 12,962 had migrated clandestinely, while 2,703 men were working abroad under contracts (Borges Coelho 1993: 135).

Labour migration remained important in the Dedza–Angónia borderland until the 1970s. In 1952, for example, when major roadworks were finally commenced in Tete, only 19 per cent of Angónia's male labour force were present in the district, according to an official estimate (Borges Coelho 1993: 138). With independence in Malawi and Mozambique came changes in the recruitment of labour migrants. In 1965, the new government of Malawi prohibited direct recruitment by WNLA and sought to participate in transporting labourers to South Africa, without setting any limit to their numbers (Boeder 1974: 236). In 1974, after a plane crash in which several Malawians were killed, Malawi imposed an embargo on all recruitment (White 1987: 232; Mtukulo 1995; Chirwa 1996).[10] After 1975, the Frelimo government's uncompromising opposition to the apartheid state cut the flow of authorised migrants to a trickle (Newitt 1995: 498–9). As a result, whereas 227,000 Malawians and Mozambicans were working in the mines in late 1973, six years later only 56,000 were doing so (Crush et al. 1991: 101). In the late 1980s, the South African government itself imposed severe restrictions on foreign labour.

As has been seen, labour migration on such a huge scale was in part a result of taxation and the lack of industry and commercial agriculture in the area. The impact of labour migration – which for most men was spread over several years – on the political outlooks of Dedza–Angónia borderland villagers was also significant. Malawians and Mozambicans were active not only in independent and mainstream churches (Boeder 1974: 105–16); the South African mines were also sites for the emerging nationalist agitation (Newitt 1995: 521). Even though in 1939 the Dedza District Commissioner appeared to believe that 'the health and physique of the labourers is in most cases improved out of all knowledge' (NCD 2/1/4), the labour conditions were more likely appalling enough to fire the nationalist cause (see First 1983). While various 'Native Associations' and other pressure groups had already contributed to the rise of nationalism in Malawi (see van Velsen 1966), it was the establishment of the Nyasaland African Congress, later known as the Malawi Congress Party (MCP), in 1944 that gave nationalism its sharply political edge. Predictably, the growth of the MCP did not conform to the international boundaries. As the first nationalist mass movement on both sides of the border, the MCP circulated its message in the late 1950s and the early 1960s in both Malawi and Mozambique (Borges Coelho 1993: 170). The fact that men from different colonies worked together in the South African mines also helped to spread the nationalist cause.[11]

The Dedza–Angónia borderland was, however, saved from some Portuguese and Frelimo policies which fuelled discontent in many other parts of Mozambique. Such policies, largely avoided in Angónia, concerned forced resettlement. The Portuguese administration introduced a villagisation programme (*aldeamentos*); the dual objective of this was development and counter-insurgency (Henriksen 1983: 154–8). Frelimo, as discussed in the Introduction, established 'communal villages' (*aldeias communais*) in its own quest for development and 'socialism' (Isaacman and Isaacman 1983: 152–8).

Angónia was not only a relatively peripheral area in the colonial period but also considered to be 'naturally' villagised by its compact settlements and high population density (Borges Coelho 1993: 223). In the immediate pre-independence period, there were officially eighteen *aldeamentos* in Angónia, and more than 58 per cent of the total Tete population lived within the confines of *aldeamentos* (Borges Coelho 1993: 229–31, 1998: 67). In Angónia, no actual resettlement occurred after independence. Nor were the *aldeamentos* in the district transformed by Frelimo into *aldeias communais* (Borges Coelho 1993: 377, 1998: 67). In the early 1980s, there were only two *aldeias communais* in the whole of Angónia, with just over 2 per cent of the district's population living in them (Borges Coelho 1998: 66).

Frelimo's *Luta Armada*, the armed struggle for independence, had been a remote affair which merely a few men from the local villages joined. Where the independence struggle created displacement, the southern Malawian frontier, once again, was the more important scene for the influx of refugees (e.g. 19.3–3F 14966[12]). Although thousands of Mozambican refugees were estimated to be in the Central Region in 1971 (17/2 3/10/9R[13]), only the war between Frelimo and Renamo created widespread displacement in the Dedza–Angónia borderland from the mid-1980s onwards.

Menace, even violence and killings, preceded the flight of most Angónia villagers. Yet some villages were never completely deserted in the interior of Angónia. Renamo, after entering Tete Province in 1982, established a permanent base in Angónia in 1984 (Juergensen 1994). By 1986, only Villa Ulongwe and the sub-district capital of Domwe remained under government control, but Frelimo returned in force to Angónia in 1990. Towards the end of the war, Angónia was a patchwork of Renamo-controlled zones, a dangerous 'no-man's land' and a government-held area from Domwe to Villa Ulongwe (Bonga and Wilson 1993: 7). The bulk of the Angónia population did flee, and 220,000 refugees were expected to return from Malawi in 1993 (UNHCR 1993). Angónia had expelled to Malawi by far the largest contingent of displaced persons from the whole of Mozambique. Of the Mozambican refugees in Malawi, 20 per cent were estimated to be from Angónia (Cruz e Silva 1992: 8).[14]

Apart from occasional looting at night during the late 1980s, Renamo guerrillas respected the international border and never attacked refugees in Malawi. The Malawian government, on the other hand, did not obstruct the influx of refugees. In fact, the crisis, undoubtedly a serious concern for the Malawian government, was also an opportunity for President Kamuzu Banda's autocratic regime to attract favourable international attention (Callamard 1994b). The Malawian government tested the limits of that international interest in 1988, when it proposed that a portion of the frontier area in Angónia should be brought under Malawian administration and filled with repatriated Mozambicans (Finnegan 1992: 160–1). Although the Red Cross was to make a somewhat similar suggestion later (Wilson with Nunes 1994: 189), the proposals were ignored, and the international border remained intact.

The era of democracy and liberalisation

From the perspective of villagers in the Dedza–Angónia borderland, the new era first dawned in Malawi. In March 1992, a lenten letter written by Malawi's Catholic bishops was read in all Catholic churches in the country. Although political opposition existed in exile and clandestinely in Malawi, the outspoken letter was the first time for many years that the government was publicly criticised in Malawi. Its references to the 'climate of mistrust and fear' and to the 'growing gap between the rich and the poor' struck a chord among Dedza–Angónia borderland villagers, but few thought that President Banda or the ruling Malawi Congress Party had been wholly discredited (see Englund 1996a). It was the government's over-reaction against the bishops that inadvertently undermined its legitimacy. The bishops' arrests, and the insults, even threats to their lives, which some party zealots hurled against them were widely seen as assaults on the Catholic Church. Shocked by this insolence towards the church of God, most villagers around the Bembeke parish voted for multipartyism in the 1993 referendum on the system of government.

The referendum in June 1993 coincided with the return of refugees from Malawi to Mozambique. In fact, most refugees in the Dedza–Angónia borderland wanted to ensure that they had completed their repatriation before the referendum, because violence was widely expected to erupt. Refugees received the news of the Mozambican peace treaty with cautious optimism and began building their houses in Mozambique as soon as the rains eased, although many thought that they would build bigger and more permanent houses after some two years of peace in the country. The will to return was great, in any case, and most refugees from Dedza District had completed their repatriation before official programmes had even started. By the end of 1993, virtually all the refugees in the area covered by this study had returned, and the delivery of their relief aid in Malawi had stopped.

For the rest of the 1990s, despite apparently profound changes, Dedza–Angónia borderland villagers were spared political violence. A sense of marginalisation has come to replace the official attention which the area received during the refugee crisis. One source of marginalisation was the fact that both sides of the border came to be in the orbit of political opposition after the transition. In Malawi, the United Democratic Front, the new party which won both the 1994 and 1999 multiparty elections, did not establish a viable party organisation in rural Dedza. The election results showed a clear regional pattern of support (Kaspin 1995; van Donge 1995), and villagers in the southern part of Dedza District fell into the 'power base' of the Malawi Congress Party in the Central Region. The re-election to parliament of John Tembo, the Minister of State in the outgoing MCP government and Banda's close aide, both in 1994 and 1999 indicated more lack of challenge than popular trust.

In Mozambique, the links of border villagers to their parliamentary representative are even more tenuous. A Renamo candidate was elected from Angónia in the 1994 multiparty elections. Despite the considerable strides which Renamo made to establish itself as a political party (Manning 1998), most villagers on the Angónia frontier were unaware of their parliamentarian's name and personality. They insisted, in all seriousness, that the area had no representative in the Mozambican parliament.

The Epilogue returns to the Dedza–Angónia borderland in 1996–7 when the sense of marginalisation had begun to haunt villagers. Economic problems, experienced as lack of 'development' (*chitukuko*), preoccupied villagers more than the apparent benefits of political pluralism. The economic crisis has been particularly dramatic in Malawi, where the rate of inflation rose to 115.9 per cent in 1994 and has remained a problem ever since (Banda et al. 1998: 78). The removal of subsidies on agricultural inputs as a part of Structural Adjustment has made chemical fertiliser a commodity beyond the means of the villagers, and the prices of the villagers' own products have not kept up with the increasing cost of living.

In Mozambique, the success of the peace treaty has not failed to produce an impressive growth in the economy, but this has had little impact on the Angónia borderland. Villagers have continued to rely on markets and hospitals in Malawi. In the Epilogue, I describe the effects of this predicament on the villagers' relationships and on their ideas about Frelimo and the government.

MFUNO AND CHITIMA
Land and livelihoods

From the international slave trade to Catholicism, from the postcolonial war to multipartyism, many historical currents have flowed through the Dedza–Angónia borderland. The aim of this book is to show how personal relationships have mediated, and have themselves been shaped by, translocal historical forces. Although various 'absent' relationships will prove to be significant, this book is primarily a study of locals and refugees, all of whom lived at one point in the Malawian border village of Mfuno (see Map 2).[15] With the exception of those in Chapter 3, the Mozambicans in the case studies are from Chitima, the village immediately opposite Mfuno on the Mozambican side of the border. During fieldwork, the population of Chitima was around 3,000 persons, and that of Mfuno, excluding refugees, well above 1,000. Historically, too, Ngoni villages have been large and compact settlements (Barnes 1954: 11–12). This form of settlement ensured that the villagisation programmes of both the Portuguese and Frelimo never reached the area.

Until the early 1970s, male labour migration to South Africa, Zambia and present-day Zimbabwe had a profound impact on the local economy.

After that, the Dedza–Angónia borderland has been renowned for its supply of vegetables and potatoes, with tomatoes, in particular, being an important source of cash. Tomatoes and other vegetables are grown, mainly, in wet gardens known as *madimba* (sing. *dimba*), watered from nearby streams or wells and cultivated especially during the dry season. In contrast to a finding in southern Malawi in the early 1980s, *madimba* are not considered to be 'women's gardens' (Hirschmann and Vaughan 1983: 94). Instead, in households where both spouses are present, men tend to engage in the cultivation of tomatoes, whereas women concentrate more on the cultivation of maize, the staple crop. The extent to which this allocation of labour is reflected in the pooling of cash income within households varies greatly. An exclusively female source of cash is the brewing and sale of *masese* beer, made of maize and millet, and strong *kachasu* liquor (see Englund 1996b: 268–71).

Most of the maize, the staple crop, is cultivated in dryland gardens known as *minda* (sing. *munda*). Beans, pumpkins, pigeon peas, millet, potatoes and, on the fringes, cassava are also commonly planted in *minda* where the crops are dependent on rainfall. Both *minda* and *madimba* gardens are also cultivated in seasonal swamps (*madambo*, sing. *dambo*). Because the villages in the area are compact settlements, with populations requiring a considerable acreage of arable land, gardens lie at a distance of up to eight kilometres from dwellings.

According to my fieldwork in 1992–3, with invested capital, diligence and good luck, a farmer could sell tomatoes worth over 2,000 kwacha (US$460), but an annual tomato-based income of around 800 kwacha (US$184) was much more common.[16] Very rarely did the owner of the crop find the necessary transport and time to go to the market. Instead, middlemen from the major Malawian towns of Lilongwe and Blantyre often came personally to collect the produce from the villages. This represented a change from the pattern of trade before Mozambique's independence, when the traders and middlemen were usually Portuguese, and the major destinations were the markets in Villa Ulongwe and Tete, the district and provincial capitals, respectively.

The Frelimo–Renamo war severed such ties to markets and services in Mozambique, ties that had begun to erode on the eve of the country's independence. During the period of my fieldwork, the Mozambican currency, metical, was an object of some curiosity for Malawians and Mozambicans alike. All the monetary transactions were made in kwacha, except in Villa Ulongwe, where kwacha had to be changed into meticais. Even before the Frelimo–Renamo war, the district hospital in Dedza town had already come to be a major source of health services for both Malawians and Mozambicans. Formal education has remained the most obvious divide between the two countries. Primary schools have long been situated in, or near, Mfuno and Chitima villages on both sides of the border. These schools have taught different curricula in Malawi and Mozambique.

Since the end of labour migration, opportunities for employment outside the villages have been very limited. Some young men, mainly unmarried, work on the tobacco estates elsewhere in central Malawi or find employment in Malawian towns, but their annual income in 1992–3 was often as low as 600 kwacha (US$140). Villagers in the area do not grow such cash crops as coffee and tobacco. Low prices offered to producers by the Agricultural Development and Marketing Corporation (Admarc), moreover, effectively discouraged the adoption of maize as a cash crop during President Kamuzu Banda's regime. Because the bulk of the vegetable produce is also not sold to Admarc, the local agribusiness functions largely beyond the direct control of the Malawian and Mozambican governments. However, virtually every crop, with the exception of such undervalued crops as cassava, sweet potatoes and various green leaves, is thought to need chemical fertiliser and pesticides. In 1992–3, the villagers accused the Malawian government of making excessive profits by its offer of fertiliser on credit which provided for an interest rate of 18 per cent. As mentioned above, after the removal of subsidies on agricultural inputs in 1994, chemical fertiliser has become an ever more precious commodity, deepening villagers' discontent with political reforms in both countries.

Environmental conditions for agriculture, on the whole, are favourable. In scholarly opinion, this area has long been considered to be one of the most fertile in central Malawi and northern Mozambique (see Rimmington 1963: 40; Wilson et al. 1989: 178). The garden land is mainly rich red loam, although clay and sandy soils are also common in parts on the Malawian side of the border. The altitude in this highland area is around 1,600 metres, and the rains are often plentiful, at least 900 mm per season.[17] Even though most villagers perceive an acute need for fertilisers and pesticides, the agricultural potential on each side of the border is also widely thought to be disparate. Villagers attribute the perceived difference in fertility to the 'old soil' (*nthaka yakale*) in Malawi. Indeed, villagers usually cultivate the same gardens for several years in Malawi, whereas in Mozambique they permit their land to lie fallow more often.[18] In line with this scarcity of land, refugees' access to land on the Malawian side was often restricted to the opportunities that marriage and piece-work (*ganyu*) presented. Many Mozambicans from nearby villages continued to cultivate part of their land throughout displacement. Subsequent chapters of this book demonstrate how, rather than being the inevitable consequences of exile, disputes over land were contingent upon refugees' and their hosts' particular configurations of relationships.

Locals and refugees in Mfuno village

Displacement in the Dedza–Angónia borderland began around 1985, and Mfuno village endured its most intensive influx of refugees during 1986. There were three ways in which a refugee could find a place to build a house in Mfuno. First, some Chitima villagers, emigrants to Mozambique in the early 1950s, returned to their old sites in Mfuno. Second, some refugees used their prior links to the village to gain a fresh site. Third, the headman of Mfuno allocated places for newcomers lacking prior links. The headman had the duty – before the Malawi government had installed a Relief Clerk, an outsider to the area, in each refugee settlement – of seeing that the refugees reported their arrival in Malawi to the police in Dedza town.

The fortnightly deliveries of food aid, largely provided by the World Food Programme but distributed by the UNHCR and the Red Cross, became the most significant forms of external support for such 'self-settled' refugees. The fortnightly refugee food basket included maize flour (6,300 g per person), pulses (560 g), groundnuts (280 g), sugar (280 g) and salt (70 g). In addition, cooking oil and soap were given at longer intervals. However, although the distribution took place fairly regularly – generally every fortnight – there was a widespread belief among refugees that they were not receiving their due amounts of aid. They constantly suspected the distributors, themselves refugees and local villagers selected by the Relief Clerk, of stealing a portion of the aid. Some items, such as sugar, were for long periods not delivered at all. Women's needlework classes, which never made a significant contribution to income generation, a primary school which taught the Mozambican curriculum, a Health Officer employed by the Malawi government and occasional censuses were the other aspects of the official attention paid to Mfuno as a consequence of the refugee influx. One result was that 'refugees' (*malefuchi*) became a common concept in the villagers' own vocabulary.

In 1992, according to the Relief Clerk's calculations, nearly 3,000 persons were entitled to receive food aid in Mfuno. Not all of them actually lived in Mfuno, because some men had married into other Malawian villages. Chitima villagers settled, in the main, in three different villages along the Malawian side of the border: in Mtunda, Mfuno and a village in the neighbouring Ntcheu District. Those refugees, including Chitima villagers, who settled in Ntcheu District received their relief aid there, not in Mfuno. Roughly 20 per cent of the refugees in Mfuno were from elsewhere in Angónia, the most distant originating from about thirty kilometres away in the interior.

Mfuno's refugee population shared a number of characteristics, not merely among themselves but also with Mfuno's own villagers. Everyone spoke Chichewa and usually considered themselves to be Ngoni. An over-whelming majority of locals and refugees were Roman Catholics, the second

Table 1.1 Investment in livestock among local and refugee households in Mfuno village, 1992

	Locals % (N)		Refugees % (N)	
No livestock	39	(67)	39	(68)
Less than K120 invested	29	(51)	43	(75)
K120–400 invested	23	(39)	14	(25)
More than K400 invested	9	(16)	4	(8)
Total	100	(173)	100	(176)

significant congregation being, in both Mfuno and Chitima, the African Church, the independent church mentioned above. Chapter 5 of this book also describes the emergence of a small congregation of Jehovah's Witnesses.

The local and refugee populations of Mfuno were also remarkably similar in other respects. Both populations contained a large number of young people, the refugee population having a slightly larger proportion of under-five-year olds (22 per cent) than the local population (18 per cent).[19] The proportion of females was 51 per cent among the refugee population, and 53 per cent among the local population, both children and adults included. Table 1.1 uses investment in livestock as an indicator of relative affluence among the two populations.[20] The ownership of livestock is generally considered a safety net against crop losses and other hardships, because livestock can be eaten or sold for money. The income from formal employment and commercial farming, therefore, tends to be invested in livestock.

As Table 1.1 indicates, very small numbers of livestock were owned among both populations. Of the sample households, 68 per cent among the locals either had no livestock or had invested less than 120 kwacha (US$28); the figure for the refugees was 82 per cent. The livestock owned in this category included, for example, less than ten chickens, ducks, pigeons, rabbits or guinea pigs, or not more than two goats or pigs. By contrast, only the last category, the owners of livestock worth more than 400 kwacha (US$93), included cattle or, for example, more than seven goats or pigs.

The largest herd of cattle in the sample was eight head for a local household and five head for a refugee household. This contrasts sharply with villagers' reminiscences of the huge cattle herds kept during the colonial times. Before the Frelimo–Renamo war, the herds of cattle were still considerably larger than during the period of my fieldwork; the most affluent villagers are reputed to have possessed herds of some hundred head. Villagers attribute the collapse of herding unequivocally to Renamo's impact. The Renamo guerrillas, who looted herds on both sides of the border, reduced, in particular, the numbers of cattle, pigs and goats. The end of labour migration to South Africa and the collapse of commercial farming by the Portuguese made it impossible for the vast majority of

Table 1.2 Female-headed households and the investment in livestock among locals and refugees in Mfuno village, 1992

	Locals % (N)	Refugees % (N)
Female-headed households of all households	18 (31)	20 (35)
Female-headed households of all households with no livestock	27 (18)	37 (25)
Female-headed households of all female-headed households with no livestock	58 (18)	71 (25)

villagers to restock their herds of large animals. Table 1.2 shows that this predicament was not confined to female-headed households, although the majority of such households did not own livestock. The proportion of female-headed households among all sample households does not differ significantly between the local and refugee populations.[21]

As these figures suggest, in the diet of the Dedza–Angónia borderland villagers, meat is a very rare item, usually consumed on major ceremonial occasions only, such as funerals and weddings. Bush-rats (*mbewa*) are caught throughout the year, but borderland men organise hunting parties for larger game only during the dry season. Although Mozambique is considered to have more game than Malawi, the war prevented hunting in the interior for several years. Even after the end of the war, hunting has not contributed substantially to most villagers' diet. Large game – such as duikers (*huluku*), bushbuck (*ambawala*) and wild pigs (*anguluwe*) – are rare, and, after the more usual game – rabbits (*kalulu*) – have been shared between the hunters, the meat is seldom enough to last for more than one meal.

A slightly more common item in the diet is fish, obtained from fishermen in Lake Malawi and resold in the villages. During the scarcity months before the new harvest, many households subsist for several weeks on a diet of stiff maize porridge (*nsima*) and the relish of turnips or rape. Refugees' relief aid brought little variation – it provided only beans as relish. As a consequence, refugees often sought to sell or exchange beans for other relish (cf. Callamard 1994a). Although illegal in principle, the small-scale trade in relief items was seldom obstructed by the authorities. The more fortunate refugees, who harvested maize in Mozambique, also used the yellow relief flour (*deneka*) as a payment for piece-labour or as forage for domestic animals, preferring the flour made of their own maize.

Cognatic kinship

Kinship (*ubale*), the most common domain for Dedza–Angónia borderland villagers' valued relationships, extends to both maternal and paternal ties without distinction and, therefore, it is cognatic rather than unilineal in nature (Englund 1999; on cognatic kinship, see e.g. Fortes 1970: 49; Scheffler 1985; Strathern 1992). Throughout the life-cycle, every person carries a *mfunda* (or *chiwongo*), variously referred to as 'clan-name' (Mair 1951: 103) or 'descent-name' (Barnes 1959: 226) in earlier ethnography,[22] which derives from his or her father. The father is the man who is thought to have begotten the child, not necessarily the mother's current husband, who may be a different person and the one who supports the children.[23] This is significant, because the name recognises the person as a child of a particular man, even if the person's parents were not married. Hence the person is able, at least under favourable circumstances, to claim relationships in the potentially very wide social field which his or her agnatic links provide.

Residence, as a rule, is uxorilocal in the Dedza–Angónia borderland, and the management of the garden land is vested in women's brothers. Because it is men who move when they marry, women cultivate the bulk of the family land and commonly see their mothers and grandmothers as the sources of their land.

The mother's brother, known as the 'guardian' (*nkhoswe*), is nevertheless an important figure who, among other things, represents his sisters and their children in litigation. Among villagers in the Dedza–Angónia borderland, the patrilateral inheritance of land and property is also practised, especially among men. A wealthy man's land is often divided between his sisters' daughters and his own sons, and both women and men inherit *minda* and *madimba* gardens. Men's inheritance of property should not be read as direct evidence of collapsing matrilateral ties, with men exhibiting an increasing preference for supporting their own children rather than their sisters' children. This teleological view has long promised a victory for the male line over the female, and for the nuclear family over the extended family under 'modern' economic conditions (see e.g. Gough 1961; Douglas 1969; Poewe 1981). The imagery of collapse and doom belongs, however, to a discourse on 'total kinship systems', a form of holism thought to be obsolete in current anthropology (see Peters 1997a; Englund 1999). Recent evidence from Malawi, moreover, shows the continuing importance of various 'matrilineal' features (see Davison 1993; Peters 1997b).

When studying Dedza–Angónia borderland villagers' relationships – in war, exile and beyond – the challenge is to understand the value of multiple and ramifying ties, traced through different 'lines' and put into play in various contexts. For example, one consequence of uxorilocal residence, men's continued relations to their sisters' families and men's inheritance of land is that men, rather than women, can have multiple claims in various neighbourhoods and villages. Because most marriages remain uxorilocal in the area, a man's links to his father's village may have remained rudimentary. In the course of time, therefore, men can even inherit land in villages where they have previously had few personal ties. On the other hand, a man can marry in a village which is different from that of both his mother and father. In such a case, he may have a garden in one village, sisters and their children in another and his own children in a third. If his sons inherit his land, they will have an even wider range of claims. The case studies in this book show how such extended ties of kinship, rather than the attempts to scale them down, may be compatible with economic aspirations.

Both patrilateral and matrilateral ties are recognised in the patterns of succession and inheritance among Dedza–Angónia borderland villagers. The village headman, his councillors and the guardians of families are succeeded by relatives, whereas candidates are elected to the offices in the local church and party organisations. The different domains of authority vary, however, according to the patterns of succession. The village headman (*mfumu*) and his councillors (*nyakwawa*) are succeeded by their own sons, patrilateral brothers or brothers' sons, whereas the guardian (*nkhoswe*) of a family group is succeeded by a matrilateral brother, a sister's son or a sister's daughter's son.[24]

The patrilateral succession of headmen and councillors, for both previous ethnographers (see Mair 1951) and current village headmen in the Dedza–Angónia borderland, is the most reliable way to distinguish 'the Ngoni' from 'the Chewa'. The patrilateral principle appears to be rigorously applied, but it alone is rarely sufficient for the actual selection of the headman. Not only polygynous headmen create multiple lines for the choice of a successor; the deceased headman may have left brothers in addition to his own sons, all of whom may have sons who can also emerge as potential successors. Although the principle of seniority should be followed, the practice often shows little consistency in this regard. Only the bare limits of possible decisions are enshrined by the principles of succession. It is the active cultivation of ties, always within historical contingencies, that under-lies personal trajectories. The extended cases of the following chapters show the impact of nationalism, war, exile and repatriation on this dynamic.

2

THE PATHS TO WAR

Before Renamo guerrillas reached border villages in Angónia, Rafaelo, the deposed headman of Chitima village, paid a visit to their base. He made a simple request: the guerrillas should advance to Chitima to end the Frelimo rule. An obvious act of a disgruntled headman? Although Frelimo's early policies excluded important strata of rural communities, local studies of the war, as shown in the Introduction, advise wariness of quick conclusions. The local reach and significance of the postcolonial state interventions were by no means predetermined.

Accordingly, Rafaelo's act occurred at the interface of apparently separate histories. On the one hand, there is the economic and political history of the Dedza–Angónia borderland, which shows the encroachment of nationalism, Frelimo's state and Renamo's counter-revolution. On the other hand, there is the history of Chitima village, which chronicles the emergence of schisms and struggles for various positions of authority. When the analytical focus is on personal relationships, the two sets of histories can be shown to be entwined. In order to discern the processes that led to Rafaelo's act, this chapter presents an extended-case study of Chitima village, of the relationships which have shaped local politics from the early formation of the village to the promises and agonies of the postcolonial war.

The contribution of local studies has been to highlight complexity in the actual circumstances in which various subjects came to participate in, and to flee from, the war. It is complexity which necessarily demands historical nuances in analysis, an appreciation of the processes by which 'traditional' authorities, party officials, ethnic identities, differences in wealth and so on gained locally variable relevance before and during the war.

One analytical strategy is to look for determining factors in the social fabric in which the war came to be embedded. The role of kinship and affinity in Chitima village politics, for example, might be seen to lend itself to the conclusion that the local impact of the war must be explained in terms of a kinship system. Recurrent cleavages between kin-groups, not least the fact that the opposing causes of Frelimo and Renamo came to be personified by two full brothers, would seem to support this conclusion.

This, most emphatically, is not the analytical strategy in this book. The extended-case method, designed to disclose intricate processes in social life, would become redundant if the repetition of abstract structural principles was the fate of human societies. Oddly, Barnes, the first to highlight heterogeneity in the Ngoni 'snowball' state, appeared to forget the contribution of the extended-case method when he described Africa, in contrast to Melanesia, as an ethnographic region where the segmentation of 'determinate unilineal societies' (1962: 7) took an 'inexorable form' (1962: 9). For Barnes, the line of cleavage in a patrilineage could already be seen when two brothers '[were] still lying in their cradle' (1962: 9).

The early Ngoni migrations indicated, rather, a pattern whereby social capital emerged in clusters of relationships around competing protagonists. The emergence and trajectory of Chitima village, like those of earlier Ngoni polities, have been shaped by historical contingencies. The postcolonial conflict personified by two brothers was predicated on the emergence of Jeremiya, their father, as a leading figure in the village. The youngest son of his father's youngest wife, Jeremiya would not have advanced his standing in the village without the historical contingency of the colonial boundary-making. The analytical challenge, in contrast to both structural determinism and historical particularism, is to understand the historical conditions in which the patrimonial logic of social capital is feasible, and, on the contrary, those in which it ceases to organise social relationships. The postcolonial war, despite the paths that led villagers to participate in it, is a striking example of the latter condition.

FORMATIVE MOVES

Chitima village and its Malawian neighbour, Mfuno village, have somewhat different histories despite their geographical proximity to one another (see Map 2).[1] Mfuno was established on its current site around 1916, after the founding of Bembeke parish had reduced grazing-land for cattle on the village's previous site. Amfuno, the founder of the village, had moved widely with his followers during the early years of 1900, and the reputed number of his wives is stunning. As a consequence, many villages near Mfuno are said to contain his descendants, and a part of his group settled in the Linthipe area of Dedza District, some twenty-five kilometres from the present-day Mfuno village. As will be seen in subsequent case studies, some Mfuno and Chitima villagers still maintain active ties to this area.

Chitima village, on the other hand, only came into being in the early 1930s, when Achitima led his late father's three wives, their children and grandchildren and some affines away from Domwe mountain (see Figure 2.1). Achingano, Achitima's father, had been a headman's councillor in Njerwa village at Domwe, and the move took place after his death. Chitima elders' recollections convey that forced labour recruitment, possibly by the Sena Sugar Estates, had caused the group to flee from Domwe. The uterine brother and sister Mariki and Lustiko are recalled as having proceeded

Figure 2.1 Achingano's wives and children who migrated from Domwe

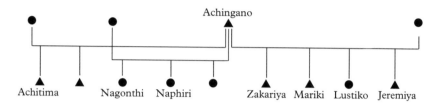

directly from Domwe to the present-day Ntcheu District of Malawi, because they wanted to escape from the Portuguese (*Apwitikizi*) once and for all. Of their children, only Lustiko's daughter Deliya returned to live in Chitima. She subsequently married her cross-cousin Rafaelo, the future headman.

Chitima village, despite emerging as one cluster, came to contain five divisions: Zakariya, Maphiri, Manguluwe, Machanza and Mtunda (see Map 3). The villagers in three of these – Zakariya, Maphiri and Manguluwe – had never resided in Malawi before the Frelimo–Renamo war, whereas the names of Mtunda and Machanza indicate historical links to two Malawian villages. Mtunda derives its name from Mtunda village; Machanza from a similarly named division in Mfuno village. These divisions came into being in Chitima when, following the Portuguese ordinance mentioned in the previous chapter, the British subjects cultivating in the Portuguese territory moved to that territory in 1950–1. To speak of Mtunda and Machanza as 'being from' (*kuchokera*) Malawi is considered divisive in Chitima village politics. Mtunda and Machanza are integral to the village, with represent- atives in all the main spheres of village politics: the headman's councillors, Frelimo and the Catholic Church.

If Achitima founded his village as one cluster, without recognised divisions, how then did the Zakariya, Maphiri and Manguluwe divisions come into existence? The question is critical, for its answer leads to an appreciation of nationalism and war in Chitima. After leaving Domwe, Achitima's cluster settled for almost ten years by the Mawe river, about fifteen kilometres from Domwe. They believed, Chitima elders recall, that they had reached the boundary between the Portuguese and British territories. Perhaps this belief proved to be erroneous, or some other reason drove the villagers to move to the present-day site of the Zakariya division in the early 1940s. Achitima died soon thereafter, and Zakariya performed the headman's duties for a number of years before a new headman was formally installed. Zakariya's authority was challenged most vigorously by the wayward habits of his younger brother, Jeremiya. The two men 'did not see each other well' (*sanaonane bwino*), Chitima elders recall. It is not clear how

Figure 2.2 Ferdinand and persons in Jeremiya's group

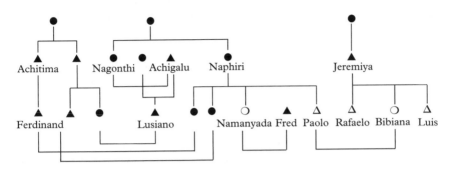

consciously the Chitima elders of that period attempted to safeguard the unity of the village, but they eventually selected Ferdinand – Achitima's son and Naphiri's daughter's husband – as the new headman. Zakariya remained, however, a prominent councillor.

Ferdinand's nomination followed an event which demonstrated Jeremiya's potential for dividing the village. Jeremiya left the original cluster and settled on a new site about a kilometre away. He was accompanied by two of his wives and their children, his sister Naphiri, who had recently been widowed, and two of her youngest children, Namanyada and Paolo (see Figure 2.2). Of the children in Jeremiya's group, only Namanyada was married at the time. Fred, her husband, was a Mfuno villager who had a senior wife in Mfuno. Soon after Jeremiya's group moved, the cross-cousins Paolo and Bibiana married. Naphiri's oldest daughters had married before Jeremiya moved, and they stayed with their families in the original cluster. Four of Jeremiya's six wives did not join him in the new cluster. They remained scattered in other villages in Malawi and Mozambique.

Jeremiya's decision to move did not break the village; nor did it lead to an immediate recognition of separate divisions within it. The different divisions came to be recognised as such only in the 1950s, and moves by other groups were necessary to enhance Jeremiya's cluster as the emergent centre of the village. Already during the 1940s, soon after Ferdinand's accession to the headmanship, Nagonthi also left the original cluster to live near Jeremiya and Naphiri. Nagonthi arrived with her children and her husband Achigalu. Achigalu's other wives and children soon followed, thereby underscoring the significance of affinity in the growth of Jeremiya's prominence. Given the fact that Achigalu later came to be seen as the founder of the Manguluwe division, his son Lusiano becoming its first councillor, affinity provided new opportunities also the other way around. Achigalu's marriage to Jeremiya's sister not only enabled him to leave the original cluster, it also made possible the eventual emergence of *his* cluster in Jeremiya's neighbourhood.

In 1950–1, several families crossed the international border to settle in Chitima in order to be able to continue cultivating in the Portuguese territory. They found a new site a few hundred metres away opposite their former dwellings in the British territory. Because there were no settlements opposite the original cluster, only Jeremiya's neighbourhood received immigrants. It was a unique stroke of luck in a setting in which authority was made visible by the number of one's dependants. Although the immigrants already had their gardens, Jeremiya is recalled to have acted as a virtual headman, showing them where to build houses and eventually hearing disputes which involved them. Already during this early period, therefore, crossing the international border was not an act of obedience to inherently meaningless rulings by foreign authorities. Such an act would have been devoid of a sense of territory on the part of Mfuno and Chitima villagers – a sense which was likely to be well developed in the tense village and colonial politics of the time. Whatever allegiance the newcomers might have continued to profess to their former village, both Chitima and Portuguese authorities made it clear that they had entered another village and, indeed, another country.

At the time of Ferdinand's premature death in 1953 or 1954, the numbers of the people outside the original cluster far exceeded its own numbers. Even more, Jeremiya's prominence had grown in tandem with the decreasing importance of the original cluster. He was a popular character, Chitima elders recall, and Zakariya's ill-health and the absence of Zakariya's sons because they were labour migrants did little to improve the status of the original cluster in the search for a new headman. In 1955, villagers asked Jeremiya to ascend to the headmanship. He declined, however, and insisted that the office should pass directly to his eldest son Rafaelo. The villagers accepted his decision. According to Rafaelo's interpretation, Jeremiya wanted the headman to remain, as Ferdinand had been, a 'child' (*mwana*) to him. Although Jeremiya remained a popular and venerable elder for the rest of his long life, he was soon overshadowed by a new generation. His fame was briefly reasserted after his death in 1985 when Rafaelo had a memorial erected on Jeremiya's grave in Chitima. As is discussed below, Rafaelo's act itself was extraordinary, best understood within the tumultuous political context of the mid-1980s.

The recognition of the five divisions in the village followed Rafaelo's accession to the headmanship, with each division nominating councillors for the headman. Every division (*chigawo*, pl. *zigawo*) can be considered a 'family' (*banja*, pl. *mabanja*), although this encompassing notion includes several families of a narrower scope, also spoken of as *mabanja*. Even the Maphiri division, which Jeremiya founded, and the Zakariya division are usually considered separate families, despite having been formed, in the main, by the children and grandchildren of Achingano.[2] Every division also has a corresponding unit in the Catholic Church organisation, known as *Limana*, a group which combines praying and religious teaching with assistance to its members in times of trouble (Englund 1996a: 123). In 1975, the village headman and his councillors were replaced in every division by Frelimo officials.

POLITICS BEFORE INDEPENDENCE

Of Jeremiya's children, only those whom his first wife had borne became prominent figures in Chitima village politics. The rest of his children either died before adulthood or remained in other Mozambican and Malawian villages. Three of the first wife's children survived to adulthood: Rafaelo, who was born in 1922; Bibiana, born in 1924; and Luis, born in 1927. They, together with Paolo, their cross-cousin and Bibiana's husband, born in 1923, were highly active elders during the Frelimo–Renamo war and its aftermath. All four were of unusual height, and the exceptional stature of Rafaelo and Luis, in particular, was matched by strong, deep voices. The charismatic four consolidated, before the war, the position of the Maphiri division in the village by assuming leadership in every major sphere of local politics: the headmanship, the Catholic Church and Frelimo.

Large numbers of children have been integral to their prominence. Bibiana gave birth to thirteen children, and in the early 1990s she and Paolo had eleven surviving children and forty surviving grandchildren. Many of their children are relatively well educated and have married in far-away districts in Mozambique and Malawi. An exception is their son Stefano, who married in the Machanza division of Chitima and became, especially after independence, Rafaelo's henchman.

Rafaelo's own sons are considerably younger than Stefano, because Deliya, Rafaelo's first wife and cross-cousin, gave birth to daughters only. According to Rafaelo, this was the reason why he decided to have two wives, the second wife being from Mfuno village but living in Chitima in a virilocal (*chitengwa*) pattern of residence. Two of her eldest sons had married by the early 1990s, both in Malawi, far from Chitima, and had little to do with the events at their father's home.

By contrast, Luis's eldest sons, whom Skolastika had borne, married in Chitima and Mfuno, and supported Frelimo. Skolastika, Luis's classificatory child (see Figure 2.3), is the first of Luis's five wives, of whom one had died and one had divorced him by the early 1980s. The second remaining wife is Nasoweka, who was born in Mfuno village but belongs to the Machanza division of Chitima. The third wife is Namadzi, Luis's classificatory grand-child and a member of the Zakariya division.

By the time Rafaelo became headman, Paolo had assumed important positions in the local Catholic Church organisation. During the 1960s, he became the 'shepherd' (*mbusa*) in Chitima, the highest Church official in

Figure 2.3 Key actors in Chitima politics

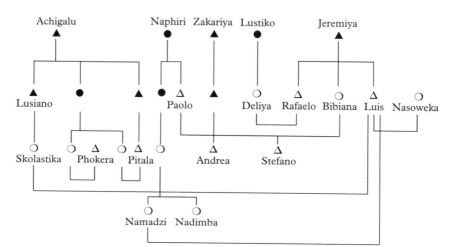

the village. He retained this position until the mid-1990s. Bibiana was long the leader of the Catholic women's group in Chitima, *Azimayi Achikatolika*. Like many other polygynous men, Rafaelo and Luis joined the African Church after having originally been Catholics. Of their wives, only Nasoweka also belongs to the African Church, the rest being Catholics. Rafaelo and Luis are active elders in the African Church, but, probably because of its smallness, neither has ever envisioned it as his principal sphere of public activity.

It was, instead, the nationalist cause that came to define Luis's field of political prominence. In 1958, in the immediate aftermath of Kamuzu Banda's return to Malawi, he was among the first activists in Dedza to organise a nationalist movement which later became the Malawi Congress Party. In 1964, he became active in the Mozambican nationalist campaigns. He started to organise clandestine Frelimo meetings, usually around Dedza town in Malawi. In a common pattern that was intended to defuse suspicions, the participants crossed the border at different places and in small groups. Luis appears to have been the unchallenged leader of the nationalist cause within Chitima village, but his agitation took place in close co-operation with other activists in nearby villages in the frontier area. Poorly educated in comparison with other activists, Luis never became a Frelimo leader outside Chitima village.

According to Luis, the years he spent as a labour migrant in South Africa introduced him to the nationalist cause. Luis, Rafaelo and Paolo began their careers as labour migrants in the South African mines in the 1940s, but only Luis continued to go there, with brief interludes at home, until the late

1950s. Together with Phokera, the husband of Skolastika's cross-cousin (see Figure 2.3 above), he embarked on nationalist politics before anyone else in Chitima. Phokera was originally from Mtengo Wa Mbalame, an area currently in Angónia's neighbouring Tsangano District, and he came to marry Skolastika's cross-cousin in the same year as Skolastika and Luis married. During the nationalist campaign, Luis and Phokera were frequently detained. In the late 1960s, this forced Phokera to leave Mozambique and to move with his family to the Linthipe area in Dedza District, some twenty-five kilometres from Chitima. Although Phokera eventually gave up his involvement in Mozambican politics, he and Luis remained close friends. During Renamo's war, for example, Luis took his cattle to safety at Phokera's household in Malawi.

Luis, enduring much hardship before independence, did not seek asylum until Renamo's arrival. His harrowing experiences were unique in Chitima, although he did not join Frelimo's armed struggle as a few men in Chitima, probably less than ten, did later. Instead, Luis spent long periods in detention in the district capital Villa Ulongwe, the provincial capital Tete and the national capital Maputo. In Maputo alone, he was detained for three years. Decades later, he recounted keenly his memories of Villa Ulongwe and Tete as 'bad places' (koipa), because there the Portuguese authorities were particularly likely to beat and torture the nationalists. Maputo, on the other hand, was 'good' (kwabwino), because there the Portuguese were more inclined merely to question the nationalists.

Luis's oratory aroused widespread excitement, Chitima villagers recall. From the outset, it appeared to compete with Rafaelo's authority. Rafaelo is recalled to have been the Chitima villager who never showed enthusiasm for the nationalist cause. Many villagers remember that Rafaelo gave the Portuguese authorities in Villa Ulongwe the names of some nationalist activists in the area, and many were questioned, or even detained, as a result of information he supplied. The Portuguese authorities also gave him a gun, but he is not recalled as having made use of it.

In many Frelimo activists' reminiscences, however, Rafaelo is closely associated with experiences of torture. He is said to have 'sold' (anagulitsa) villagers to the colonial authorities for the sake of his own position and enrichment. Once the police had taken nationalists to Villa Ulongwe or Tete, they were asked to present each of their hands in turn, and both hands were beaten with a palmatória. A notorious instrument of Portuguese colonialism, palmatória was a paddle with holes which were designed to raise weals. Among detainees, a routine soon developed in which those who had arrived earlier prepared hot water to nurse the newcomers' weals. Immediately after Mozambique had been declared independent, a group of Frelimo activists in Chitima broke into Rafaelo's house at night and took him and Deliya to the nearest border post. After levelling accusations of torture and murder against Rafaelo and Deliya, they asked the customs officials to despatch them to the police. Only three days later, the couple returned to the village. Rafaelo was cleared of all charges, but he was deposed.

Despite the violence that accompanied Rafaelo's position before independence, two points are particularly salient in understanding his action. First, he was not a mere marionette installed by the Portuguese administration to collect taxes and harass nationalists as is said to have been the case for the so-called *régulos* in other areas (see e.g. Isaacman 1985; Newitt 1995: 387). As described above, Rafaelo's installation was the culmination of several processes in Chitima village and beyond, processes which, despite Jeremiya's decisions and colonial interventions, were not orchestrated by any one subject. Second, and in line with the first point, it appears that Rafaelo gave names to the Portuguese authorities selectively. Luis and his closest companions, such as Phokera, were frequently detained or questioned as a result of information Rafaelo supplied, whereas the names of several other villagers, who, according to their own testimony, were at first greatly intrigued with the nationalist cause, were never given by Rafaelo. These included Paolo, Lusiano and Pitala, all of whom are hailed by Luis as Frelimo veterans, while they have also remained Rafaelo's close companions and supporters. Another interesting case is Zakariya's grandson Andrea, who was Rafaelo's councillor for the Zakariya division, the highest village authority in Rafaelo's Maphiri division's historical rival. He engaged in nationalist politics and was apparently detained at least once on information Rafaelo supplied.[3]

Rafaelo's collaboration with the Portuguese administration, therefore, was a means by which he managed his own authority in Chitima. Because Rafaelo's authority did not *derive* from the colonial administration, his agenda in harassing the nationalists was not identical to the agenda of the administration. His agenda took shape, in effect, within the constraints of his authority in Chitima. The paths of the village from revolution to counter-revolution should not be seen as struggles between two great men, Rafaelo and Luis, in isolation from the social fabric in which those struggles were embedded. Their authority was subject to the vacillation of other villagers between the causes they personified. The patrimonial logic of social capital had a dynamic of its own, a dynamic in which processes at once internal and external to the village generated schisms, aspirations and allegiances.

LIVING WITH THE PORTUGUESE

When Luis began his nationalist campaigning, Chitima villagers had already lived for some years with Portuguese farmers and shop-owners in their vicinity. From the 1950s onwards, there was a steady distribution of Portuguese shops on the Mozambican side of the border along the main Malawian highway in Dedza and Ntcheu Districts. A brief discussion of the local position of the Portuguese entrepreneurs highlights the complex sources of patronage before independence, and, moreover, provides an understanding of the ways in which Luis and other activists expressed the nationalist cause. In a marked contrast to their views of the Portuguese colonial administration, most adults in Chitima village insist that these Portuguese entrepreneurs were more beneficial to local welfare than anything that came after them.

Many Portuguese shop-owners cultivated vegetables, potatoes and maize for markets in Tete town and Malawi. Although the land on which the Portuguese established their farms had been alienated by the colonial administration, in the villagers' view the gardens of the Portuguese remained within the territory of specific villages, even if they often cut across the land of several families. Both Mozambicans and Malawians were employed on the farms, which provided agricultural work for men throughout the year, while women were usually employed only during the harvesting season. The Portuguese also purchased the villagers' own produce. Through this trade, they are recalled to have initiated the current importance of the wet garden (*dimba*) cultivation as a source of income. Moreover, from clothes to spices, including the kinds of beer and spirits which men had tasted in South Africa, the Portuguese shops had goods which villagers have not been able to find locally, let alone to buy, ever since the Portuguese left the area.

In the villagers' recollections, the period is often represented as one of mutual assistance and exchange. A Portuguese shop-owner and farmer, known as Leonardo but addressed as *o senhor*, lived in Chitima with his Portuguese wife and child for almost two decades before independence. His wealth (*chuma*) is recalled with awe; he is said to have had three kraals of cattle, some hundred head in each kraal. His 'love' (*chikondi*) towards the villagers, displayed in very mundane ways, is another common theme in these recollections. Those who worked on his farm had their own gardens prepared by his tractor and plough; wages were paid not only in money but also in clothes, soap, salt and so on. When a cow died before it had been sold, Leonardo donated it as a contribution to a village feast. When a prominent villager died, he donated a coffin; and when people were ill, he took them in his car to a hospital. If a woman wanted to have her corn ground in Leonardo's grinding-mill, she would be given a bucket to draw water for Leonardo's family. After she had finished, she would find her flour ready waiting for her, without being asked to pay for it. Above all, Leonardo's presence is associated with the years of plenty. 'There was never hunger' (*kunalibe njala*), many Chitima villagers recall.

Given this favourable, if now nostalgic, view of the local Portuguese, it is unlikely that Chitima villagers advocated nationalism from an unqualified anti-Portuguese standpoint. This is so despite the fact that they were familiar with the stories of the Portuguese methods of torture and punishment, and that some villagers, like Luis, had suffered personally from such maltreatment. The Portuguese entrepreneurs in the area were not inclined to get involved in colonial politics, or to show any difference in their attitudes towards the headman and the nationalists. The Portuguese entrepreneurs were competing among themselves for a clientele which would buy and sell through their own enterprises rather than through those of their rivals. Luis himself keenly recounts his favourable memories of the local Portuguese. It is clear that he, along with Rafaelo, was recognised as an influential villager by Leonardo. For instance, Luis received considerable support from Leonardo in the form of pesticides, fertiliser and even livestock.

Already before independence, Luis often arranged feasts (*phwando*) at which beer and food were provided. Some villagers tell a story of how he sometimes asked every household in the village to contribute money to help him to obtain beef for the feast. But he had received the meat that he distributed at the feast as a gift from Leonardo, who, upon hearing about the requests for money, reported the case to the police in Villa Ulongwe. For some villagers, this story was a means of expressing sarcasm about Luis's political career. They concluded the story by reflecting whether Luis's frequent detentions in Villa Ulongwe were less a consequence of his striving for an independent Mozambique than a punishment for his abuse of the gifts from the Portuguese![4]

Chitima villagers do not recall that the expulsion of the Portuguese was ever on the agenda of Luis or the other activists. The current system of taxation was the principal target of their anti-colonial agitation; even villagers, moreover, were promised positions in the 'government' (*boma*). For Chitima villagers, the closest model was Malawi, where villagers were seen to assume positions of authority in the nationalist party. The perception of the continued importance of Europeans and Asians in Malawi, particularly in commerce, also contributed to the villagers' belief that the Portuguese entrepreneurs were not going to vanish after independence.

In other words, Chitima villagers, including Luis himself, made a distinction between the Portuguese administrators and the entrepreneurs. This indicates the need for a similar subtle understanding to that in the above perspective on Rafaelo's harassment of nationalists. The Portuguese were integral to pre-independence politics in Chitima, but it appears that none of its actors perceived them as an undifferentiated mass. For Luis, the Portuguese administrators in Villa Ulongwe and elsewhere were the targets of anti-colonial agitation. Rafaelo, in turn, used their powers of enforcement selectively in managing his authority. For both Luis and Rafaelo, the special patronage they received from Leonardo and other entrepreneurs was a further confirmation of their prominence in Chitima. The Portuguese, in brief, were part and parcel of the political constellations of Chitima, but their presence and activities could not determine the specific form that the villagers' relationships took. As such, the processes which this chapter has begun to unravel also accounted for villagers' participation in the Frelimo–Renamo war.

DISCONTENTS OF INDEPENDENCE

When Frelimo achieved its revolution, however unexpectedly (see Introduction), and Mozambique became independent, Luis became the Frelimo *secretário* in Chitima. He was locally known as a 'chairman' (*mcheriman*), a term which was, and is, also widely used for party officials in Malawi. Luis was the highest Frelimo official in Chitima village, but he had his superiors at both the area and district levels. Although in the local Frelimo hierarchy the area and district organisations encompassed Chitima as a political unit, Chitima villagers had considerable autonomy in selecting their party officials in the village.

Within Chitima, every division has had several party officials since independence, also known as 'chairmen'. In line with Frelimo's policies (cf. Hanlon 1984: 147–69; Kruks and Wisner 1984), every division has had at least one female *mcheriman*. Since the early 1980s, three persons have commonly been considered as the most prominent party leaders after Luis: Nadimba, Alfredo and Sadlek. Nadimba, the sister of Luis's junior wife, oversees the Zakariya division; Alfredo, the son of Luis's second wife's mother's sister, has the highest office in both the Machanza and Manguluwe divisions by virtue of his mother's and father's origins; Sadlek, a Malawian who married in Chitima, oversees the Mtunda division. As is discussed further in Chapter 6, however, the number of 'chairmen' in the divisions is not fixed, because *mcheriman* is also a term for anyone who is thought to have been an active Frelimo member for a number of years.

After independence, in any case, the affairs of Chitima village were managed by Luis and a few other Frelimo officials whose duties and methods, in villagers' eyes, made little difference to the authority of the village headman and his councillors. As a matter of fact, most councillors simply continued to oversee their divisions as chairmen. The most dramatic transformation after independence awaited Rafaelo. He lost not only his gun, which was confiscated by the Frelimo government, but also his position as the headman. He was refused membership in Frelimo too, less because of Luis's opinion than because of the district officials' zeal for implementing the strictures against former headmen.

It is conceivable, of course, that Rafaelo would have refused party membership even if he had been offered it, although very few Chitima villagers actually did refuse membership. An exception was Stefano, Paolo's son, who may have been influenced by Rafaelo, his *malume* (mother's brother), and he became Rafaelo's closest companion after independence.

But Stefano had his own reasons for opposing Frelimo. It is said that Stefano had long suspected Luis of witchcraft against him. Stefano blamed this witchcraft for his failing at school and being considerably less educated than Paolo's other children.

Paolo and Bibiana themselves never assumed formal positions in the Frelimo organisation. Although Paolo did develop an early interest in Renamo, the Frelimo government's lukewarm attitude to religion, especially to the Catholic Church (see Vines 1991: 103–6), was not the reason for this interest. In Chitima, the churches were able to operate without hindrance throughout the post-independence period. After displacement, Paolo and Bibiana denied that they were members of any party. 'We have no party' (*tilibe chipani*) was an assertion which effectively distanced them from the ongoing tensions between Luis and Rafaelo. It also delineated the Catholic Church as the source of their prominence.

Seen from broader official and comparative viewpoints, the transition to independence in Chitima had many surprising characteristics. For example, Frelimo's official policy, during the late 1970s, was to expand the membership base of the party through numerous party cells in the countryside. Collaboration with the colonial regime and 'anti-social behaviour' (Isaacman and Isaacman 1983: 122), such as polygamy, were still thought to discredit persons as proper members of the party. In the light of this official policy, Chitima's party organisation had a definite localised flavour. At the time of independence, Luis had five wives, and most of his chairmen were former councillors of the village headman.

By its attempts to promote 'socialism', moreover, Frelimo sought to create a classless, united nation (Newitt 1995: 546–7). Although Luis and some other chairmen in Chitima were occasionally called to attend 'studies' (*maphunziro*) in Villa Ulongwe, it appears, as is described below, that only Renamo's derogatory remarks publicised the concept of 'communism' (*komunisimi*) among Chitima villagers, 'socialism' being an unknown concept to them. Above all, Frelimo, and thereby its image of a nation without divisions, never came to occupy the entire space of authority in Chitima.

Elsewhere in certain newly independent African states, the literature suggests that party cells and offices were taken over by educated 'new men', who apparently avoided being identified with particular kin-based factions but sometimes came into conflict with established village elders (see e.g. Kuper 1970: 168, 172; Moore 1978: 72). As was seen above, Luis acquired information about the nationalist cause when he was a labour migrant in South Africa. At the time of independence, however, he was hardly a 'new man' in Chitima politics, but a villager whose prominence as a nationalist was largely a concomitant of his management of relationships on the local political scene. In brief, he was as little a party stalwart as Rafaelo was a puppet of the Portuguese administration.

It would be misleading to suggest that the transition to independence entailed no shift in terms of the local discourse on politics. Clearly, 'the government' (*boma*) and 'the party' (*chipani*), understood as virtual synonyms, came to be viewed as important loci of authority. This added another localised flavour to the official rhetoric. The corporate nature suggested, for example, by Frelimo's Portuguese slogan *povo* (the common people) and the Chichewa slogan *ife tonse – boma* (all of us – the government) of the Malawi Congress Party did not concur with villagers' perceptions of party offices. A close identification with *boma* and *chipani* implied superior authority and access to the measures of enforcement.

During heated arguments at beer parties, for example, it was not uncommon for a villager to produce his or her Frelimo membership card and announce 'I am the government' (*boma ndine*) in order to press home his or her argument.[5] In a similar vein, after the return from exile in Malawi, Luis launched a rumour of his imminent transfer to join the government 'in Maputo' (*ku Maputo*). This countered the challenge other chairmen in Chitima were beginning to pose to him. His identification with Maputo, the ultimate source and symbol of the government, underlined the uniqueness of his position in the party.

Boma and *chipani*, if important, did not exhaust Chitima villagers' discourse on politics after independence. Rafaelo's exclusion from the new framework, in particular, inadvertently maintained a significant contrast to Luis's prominence. Even though Luis, who also took over the leadership of the headman's court (*bwalo*), did not grant Rafaelo any formal status in judging the court cases, he could not obliterate Rafaelo's seniority and relative affluence. Rafaelo ceased to work in South Africa earlier than Luis, but his savings, Jeremiya's command of vast areas of land and Leonardo's patronage gave him resources to engage in his own patronage and extensive feasts. Chitima villagers recall that Luis's and Rafaelo's feasts began 'to compete' (*kupikisana*) in their lavishness, but Luis's feasts soon became more extravagant than any others in Chitima. The whole village was expected to attend, and every household was asked to contribute beer, maize flour and other food.

During such feasts, on a table, standing in a central place, was a plate into which all villagers were expected to put some coins to 'help' (*kuthandiza*) and to show 'respect' (*ulemu*) towards the 'party' (*chipani*) and the 'government' (*boma*). Luis's ruling that such gestures of 'help' and 'respect' were allowed only during his feasts ensured that the party and the government became personified, above all, by Luis himself. He used much of this money for his own patronage. In particular, the performance of piece-work (*ganyu*) in his gardens was a well-paid and popular option for many villagers. Luis himself merely worked on his tomatoes in *madimba* gardens after independence, and often all the other farming was performed by *ganyu* labour in his gardens, while his wives cultivated their gardens, with occasional *ganyu* labour paid by Luis. As a leader, Luis appears to have enjoyed a fair measure of popular support. His management of the court, for example, has not led to negative recollections, and most villagers maintain that Frelimo never really troubled them.

Nevertheless, Frelimo's early rulings *are* recalled with bewilderment by most adult villagers. It is unlikely that Chitima villagers, including Luis, embarked on nationalist campaigning with a desire to depose the headman of their village. The model was Malawi, where nothing suggested that village headmen were incompatible with the independent state. An even greater source of bewilderment, and indeed discontent, was the flight of the Portuguese immediately after independence. Even if the issue in Frelimo's nationalism was 'oppression and not race' (Isaacman 1976: 298), and the exodus of white settlers followed rumours rather than a deliberate policy (Munslow 1983: 162), Chitima villagers insist that Frelimo 'drove away' (*anathawitsa*) the Portuguese. For a few years after independence, the Portuguese entrepreneurs came to be replaced by outsiders, in the villagers' idiom, 'from Maputo' (*a ku Maputo*). No stories about their 'love' and patronage circulate in the Dedza–Angónia borderland. On the contrary, it is recalled that the grinding-mill was not serviced, and eventually broke down; the shop began to suffer from an acute shortage of goods. As will be seen in Chapter 6, the return of the Portuguese was one of the first reforms which Luis and other Frelimo chairmen demanded from the government after the war.

INVITING RENAMO

A significant contrast in Chitima village politics was maintained by Rafaelo's exclusion from the relationships which constituted *boma*. In the history of Chitima village, the difference that such a contrast generates has consistently accounted for the logic by which political prominence has been achieved. Jeremiya's rise in prominence, for example, was predicated on his detachment from the original cluster. Achigalu, in turn, founded another village division by detaching his set of relationships from Jeremiya's neighbourhood. In a similar vein, after independence, the domain of *boma* has failed to occupy the entire political space in Chitima. Rafaelo has been the principal personification of this residual, yet significant, political space.

It was within this framework of existing constellations that Renamo came to be perceived by Chitima villagers. Their interests in Renamo, however, were divergent. For those who appear in this case study, Renamo, at least initially, was integral to the management and expansion of the village's residual political space. For others, with few prospects or aspirations in Chitima village politics, Renamo appeared precisely as a means to free themselves from the confines of the village. This category consisted, above all, of young men, married and unmarried, who, in Finnegan's words, 'were probably looking for a career behind a hoe, a life of tedium and deprivation' (1992: 71), had not Renamo guerrillas showed them avenues to wealth and authority. Still, the divergent interests in Renamo were not unchanging or endlessly incompatible. This becomes clear from the testimony of those who first joined Renamo, then discovered it could not fulfil its promises and, putting their lives at great risk, escaped to their families in exile.

Although many accounts of life with Renamo begin with the claim that the person was captured, other villagers' recollections of the same events often disclose that there was more co-operation. The problem is the same in all reports which emphasise coercion as the principal, if not the sole, method of recruitment to Renamo – they often fail to discern variation in locals' interests according to the phase of the war (see e.g. Minter 1989: 3–5). Moreover, because such reports are usually based on the testimony of those who have escaped from Renamo, they may convey the views of persons who would rather forget their early interest in Renamo. Long-term fieldwork, making possible the gradual emergence of opposing recollections of the same events, produces a more complex picture of the war.

It is clear that recruits had to follow a long and arduous path before they were granted the status of 'real' guerrillas, given a chance to carry guns and to participate in operations. The recruits from the Dedza–Angónia border-land were usually ordered to act as porters, and those who escaped stressed that they would have died of sheer hunger if they had stayed with the guerrillas. Even though the gun-wielding guerrillas and their commanders ate well – meat at virtually every meal – porters were given negligible portions of *nsima* porridge only once per day, usually late at night, after a day of extensive walking with heavy loads. Renamo guerrillas' fascination with whatever loot, even waste, they could bring with them from their assaults is a recurrent theme in villagers' accounts, as is their strategy of criss-crossing the terrain on foot for several hours every day in order to confuse possible pursuers. Villagers' accounts also attribute the Ndau identity to many guerrillas, with *Chifanikalo*, a creole spoken in South African mines, as the principal language between them and local recruits.

The collaborators who remained in Chitima village consisted, according to a popular view, of a few men led by Rafaelo. In this view, Rafaelo 'invited' (*anaitana*) Renamo to Chitima village and was supported by Paolo, Stefano, Andrea, Lusiano and Pitala. Although most of them withdrew from collab-oration very soon after the arrival of Renamo, their plot in late 1985 was still recalled during fieldwork as the ultimate cause of the war reaching Chitima. According to many villagers, Renamo guerrillas were completely unaware of Chitima before Rafaelo's invitation. They had displayed, popular recollec-tions assert, much reluctance to proceed to the Dedza–Angónia borderland, viewing it as part of Malawi.

Rafaelo visited a Renamo base before its guerrillas had reached the frontier in Angónia. Before he went to see them, he sold a cow and persuaded the aforementioned collaborators to contribute money. For the first visit, he had acquired 400 kwacha, and, when handing them over to Renamo, he had allegedly asked them to come to Chitima, saying 'people are behind the *Machanga*' (*anthu ali pambuyo pa Machanga*). He was apparently told to collect more money to prove that his people really supported the *Machanga*. The next time he went, he had with him, after further persuasion and personal investment, 500 kwacha.

There is widespread consensus among Chitima villagers that Rafaelo 'invited' the *Machanga* because 'he wanted a territory' (*anafuna dziko*), a village of his own. During my fieldwork, Rafaelo would neither confirm nor deny that his visits had taken place. Some of his supporters, however, openly regretted that they had contributed money to his plot. Paolo, Lusiano and Pitala in particular became vociferous critics of Renamo, whereas Andrea and Stefano continued their collaboration even after Renamo's menace and arrogance had become evident. As mentioned before, Andrea had been Rafaelo's councillor for the Zakariya division before independence; he then became an active Frelimo member and was overshadowed by Nadimba, the most popular Frelimo official in Zakariya. Stefano, in turn, was never active in the party, apparently because of his long-standing resentment against Luis, mentioned above. Yet because Renamo was, at first, understood to be another 'party' (*chipani*), its appeal initially went beyond these collaborators. Many Chitima villagers admit that they were intrigued by the newcomers. To their horror, they soon discovered that the guerrillas' approach to the villagers was more unreasonable than anyone else's within living memory had been.

THE PHASES OF THE WAR

Before their flight in mid-1986, Chitima villagers had been subject for several months to extensive extraction of food and money by the *Machanga*. Many had also left their houses for the night in order to sleep on the border, thereby being able to flee if the *Machanga* attacked the village during the night. It had taken some time, however, before the *Machanga* guerrillas had started to visit the village openly. Elderly villagers recall that the presence of the *Machanga* was first felt when Rafaelo invited elders, with the exception of some Frelimo chairmen, to attend meetings in the bush. There the *Machanga* were supposed to give information on the situation. In retrospect, these meetings seemed to the elders to have been a mere prelude to the more extensive extraction of tribute. Before the meetings, Rafaelo announced what was expected to be given during the meeting; for example, five flat baskets (*malichero*) of roasted chicken, and these had to be prepared by those who were going to attend the meeting. In the bush, people were asked to sit on the ground before a few chairs on which the guerrillas were subsequently seated. When the guerrillas appeared, everyone had to clap their hands to show respect – an awkward routine, for the mere sight of the guerrillas' guns made villagers tremble.

A sign of horrors to come, the guerrillas never showed their faces but always kept them hidden behind pieces of cloth. In a particularly 'strange' (wodabwitsa) and 'frightening' (wochititsa mantha) meeting, the face of one guerrilla was revealed. Not uttering a word, his beard and hair wild and long uncut, the sight was disgusting and terrible. Worse still, people had to pay this guerrilla because they had seen his face. The revelation of the face hardly dispelled the anxieties that the earlier concealment had created. For some villagers, this face became a symbol for all the Machanga. Its savagery anticipated 'animality' (chilombo) in subsequent encounters between villagers and the Machanga.

During the first meetings, the guerrillas insisted that the Frelimo government was no longer in office and that people should give up their positions in the party. It was never explained what had come to replace Frelimo and what the situation was elsewhere in the country. Few villagers took seriously the claim that the Frelimo government had vanished. Luis and other chairmen continued to conduct Frelimo meetings, and a school was in operation on the Mozambican side of the border until the flight. In any case, it was during the early meetings that Chitima villagers were told, for the first time, that Frelimo represented 'communism' (komunisimi). It appears that Chitima villagers were never taught what the term 'communism' actually meant. It is rage, rather than conceptual niceties, that emerges most vividly from villagers' accounts. They describe the guerrillas' rage at Frelimo, at the low turnout of people, in their questions about the rest of the villagers. Unhappy with the villagers' replies, the guerrillas sometimes shot in the air, threatening that the whole village would be burnt, if more people did not turn out in future.

These 'meetings' (misonkhano) were soon abandoned, and the relations between the Machanga and Chitima village assumed a straightforward pattern of the former extracting tribute from villagers. This, in turn, can be divided into two phases according to Rafaelo's role and the extent of the violence. At first, Rafaelo assumed the responsibility for announcing what the Machanga needed, and the tribute was brought to his house. There the Machanga would collect it during the night and eat the food with Rafaelo, or in the nearby bush, or even in a graveyard. Like many other Malawians and Mozambicans, Dedza–Angónia borderland villagers commonly think that only witches visit graveyards outside burial ceremonies. The fact that the Machanga had a meal in a graveyard was, therefore, a further proof of their evil nature.

For many villagers, it was clear that Rafaelo also 'ate well' (anadyera *bwino*) at that time. Sometimes when meat had not been provided, Rafaelo escorted the guerrillas to a villager who he knew had cattle. The villager was then forced to give a cow to the guerrillas. Some villagers remember with particular contempt Rafaelo's ruling that every household in the village was expected to give ten kwacha, because 'the *Machanga* needed clothes' (*Machanga akufuna zovala*). Some villagers had sold maize in order to find the money. For the first time in years, Rafaelo was also heard to refer to Chitima villagers as 'my people' (*anthu anga*).

If Rafaelo did receive any benefits from the *Machanga*, it is doubtful that he ever redistributed them in the village – no one recalled any such patronage. However, the guerrillas' extraction of tribute through Rafaelo lasted hardly longer than a couple of months, because the guerrillas soon adopted a more direct, and more violent, method. This, in turn, introduced the widespread view of the *Machanga* as 'thieves' (*okuba*) and 'wild animals' (*zilombo*).[6] The guerrillas would come to the village at any time, or take people by surprise in their gardens. Whatever the guerrillas wanted had to be surrendered, and if people tried to hide in their houses, the guerrillas would shoot the door open. This was also the phase when villagers' recruitment to the *Machanga* began to show definite signs of coercion. Although several persons were beaten or captured, and some women even raped, there were no killings or mutilations in Chitima.

Chitima villagers had hoped that 'the *Machanga* war' (*nkhondo ya Machanga*) was merely a passing ordeal and had preferred to sleep on the border rather than flee to Malawi. By mid-1986, however, the intensity of the raids had become so severe that people did start to flee. By that time, the Malawian villages along the border had also begun to receive refugees from elsewhere in Angónia, people who told stories of unparalleled atrocities.

Before the flight, an attempt had been made to resettle villagers. Rafaelo, acting on orders from the *Machanga*, demanded that the most distant divisions of the village, Mtunda and Zakariya, leave their sites and resettle near his own Maphiri division. The resentment in those divisions was great, and Luis announced that Rafaelo's order was invalid and that no one had to leave his or her house. The members of Mtunda and Zakariya consequently ignored Rafaelo's demand, and Luis's intervention in the matter was still widely cherished and praised during their displacement in Malawi.

Luis and his closest Frelimo officials were the early targets of harassment. As described in the Introduction, in a particularly humiliating incident, Luis and Alfredo were made to sit a whole day among Rafaelo's goats in their enclosure. On that day, the wives of Luis and Alfredo had not cooked *nsima* for them, because they had thought that the men were going to be killed. An unusually violent incident finally made Luis flee to Malawi. During this incident, along with many other villagers, including men and women, boys and girls, Luis was badly beaten by guerrillas using sticks and guns. The villagers were captured in their gardens, brought together, stripped naked or half-naked, beaten, robbed of their clothes and abandoned, bleeding and terrorised. Luis, like the other victims of this assault, decided to flee to Malawi, seeking asylum in Mfuno village. Soon afterwards, Luis announced as an order from Frelimo that the villagers still in Chitima were liable to pay a fine of 30 kwacha if they did not move to Malawi.

After the flight of several Chitima villagers, Rafaelo himself was captured at his house by the *Machanga*, taken to the bush and severely beaten. Asked to explain why so many of his villagers had fled, he was unable to provide a satisfactory answer and was told to call his people back. This he never attempted to do, but instead followed them himself into exile in Mfuno. Chitima was deserted. The vast majority of its population fled to Malawi, and only a few left with the *Machanga*. The guerrillas burnt the houses of the village and looted or destroyed the remaining property.

Soon after his flight, Rafaelo returned briefly to Chitima, with a few villagers, to supervise the erection of a memorial, made of cement, on his parents' graves. Both had died in 1985, Jeremiya first and his wife soon thereafter. Rafaelo had decided to place their graves on a site near Deliya's house where no one had been buried before. All the previous headmen of Chitima had been buried in the graveyard of the Zakariya division. Rafaelo's choice of the burial place, supported by many elders in the Maphiri division, was made when he was reasserting his authority with the aid of Renamo. After the humiliating flight, the building of the memorial, in turn, revised his image, which had been tarnished by his collaboration with Renamo.

Generally only headmen have memorials on their graves in Chitima, and Rafaelo himself believes that he will be buried on this new site. In effect, his decision opened a new headman's graveyard in Chitima, inscribing in the landscape the shift of the village centre from Zakariya to Maphiri. The point needs to be reiterated – it is crucial to understand the context in which he made the decision. Above all, he did not build a shrine to commemorate his father, Jeremiya, or to stay in communication with him. Rafaelo's was an extraordinary action of a prominent villager, a concomitant of his attempts to reassert himself as the headman in the tumultuous political context of the mid-1980s. His action anticipated his own burial, the burial of a headman.[7]

During fieldwork, Rafaelo openly insisted that the war had proved that 'people do not want communism' (*anthu safuna komunisimi*). When sober, he never showed a particular bias towards the *Machanga*, although his contempt for Frelimo was evident. Yet he commented on the political prospects of Mozambique only by saying 'we shall see' (*tidzaona*). On the eve of the return to Chitima, he said that he was pleased with the fact that the Frelimo government had now 'returned' (*anabweretsa*) his headmanship. In the gesture of a self-conscious headman, he was the first to start building a house in Chitima after the war, often appealing for the need, undoubtedly in a very wide sense, to 'repair' (*kukonza*) the village.

CONTINGENCIES, POWER RELATIONS AND SOCIAL CAPITAL

If seen in the light of their area's general characteristics, villagers' desire to participate in the postcolonial war was somewhat improbable. For instance, Chitima village avoided the unpopular villagisation programmes that created a constituency for Renamo in some areas. Yet Renamo did find willing collaborators among Chitima villagers. Even more, while villagers acknowledged the Ndau ethnic identity of many guerrillas, this did not reduce their willingness to collaborate. Nor were wealthy villagers deterred from assisting Renamo – wealth differences did not divide villagers neatly into Frelimo and Renamo supporters. The roots of Renamo's initial appeal defy such simple variables. They lie, instead, in the processes by which Chitima's political constellations have taken shape from the inception of the village to its postcolonial predicaments.

The relationships through which Chitima villagers engaged with, and disengaged from, nationalism and the war were the outcomes of several entwined processes. One example of the surprising consequences of those processes was Jeremiya's challenge to the original cluster in a setting in which seniority imparted, in principle, authority. Despite being the last-born son of Achingano's youngest wife, he achieved prominence worthy of the village headmanship. His move from the original cluster was a precondition for his prominence, and the move of Achigalu's families considerably enhanced his neighbourhood. Jeremiya's achievement followed from the active management of relationships *within* the contingencies that translocal historical forces brought to Chitima village. For example, he hardly anticipated the Portuguese ruling that forced several Malawian families to settle near him. This historical contingency, combined with his popularity, created the conditions under which he appeared more suitable to be the headman than anyone in the original cluster.

The Portuguese administration and entrepreneurs, and Frelimo and Renamo, were not simply 'external' to Dedza–Angónia borderland villagers' relationships, and were not enmeshed in the local battles over 'modernity' and 'tradition'. Transformations in Chitima's political constellations have been inseparable from transformations in national and international politics. Labour recruiters pushed Achitima's group to flee; the Portuguese ordinance enhanced Jeremiya's neighbourhood; Portuguese entrepreneurs gave Luis and Rafaelo resources to engage in their own patronage; and Renamo provided an opportunity to pursue agendas that opposed Frelimo's power.

A corollary is that such 'external' forces have become internal to villagers' own ways of describing and assessing their relationships. When a villager asserts, for instance, that he or she is the government (*boma*), a mere metaphor, or an allegiance to an external force, is not at issue. The 'chairmen' in Chitima *are* the government, their chairmanship is a consequence of prominence *within* Chitima village. Accordingly, collaboration with Renamo was an attempt not to overthrow an alien force but to manage relationships within the same field of political prominence. True, Rafaelo dismissed Frelimo as 'communism', but this view arose in tandem with the quality of his relationships to Luis and certain other chairmen. In other words, he made no distinction between Frelimo, and hence 'communism', and those villagers who personified it.

Nevertheless, some distinction between the 'external' and the 'internal' must be retained – otherwise Chitima villagers' aspirations would appear to be simple extensions of colonial, revolutionary and counter-revolutionary agendas. Perhaps the most dramatic consequence of the ultimate or, rather, transient incompatibility of agendas is the Chitima villagers' displacement. Renamo's violence was not anticipated by those villagers who supported it at first. Nor, on the other hand, were Frelimo's policy of deposing headmen, and the exodus of the Portuguese settlers, anticipated by the nationalists in Chitima. The distinction between the 'internal' and the 'external', as is discussed further in Chapter 7, best describes power relations, not a cleavage between the 'peasantry' and the external world. A critical question revolves around the extent to which external power relations have enabled villagers to disengage from internal power relations. An example, to be discussed later, is the close association between Rafaelo's position and the use of violence, in his collaboration first with the Portuguese colonial authorities and then with Renamo. Not unlike the contradictions which the international slave trade imposed on the early Ngoni migrations, collaboration with Renamo introduced, at least momentarily, another logic of power.

The conclusion of this chapter, to be elaborated with other case studies, thus demands that the patrimonial logic of social capital is viewed through specific power relations. The dynamic of those power relations also undermines any attempt to attribute some inherent and primordial cultural disposition to the patrimonial logic of social capital.

Rafaelo and Luis have consistently personified the authority associated with the headmanship and the chairmanship, and Renamo and Frelimo, in Chitima village. As such, they have been the main parameters of the villagers' political discourses. This does not mean, however, that the villagers' loyalties have been fixed. On the contrary, Rafaelo's and Luis's fields of prominence must be understood as processes precisely because Chitima politics has consisted of the villagers' dynamic vacillation between these parameters. The villagers have managed their specific sets of relationships through these parameters of authority. An example is Andrea, who, in the course of several years, has been a councillor, a chairman and a Renamo collaborator. Chapter 6 analyses the transformations that took place after the return to Mozambique. The positions of Rafaelo and Luis as the personifications of contrasting authorities appeared obsolete in the post-war context, and an identity emerged between the authorities of the headman and the chairman. As a consequence, some villagers gained prominence by distancing themselves from both Rafaelo and Luis, now regarded as one clique with shared interests.

3

REFUGEES FROM AFAR

Towards the end of the refugee crisis in Malawi, an expatriate official in the World Food Programme offered me a lunch in Lilongwe. From the outset, he made it clear that my views would make no difference to the decisions already made by his superiors from Rome. They had recently toured refugee settlements in Malawi and chosen the aid delivery centres which would be closed down by the end of 1993. My host told me that the centres in the area of my research were on the list. Changing the subject somewhat, he went on to explain his personal interest in 'culture', how he had become fascinated with the apparent harmony between Malawians and Mozambicans. I did not need further persuasion to begin expounding the benefits of a local study.

Even in a border village, I said, there are great variations in the extent to which locals and refugees regard themselves as 'Malawians' and 'Mozambicans', and conflicts are often expressed in those terms, if only situationally. Besides, I added, sensing my host's impatience with situational and processual analysis, there are refugees from afar in the border village of my study. 'How far?', my host wanted to know. 'About thirty kilometres from the border', I replied. 'That is not a significant distance', my host snapped, and began his own lecture on the formation of a common cultural heritage in Malawi and Mozambique over the aeons.

What is a significant spatial distance in the dynamic of social relationships? The fact of spatial dispersal plays a crucial role in the notion that refugees find themselves in the throes of social disruption. Sweeping generalisations about the 'refugee experience' come to replace descriptive accounts. An example of a descriptive statement is Elizabeth Colson's observation on the effects of spatial dispersal during the resettlement of Gwembe Tonga in Zambia. She noted that people's contact with those relatives who were torn from the fabric of everyday interaction tended to diminish (Colson 1971: 88). A far more problematic proposition is given by the commonplace observation that stresses that the *experience* of spatial dispersal is a universal predicament among refugees. The key metaphor is 'uprootedness' (see Malkki 1992, 1995a, for a critique). In this perspective, displacement and repatriation follow a 'home–out–home' sequence (cf. Sorensen 1997: 145), in which the 'normal' state finds persons 'rooted' in particular localities. Displacement, by contrast, represents the pathological condition of disintegrating selves and cultures.

One response to this imagery is to place refugees in 'the migrant culture of the "in-between"' (Bhabha 1994: 224; cf. Preis 1997: 97), so as to high-light the refugees' creative engagement with apparently disparate worlds. As my critique of 'border culture' has already suggested, however, the degree of a person's belonging to any location, or even to the 'in-between' condition, is best left open to investigation. Accordingly, spatially bound identities, from national identities to refugees belonging to their villages of origin, are to be studied from the processual viewpoint which, in the previous chapter, showed the dynamic of political participation in Chitima village. The aim of this chapter is to highlight variations in refugees' spatial belonging, no less than the constraints of those variations. The purpose, following Akhil Gupta, is 'to investigate processes of place-making, of how feelings of belonging to an imagined community bind identity to spatial location such that differences between communities and places are created' (1992: 62).

Such research questions have emerged in recent years to challenge the anthropological tradition of fieldwork in clearly demarcated localities (see e.g. Gupta and Ferguson 1997; Olwig and Hastrup 1997). For migrants and refugees, it is now argued, the electronic media, such as home videos (see Preis 1997), provide new opportunities to maintain multiple 'homes'. Even though the increase in the use of the electronic media in many parts of the world is beyond dispute, and hence constitutes a worthy subject for anthropological research, it is also important to realise how swiftly this new subject may introduce spurious assumptions into research. For one sociologist, at least, at issue is one of the defining ruptures of modernity. 'In pre-modern societies, space and place largely coincide', he contends (Giddens 1990: 18). We are told that it is 'the advent of modernity' (Giddens 1990: 18) that heralds their separation and the relations between absent others. To the extent that the disconnection between space and place is thought to define 'modernity', and is seen to be intensified by the use of the electronic media, earlier African anthropology may well give cause to rethink the paradigm. Turner (1957: 173), for example, suggested intriguing discrep-ancies in the spatial attachments among Ndembu and Tallensi. The former brought their 'ancestors' to new places, while the ancestor cult tied Tallensi to particular places. Ndembu, in other words, were less compelled than Tallensi to occupy the same settlements for long periods.

In a similar vein, though in a radically different historical setting, this chapter shows how the separation of space and place is intrinsic to the dynamic of social relationships and quite feasible, moreover, despite the scantiest input of modern technology. This chapter presents an extended-case study of refugees who were regarded, both by themselves and by their local hosts in the border village of Mfuno, as being 'from afar' (*kutali*). A 'significant distance' was an issue for refugees and locals themselves, but this chapter shows how the notions of spatial distance and belonging could change over time under the historical contingencies of war and exile. The effects of these contingencies on villagers' personal relationships were variable, if only because of pre-existing variations in the relationships which constituted them as persons.

The group of refugees were from Lumbe village in Angónia, some thirty kilometres from Mfuno towards Villa Ulongwe (see Map 4). Even though the refugees from Chitima village, as described in the previous chapter, had also tried to cope with the menace of the Renamo guerrillas for months before their flight, the experiences of violence were clearly more searing among Lumbe villagers. Lumbe fell into the hotly contested hinterland of Villa Ulongwe. In 1984–5, both Frelimo and Renamo appeared as aggressors, with Frelimo pursuing suspected collaborators and Renamo trying to win control over the area. Shadowy 'third parties', believed to be thugs from both Frelimo and Renamo, also harassed the villagers, especially at night. Unlike in Chitima, even killings occurred in Lumbe. Some refugees had witnessed their fellow villagers being burnt alive, trapped in their scorched houses. During their displacement, refugees would not always agree about who the perpetrators of such atrocities had been.

For most years of the war, Lumbe was under Renamo control, but, after Frelimo's counter-offensive in 1990, the village appeared to be in a 'no-man's land', with more sporadic Renamo presence. Despite all that turmoil, however, the village was never completely deserted. Some, mainly elderly villagers, remained there throughout the war, maintaining vague allegiance to Renamo. Although the flight of some villagers appeared to indicate lack of trust towards Renamo, others paid clandestine visits to Lumbe from refugee settlements in Malawi, as will be seen in this chapter. The focus of this chapter is on a group of refugees who either supported Frelimo or were indifferent towards both Frelimo and Renamo. Lumbe villagers' political allegiances, like those of the Chitima villagers, had taken shape over a long period of time, at the intersection of 'external' and 'internal' dynamics. Instead of tracing the emergence of those allegiances before the war, this chapter highlights the impact of displacement, from 1986 until 1993, on refugees' personal relationships. References to the pre-war period will be necessary, but only to shed additional light on the ways in which spatial dispersal and belonging assumed a highly variable significance among this group of refugees.

THE LUMBE EXILES

In March 1986, Mfuno village received, among its first refugees, fifteen adults and sixteen youths from Lumbe village. Lumbe was to become the most distant village which had refugees in Mfuno. Other refugees from

Lumbe, a majority of the total, settled in the Lizulu area, some fifteen kilometres to the south-east of Mfuno along the border (see Map 4). The large Lizulu market had long been an important destination for Lumbe villagers' produce, with a dust road connecting the two areas. Some refugees from Lumbe also found their way to Dedza township, or became 'internally displaced' in Villa Ulongwe. In Mfuno, the Lumbe exiles were one group, and through bonds of kinship and affinity, of 'the same family' (*banja limodzi*). They were led by Evelesita, a grandmother, who wanted to spend displacement near her son John, who had emigrated to Malawi in 1969. The group built their houses around John's near the border.

Although John was the immediate reason why Evelesita decided to seek exile in Mfuno rather than in Lizulu, she also had a brother, Adasauka, living in Mfuno. Adasauka, after working in present-day Zimbabwe, had married the daughter of Amfuno, the founder of Mfuno village, in the early 1950s. Adasauka, who at that time had no relatives or other Lumbe villagers in Mfuno, had been influenced in his decision to settle there by the Mfuno villagers he had met in Zimbabwe, one of whom acted as a go-between in his courting of his future wife. The marriage proved to be successful, not only in terms of the eight children who were born, but also because it created affinal relationships between Adasauka and the headman's family. In the 1970s, Adasauka became the chairman of the Catholic association *limana* in his village division. By the time of his sister's flight, he was one of the venerable 'elders' (*akuluakulu*) in Mfuno.

In 1986, John was the reason for Evelesita's group's decision to seek asylum in Mfuno; in 1969, John, a teenager, had followed Adasauka, his mother's brother (*malume*). John's intention had been to find employment in Malawi, but failing to do this, he had been encouraged by Adasauka to seek work in South Africa. After a period of hard work in the mines, complemented by an austere life-style, John came back as a successful returning migrant to marry in Mfuno in 1974. His wife was given two gardens by her mother, whereas John received one garden from his mother's father in Lumbe. John also set up a joint business venture with Adasauka; they opened a grocery store next to John's house. Several years later, after the arrival of Evelesita's group, the store was looted by thugs thought to be Renamo guerrillas, and it remained closed throughout the villagers' displacement.

John's garden in Lumbe ensured that he retained links to his village of origin during the many years before the war. He also built a small hut for himself in Lumbe where he slept when he came to work in his garden. Most of its maize was never taken to his wife's granary in Mfuno, ostensibly because of transport problems. Instead, that maize was consumed, in the main, by his mother and her sisters. The death of John's first wife in 1984 did not make him abandon Mfuno village. His deceased wife's family

Figure 3.1 The adult refugees from Lumbe in Mfuno

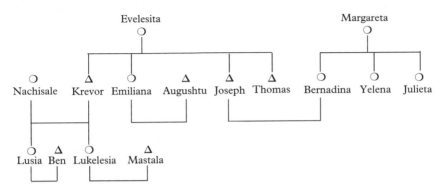

permitted him to continue cultivating her two gardens, and his second wife, a Malawian from a nearby village, came to live with him and his children in Mfuno in a virilocal (*chitengwa*) pattern of residence. As a consequence of John's access to land, she was not given gardens by her own family. John's ties to his second wife's family never became as close as his relationships to his affines in Mfuno. As is described below, John's plan to return to Lumbe in 1993 infuriated the second wife's relatives, a sentiment that owed much to John's neglect of these relationships.

Evelesita's group thus found two Lumbe villagers in relatively prominent positions in Mfuno: Adasauka, a venerable elder, and John, a diligent farmer and successful labour migrant whose spacious, iron-roofed brick house radiated unusual affluence. It appears from all accounts, however, that it was John who took the responsibility for the well-being of Evelesita's group, supporting them single-handedly for a couple of months before the delivery of food aid commenced in Mfuno. Even afterwards, he continued to supply them with relish from his vegetable produce. Adasauka's house was on the other side of Mfuno, but, more significantly, his invisibility in the Lumbe exiles' lives was consistent with his diminished involvement with Lumbe village. Unlike John, he had no garden there, and since the early 1980s, he had not even attended funerals in Lumbe. The houses of Evelesita's group – modest, grass-thatched dwellings made of soil – remained clustered around John's house throughout the period of displacement.

Evelesita's group consisted of four of her children, their spouses and children, as well as the mother and sisters of one of her daughters-in-law (see Figure 3.1). Years before the flight, Evelesita's husband had begun to live with another woman in Lumbe, and, during his exile in Lizulu, he apparently never visited his children in Mfuno. Everyone in Evelesita's group was born in Lumbe. It was the killing of Patrick, Evelesita's son, that pushed them to flee earlier than most other Lumbe villagers. Patrick went to

collect his cattle outside the village one evening. He found a horrified
herdsboy, Patrick's son, surrounded by Renamo guerrillas, who demanded
that the boy reveal to them the identity of the owner of the cattle.
Undeterred, Patrick ordered the guerrillas to give way so that he could take
the cattle to Lumbe. Thus Patrick's son was the witness to one of the first
murders in Lumbe. The gunshots ringing in his ears, he ran to the village to
announce the tragedy. A group of men brought Patrick's corpse to the
village, and soon after the burial, Evelesita called together those relatives
and affines who were, in terms of valued relationships, 'closest' to her. She
observed that the war had now reached Lumbe and insisted that they should
flee to John's place in Mfuno. Without further consultations or announcements, they embarked with very few possessions on the journey, and, under
cover of darkness, avoided contacts with guerrillas.[1]

DISPERSAL ACCEPTED, DISPERSAL DEFIED

Evelesita's exile

Evelesita took her family to Mfuno as one group – as a corporate group, one
might add, bearing in mind their very uniform pattern of flight from Lumbe
and settlement in Mfuno. Different persons were constituted by different
sets of relationships, however, and displacement continued to shape their
relationships in different ways. It was Evelesita who had 'led the way'
(*adatsogola*) to Mfuno. Some of those who went with her would have preferred
to flee to Lizulu, where many other Lumbe villagers settled. In 1991, the
young husband Mastala and his wife did just that.[2] Many others lived in
Mfuno throughout displacement, but their ties in Lizulu to fellow villagers
from Lumbe were subject to highly variable sentiments, thereby indicating
variation in different persons' constitutive relationships.

I can make this variation apparent only through shifts in the focus of my
analysis. Hence I begin with Evelesita herself and trace the configuration of
her valued relationships. Thereafter, the relationships of Nachisale and Ben,
Evelesita's daughter-in-law and this daughter-in-law's son-in-law, provide a
contrasting perspective on the experience of exile among an apparent corporate group.

The early flight both stemmed from and reinforced an incipient cleavage
between the families of Evelesita and some of her siblings. In an important
sense, this cleavage revolved around contrasting allegiances to Frelimo and
Renamo. Krevor, Evelesita's eldest son, was a Frelimo official in Lumbe.
Moreover, when Renamo arrived in the village, rumours suggested that
Joseph, Krevor's younger brother and a primary school teacher, would be
singled out, along with his colleagues, for Renamo's attacks. Although they
had, with the rest of the village, endured Renamo's ominous presence for
several months, Evelesita and her companions made their mistrust of
Renamo evident by their sudden and secretive flight. Mbewe, Evelesita's

father and the headman of Lumbe, died soon after their flight, but none of them returned to attend his funeral, fearing a backlash from both Renamo and the villagers left behind.

The Lumbe exiles in Mfuno and Lizulu had very different opinions of the way in which Mbewe died. Evelesita and her children claimed that Renamo killed him. Evelesita's sisters' children, witnesses of Mbewe's death before their flight to Lizulu, told me that he had suffered a natural death, although he had been distressed by the events taking place around him. Evelesita's siblings never fled Lumbe, because, their children in Lizulu explained, they wanted to 'look after' (kuyang'anira) the village after the headman's death. Even more, some of their children appeared to have visited them from Lizulu in order to distribute blankets and other relief items which they had received in Malawi. It is unlikely that this 'smuggling' of relief items could have taken place without paying some tribute to Renamo. Such visits, although rare in the dangerous war zone, mitigated the contrast between flight and collaboration among Evelesita's siblings and their children.

When Evelesita's siblings' children began to flee, the emerging cleavage did not inhibit them from following Evelesita to Mfuno. There they found that John was in no mood to receive more refugees from Lumbe. Before relief aid was introduced, John felt he had stretched his resources to their limits, but even afterwards he did not accept any encroachments by other refugees. He argued, ignoring his continuing favours to Evelesita's group, that all refugees were now in the hands of relief agencies. Inadvertently, as is discussed later in this chapter, John's attitude deepened the cleavage between the different sets of Lumbe villagers and had important repercussions on his attempt to return to Lumbe. Evelesita, in turn, stopped visiting other Lumbe villagers in Lizulu and led a very confined life in Mfuno.

In this regard, her conduct stood in sharp contrast to that of Nachisale and her children, who maintained close ties to Lumbe villagers in Lizulu throughout their displacement. By the time of my fieldwork, even the conduct of many everyday routine activities had begun to suggest somewhat separate lives among the Lumbe refugees in Mfuno. Such tasks as drawing water or fetching firewood were most often performed by Evelesita, Emiliana, Margareta and her daughters as one group, and by Nachisale, her daughters and certain immediate neighbours, described below, as another.

Scattered belongings

Despite being closely associated with Krevor, a Frelimo official, Nachisale and her son-in-law Ben maintained a sceptical attitude towards both parties in the war. Ben even asserted that Lumbe villagers were harassed by Renamo and Frelimo alike. 'All of them just killed' (onse adapha basi), he once said gloomily. For Nachisale, her husband's association with Frelimo was difficult to undo, but the relationships she cultivated in Lizulu's refugee

Figure 3.2 Nachisale's cross-cousin and Ben's siblings

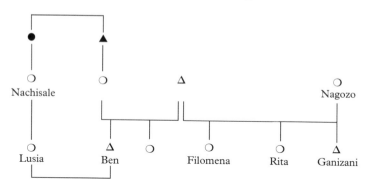

settlement were distinct from contacts with alleged Renamo sympathisers among Evelesita's siblings' children. Ben's marriage to her daughter in 1984 had enhanced Nachisale's close ties to her mother's family – Ben is the son of Nachisale's cross-cousin, the son of her *malume*'s daughter (see Figure 3.2). In the early 1980s, Ben's own parents had moved, with three of their sons and Ben's mother's brother, to work in the Mozambican port of Beira, and remained there throughout the war. Ben's closest relatives in Lizulu were his sister and the children of Nagozo, the second wife of his father. The husbands of Filomena and Rita, Nagozo's daughters, had become Ben's close friends, of whom one was captured by Renamo and the other began to work as a carpenter in Lilongwe after the flight. He sometimes lent money to Ben and brought him the seeds of tomatoes and hybrid maize from Lilongwe, when Ben resumed cultivation.

Apart from occasional visits by Nagozo's children, the most common pattern of visiting between the refugees in Mfuno and Lizulu was by Ben going on his bicycle, and by Lusia and Nachisale travelling by bus, to see people in Lizulu. A week did not pass by without at least one of them visiting Lizulu. Given the K1.20 one-way bus fare, this represented a considerable investment. While Ben and Lusia would spend time with Nagozo's children and Ben's sister, Nachisale would chat and assist in domestic routines among the families of her cross-cousins and 'sisters' (*achemwali*). With regard to the former, Nachisale never deployed the term 'cross-cousin' (*msuweni*) but spoke of them as *akulu anzanga*, the mother-in-law or father-in-law of her child. Among villagers in Dedza and Angónia, being cross-cousins often entails a joking relationship, with its properties ranging from verbal abuse to trust and intimacy. Among *akulu anzanga*, on the other hand, trust appears more as mutual respect between mature people of the same age. Relaxed conviviality, in short, welcomed Nachisale among her cross-cousins and sisters in Lizulu, a sentiment that contrasted with her solemn relationships with Evelesita and Emiliana in Mfuno.

During my visit to Lumbe after repatriation, I observed that by travelling between the refugee settlements in Mfuno and Lizulu, Ben and Nachisale had reproduced their immediate neighbourhood in Lumbe. The same persons who were so frequently visited in Lizulu were also their spatially closest neighbours at home, both before and after displacement. But why did not Nachisale, Ben and Lusia move to Lizulu altogether? Here other sets of relationships constrained the pursuit of interests that some relationships motivated. For Nachisale, her husband's opinion was a paramount constraint. Although Krevor had begun to live and work in Dedza town, and gossips told of his plans to marry another woman, he did support his family in Mfuno with money during his occasional visits. He made it clear that he opposed any idea of her moving to Lizulu, apparently because of the longer distance between Dedza and Lizulu than between Dedza and Mfuno. Had Nachisale nevertheless moved to Lizulu, Krevor would have accused her of initiating procedures for divorce and insisted that she should pay him a fine for this unilateral decision. Nachisale, enmeshed in conflicting interests that various 'absent' relationships entailed, remained in a place where she had, apart from her own children, few valued relationships.

Ben and Lusia were constrained less by Krevor's opinion than by relationships that exile, almost against their own will, had created for them in Mfuno. Whenever Ben reflected on his experience as a 'refugee' – and such reflections were frequent – he always stressed that Mfuno and Chitima villagers were 'strangers all of them' (alendo okhaokha). He insisted that his 'thoughts' (maganizo) and 'soul' (mtima; 'heart') were in Lumbe throughout the seven years of his exile. He showed extremely little interest in the events in Mfuno, hardly ever volunteered to participate in funerals and even failed to attend many of them. But he felt compelled to attend the funerals of fellow Lumbe villgers in Lizulu and Dedza town. Despite these sentiments and acts that maintained his belonging to an imagined community elsewhere, he became a focus of interest for a refugee from Chitima village living next to him. When Ben and Lusia were seriously contemplating a move to Lizulu in 1991, following the move of Mastala and Lukelesia, this neighbour took an extraordinary step to keep them where they were. He offered them land to cultivate.

Solicitude among strangers

The dilemma in which Ben found himself indicates how little his own understanding of his situation could help him to anticipate events. Ben's presence was in the interests of others, however remote he felt that he was from having relationships in Mfuno's refugee settlement. The offer of land made a relationship visible, a relationship which Ben's neighbour thought had existed since their displacement began. Reduced to its basics, the gesture of offering land merely demonstrates that being human hinges on social relationships – social relationships both animate and constrain that being. This observation appears less trivial when juxtaposed with the view of refugees as victims of pathological social conditions, uprooted and individualised. Ben's longing for 'home' in Lumbe was intense; but his displacement was never devoid of relationships. Neither Ben nor his generous neighbour was pleased with the conditions of his displacement. The dilemma which made Ben abandon the idea of changing the settlement emerged from the neighbour's own discontent with displacement. The neighbour's response to adverse conditions was to engage in relationships, not to assume the pathological state of a passive victim.

When Evelesita's group fled to Mfuno, the area in which John lived had plenty of empty, uncultivated space. Only some three months later, however, it was the area most congested by refugees in Mfuno. Most of them came from Chitima village. The availability of space and the area's vicinity to the border explain this pattern of settlement. Nevertheless, not a single member of Evelesita's family, not even John, had had active ties to Chitima villagers before this influx of refugees.[3] The Lumbe refugees were suddenly surrounded by a dense concentration of huts and houses, among them the house of Nkhoma and his wife, young newlyweds from Chitima. Nkhoma built the house next to Ben's, with only a reed fence separating the houses, which were little more than a metre apart. Yunisi, his wife, had several relatives nearby, including her mother and sisters and her mother's sisters, whereas Nkhoma's relatives lived in other parts of Mfuno's refugee settlement. None of Yunisi's relatives developed with any of Evelesita's family the kind of intense neighbourliness, ranging from casual chatting to mutual assistance in coping with difficulties, that came to characterise the relationships of Nkhoma, Yunisi and Yunisi's mother to Ben, Lusia and Nachisale.

In late 1991, Nkhoma and Yunisi, like many other Chitima villagers, judged the security situation to be calm enough to allow them to resume cultivation in Mozambique virtually to the same extent as in the pre-flight period. By contrast, as is described below, no one of Evelesita's group even visited Lumbe until late 1992. This difference between refugees coming from 'near' and 'far' was already a source of some unease, or 'pity' (chisoni), for Nkhoma, and Ben's increasingly concrete plans to move to Lizulu made Nkhoma act. He and Yunisi offered Ben and Lusia two gardens (minda), an offer which was swiftly followed by Yunisi's mother's offer of one garden to Nachisale. All gardens were accepted with deep gratitude, but it was clear to everyone that the gardens were not given permanently but 'lent' (kubwereka). The agreement did not involve formal payments or extracts from the harvest.

Clearly, the arrangement brought unusual material advantages to both sides. Nkhoma's side got free labour to clear gardens which had been lying fallow since the flight. On Ben's side, their access to the land was a unique stroke of fortune, because no one else in Evelesita's group had found land during their displacement. John sometimes employed Evelesita and Emiliana to perform *ganyu* labour in his gardens, but he did not give them any land to cultivate for themselves. But the benefits from having access to land ranged far beyond material gains. When refugees in the Dedza–Angónia borderland deployed their most compelling imagery to express the problems of displacement, they spoke mostly about land, either of the barren qualities of Malawi's soil or of their lack of access to it (see Englund 1996c). By allowing his neighbours to cultivate land, Nkhoma eased their feeling of being idle, and helped them to regain an important aspect of their normal life-style.

Nkhoma's gesture, in other words, had more than narrow material consequences. It was evident that material considerations were not paramount even for Nkhoma himself. His act has to be understood in the context of a young *mkamwini* husband, whose wife's sisters were either unmarried or had husbands who were absent. In such a context, Nkhoma's conversations with Ben were a relief to Nkhoma, and Ben's departure from the neighbourhood would have threatened Nkhoma's own well-being. For Ben, Nkhoma's presence undoubtedly contributed to his ability to cope with displacement in Mfuno, and the two men addressed one another as 'brothers' (*achimwene*). As soon as repatriation commenced, however, it became clear that the value of the relationship was not the same for Ben and Nkhoma. By the end of the second season of cultivating Nkhoma's land, Ben, Lusia and Nachisale had returned to Lumbe. Their maize was harvested by Nkhoma, Yunisi and her mother, but Lusia and Nachisale returned to collect it. Despite his promises, Ben stayed in Lumbe and did not come to see Nkhoma again. The gardens were taken back by Nkhoma and Yunisi's mother.

The case of Ben and Nachisale is an example of complex space–place relations among refugees in the Dedza–Angónia borderland. For both, the space of valued relationships did not coincide with the actual place of their exile. Their 'closest' neighbours lived some fifteen kilometres away in another settlement, but they were acutely aware that the proper place to enter into these relationships was in yet another locality, some thirty kilometres away in Lumbe village. Their displacement in Mfuno contained moments when such apparently impractical sentiments could have given way to more active involvement in relationships in the immediate setting of their exile. Nkhoma's offer of land was one such moment, which, though accepted, did not seem to outlast displacement. Moreover, Ben became a famous bicycle repairer in Mfuno, and small groups of men often gathered outside his 'workshop' at his house to watch his work and to spend time chatting. More often than not, Ben appeared absent-minded and taciturn in such gatherings, showing little interest in the gossip about Mfuno and Chitima villagers.

FROM FLIGHT TO REPATRIATION
Success and failure in repatriation

Because different persons, despite the apparent uniformity of their flight, were constituted by different sets of relationships, there was much less uniformity during repatriation. For some of them, like Ben and Nachisale, displacement reinforced their existing detachment from Evelesita's family. For others, displacement entailed transformations in their attachment to the family. John, as mentioned, became so involved in these relationships that a return to Lumbe village seemed desirable. The experiences of Krevor and Joseph, Evelesita's other sons, were somewhat different. Krevor began to work in Dedza town in 1987, and he spent his time with fellow villagers from Lumbe and other Mozambicans. He did not follow his family to Lumbe during repatriation but stayed in Dedza, apparently being in the process of remarrying. Joseph, who did return to Lumbe, became a teacher in Mfuno's school for refugees and spent most of his spare time with other teachers, none of whom he had met before displacement.[4]

Repatriation from the Dedza–Angónia borderland had in most cases begun before official programmes reached the area in late 1993. But the Lumbe refugees who had settled in Lizulu and the families of Evelesita and Nachisale timed their repatriation differently. Many Lumbe refugees in Lizulu began to return to Lumbe as soon as the news of the peace accord reached them in October 1992. Around this time, Ben and Nagozo's children also visited the village for the first time since 1986. They found the sites of their houses and gardens unoccupied. Ben built a small hut for himself and started to prepare his gardens in Lumbe, while Lusia and Nachisale worked in the gardens in Chitima. With his siblings' assistance, Ben finished building houses for his family and Nachisale in late March 1993, and he took them to Lumbe in April.

John started to spend extensive periods in Lumbe in order to build houses and prepare gardens, as soon as the rains allowed him to do so in 1993. He participated, with the assistance of Joseph, of Thomas and of Emiliana's son, in building five houses: houses for his own family, Evelesita and Emiliana to live in, and separate kitchen-huts for these two women. At first, Evelesita's sisters' children were busy working on their own houses nearby and did not assist John. In June, however, they began to make their presence felt. Filipo, the son of Evelesita's sister, confronted John and brought his plans to an abrupt end. The confrontation also delayed the repatriation of Evelesita and John's siblings. Whereas the families of Ben and Nachisale moved to Lumbe in April, the rest of Evelesita's group, with the exception of Krevor, moved only in September.[5]

I discuss the failure of John's return in detail below. In order to understand the extent to which this confrontation was – and, equally important, was *not* – a simple consequence of rivalries among the families of Evelesita

Figure 3.3 Mbewe's children and heir; John and Filipo

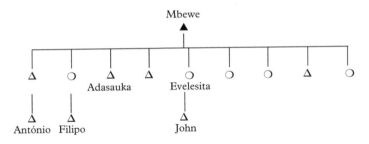

and her siblings, a brief review of the background is necessary. Evelesita had four sisters and four brothers, but only she and Adasauka were in Malawi during the war. I have already mentioned the contrasting allegiances to Frelimo and Renamo among Evelesita and her siblings. Mbewe, their father and Lumbe's headman, died soon after Evelesita's flight. He had been deposed by Frelimo, but Renamo apparently reinstated him and his councillors in their positions. During the war, while no formal installation of a new headman took place, there was widespread consensus among Lumbe villagers that António, the son of Mbewe's eldest son and a refugee in Dedza town, was going to succeed Mbewe (see Figure 3.3). He had no active ties to Evelesita's group in Mfuno. The confrontation broke out, as mentioned above, between John and his 'brother' (*mchimwene*) Filipo. It was Filipo who expressed the view, in the context of an emerging new leadership in the village, that John had left Lumbe for ever.

The confrontation merits a close study, although a facile explanation is available. The confrontation derived, so runs the explanation, from a structural cleavage between 'matrilateral segments', deepened by the rivalry over the new headman's councillors (see e.g. Marwick 1965). A rivalry may well have been at issue, but the view of a structural cleavage obscures the processes by which this particular relationship resulted in confrontation. It did not occur in abstract 'structural time' but under the historical contingencies of war and displacement. At the same time, the confrontation showed the character of moral personhood among villagers in Dedza and Angónia. John, who had distributed the harvests of his garden in Lumbe among the families of Evelesita's sisters, had had solicitous relationships with these families until the war. During displacement, he felt compelled to refuse to assist them, because the burden of playing host to Evelesita's group was demanding enough. Here lies a clue to an understanding of the confrontation. It derived largely from John's performance under the extraordinary conditions of war and displacement. Even more, an account of the confrontation must include the actual content of John's post-war aspirations, and the way in which Filipo challenged John.

Staying behind

The prospects for commercial agriculture drew John to Lumbe. The land to which he had access there contrasted, in his mind, sharply with his land in Malawi. He emphatically subscribed to the view that the soil was intrinsically better in 'Mozambique' (cf. Englund 1996c). On the other hand, the source of his land in Lumbe had been Mbewe, whose headmanship had given him the control of vast areas of uncultivated land. This was the land on which John intended to expand his garden. So large an expansion was impossible in his Malawian gardens, surrounded as they were by gardens already under cultivation. Confident and full of ideas, he made no secret of his plan to hire a tractor and a plough to open a wide farming area for himself. Fellow villagers from Lumbe, of course, were toiling away with hoes; it appears that no one else had such grandiose plans.

Before the confrontation with Filipo, John was sliding into a dispute on the domestic front. The rumour of John's imminent departure caused much dismay among the relatives of his second wife. He had already given them money when she moved to live with him as a *chitengwa*, and he openly dismissed the need to notify his affines again if he decided to move elsewhere. This infuriated her guardian (*nkhoswe*), who sent John a letter saying that he would not be allowed to take her to Mozambique. The additional gossip about John's courting of a young woman from Chitima did nothing to comfort his second wife and her relatives. John's relationship with this woman had not taken on any definite signs of a conjugal bond; for instance, he did not build a house for her when she returned to Chitima, nor did he start living with her. Nevertheless, given his affines' opposition, it was clear that a new marriage was a corollary of John's plan to move to Lumbe.

This friction was only superficially a consequence of John's decision to move to Mozambique. It indicated different qualities in John's relationships with his two sets of affines, the relatives of his first and second wives. The parents of the second wife in a nearby village often complained that John did not visit them. Moreover, John was irritated by Evelesita's and Emiliana's reports that his wife had asked for a share of food aid from them. John's household had little need for provisions from the food aid, and his wife's intent was to take these items to her own parents. John, in turn, accused her of bringing 'shame' (*manyazi*) to their house by asking for favours from his relatives. Seemingly contradicting himself, John did occasionally request Evelesita to give items of the aid to his deceased first wife's parents and grandparents in Mfuno. This disparity in John's approach to his affines did not pass unnoticed by his wife, whose protests, however, made no impact on John. His indifference to her village was exacerbated by the fact that she had not been given land when she married. The deceased wife's land, by contrast, continued to link John to his affines from the first marriage. By his occasional gestures of solicitude, John made this continuing relationship visible.

John's domestic troubles had not reached a conclusion when Filipo, in June 1993, came to see the progress of John's house in Lumbe. He found John at work with Joseph, Thomas and Emiliana's son. Filipo's confrontational disposition made it evident immediately that no compliments would be exchanged. He began to criticise John for his plan to open a farm. Filipo asserted that John had no right to prepare extensive areas of new land for himself, because he had married a Malawian and had gardens in Malawi. John, Filipo concluded, had left Lumbe and had no reason 'to claim land' (*kupempha malo*; literally 'to beg a place'). John was given no opportunity to respond, and Filipo left as soon as he had uttered an ominous threat, 'You will see' (*mudzaona*). This, in effect, suggested that Filipo had cursed (*anatemberera*) John. The implied threat was that John would be exposed to sorcery, if he still pursued his plan.[6]

John, shaken and perplexed, promptly called his friend from Chitima, a healer (*sing'anga*), to protect his houses in Lumbe against witches. After reflecting on the matter, John became convinced that he would be afflicted by Filipo's malicious activities even if he merely dwelt in Lumbe, without plans to engage in commercial farming. He decided to abandon not only his ambition to have a farm but also his desire to live in Lumbe. Filipo, in turn, continued to spread his view of John's plan among other villagers, with the result that their confrontation quickly became known among most Lumbe villagers in both Lumbe and Malawi. Joseph attempted to mediate in the argument, but to no avail. The rest of Evelesita's siblings and their children remained silent during the mounting tension, and no further hostility erupted before the end of my fieldwork. As mentioned above, however, Evelesita, Emiliana, Margareta and their children returned to Lumbe later than most other Lumbe villagers, after they had privately expressed concern over the 'troubles' (*mabvuto*) in Lumbe.

All the parties denied that Filipo had ever been known to have appropriated the powers of witches (*afiti*). John was unable to alter the terms of the argument precisely because the confrontation occurred not with a marginal person but with someone known for his propriety. Filipo was a prominent villager in Lumbe and one of Mbewe's senior grandsons. He had maintained close ties to António, Mbewe's presumed successor, throughout the displacement, and it was widely rumoured that he would be António's councillor. John, by virtue of his commercial farming, would have been another prominent son of Mbewe's daughter, and António's cross-cousin, in Lumbe. His presence would have been likely to diminish Filipo's relative prominence in the village and the family. In part, therefore, Filipo's argument may have indicated his desire to keep a rival away from Lumbe.

The structural cleavage between 'matrilateral segments', expressed through the 'idiom' of land dispute, thus appears again as an explanation. Three observations undermine this explanation, however. First, no one

defined *groups* as entities against one another. Far from suggesting that
Evelesita and her companions in exile had estranged themselves from Lumbe
villagers, Filipo depicted John as a *person* who belonged elsewhere. Second,
Filipo's argument invoked the general impropriety of expanding one's
garden after one has settled elsewhere; he did not suggest that John had no
claims to Mbewe's land. Third, and most significantly, there were a number
of other prominent matrilateral brothers to be attacked. Krevor and Joseph,
for example, were in formal employment and apparently had very different
party political allegiances from Filipo. His argument, therefore, was over the
conditions of commercial farming – the conditions under which an entrepreneur could be allowed to invest and prosper in the village.

Filipo's concentration on John must be understood in the light of John's
performance during displacement. Despite its stark contrast to John's conduct before the war, that performance was fresh in Lumbe villagers' memory
when repatriation commenced. As has been seen, during displacement John
had performed acts of unqualified solicitude towards Evelesita's group,
while he had refused to assist other Lumbe villagers. His actions, in effect,
revealed the scope of John's relationships in Lumbe. This revelation bespoke
a transformation, because John had previously supported the families of
Evelesita's sisters. The transformation, hardly intended by John, was a
consequence of the demands that exiled relatives made on his wealth under
the extraordinary conditions of displacement. Filipo's argument disclosed,
however, that a successful return to the village as a commercial farmer
would have required a much broader scope of active kin-relationships.
John's current image was that of a 'proud' (*onyada*) person encroaching on
village land with a view to enriching himself and, perhaps, only a handful of
relatives. Like the Portuguese entrepreneurs described in the previous chapter,
a local commercial farmer, hiring a tractor and a plough, is expected also to
be 'big' (*wamkulu*) as a person. John's performance during displacement
had failed to display this quality.

There was a clear, although unintended, irony in Filipo's argument that
John as a person belonged to Malawi. For John, the effect of displacement
was precisely that, for the first time since he had left Lumbe, he actually
wanted to return to live there on a permanent basis. He became so much
associated with his Lumbe relatives and his new 'wife' from Chitima that
many local Malawians started to refer to him as a 'refugee' (*lefuchi*). Before
the confrontation with Filipo, John occasionally joked about his prospects of
becoming the new headman in Lumbe, because Mbewe was his grandfather
(*gogo*), deliberately ignoring the fact that a matrilateral link related him to
Mbewe. When Evelesita and the others finally left Mfuno, John stayed
behind and continued to live with his second wife. A patriot despite his
marred repatriation, John showed in his reflections on Malawian and
Mozambican affairs a consistent bias towards Mozambique. Mozambique,

he insisted, was 'home', 'our place' (*kwathu*). He ridiculed the small size of Malawi and doubted whether such a small country was a 'country' (*dziko*) at all.

DISTANCE AND THE DIVERSITY OF 'REFUGEE' EXPERIENCES

The cases in this chapter have demonstrated that diversity was often concealed by the analytic and bureaucratic category of 'refugee'. Seen through space–place relations, the experiences of displacement among the Lumbe villagers described in this chapter exhibited considerable variation, in spite of the equally long distances which they had covered during their flight. After these cases, it is especially difficult to sustain the notion that refugees generally are 'uprooted'. The complex separations and conflations between space and place among Lumbe exiles show how spatial belonging is itself subject to the dynamic of social relationships, not an unchanging constraint in that dynamic. John, for example, maintained close ties to his village of origin before the war, but it was only during the displacement of his relatives that he began to contemplate a return to that village. Ben and Nachisale, on the other hand, did not allow displacement to have much impact on their valued relationships at 'home', even though displacement had dispersed those relationships. Evelesita's exile was spatially more confined, and an emerging conflict with relatives, though spatially absent, reduced her willingness to be mobile.

Historical contingencies intervened to shape the dynamic of relationships in ways that no actor could have anticipated. Under the conditions of displacement and repatriation, with the legacy of the war by no means beyond dispute, spatial belonging became one arena in which relationships were contested and power relations revealed. Filipo attacked John by arguing that John's proper place was in Malawi. Nachisale's husband forced her to stay in Mfuno, despite the concentration of her valued relationships elsewhere. Similarly, Ben felt compelled by Nkhoma's offer of land to postpone his departure from Mfuno. Rather than being simply 'uprooted' by translocal forces, Lumbe villagers and their local hosts had their own understandings of their predicaments. The various attempts to bind others to particular places were striking examples of villagers' capacity to depict one another as 'refugees' or as persons belonging elsewhere than to the village of origin.

The positive contribution of this chapter is to indicate the role of power relations in the patrimonial logic of social capital. A particularly illuminating example of power relations was Filipo's capacity to undermine John's aspirations. Despite John's material capital enabling him to engage in commercial farming, his stature as a Lumbe villager, and as a *person*, was found wanting. The confrontation did not indicate Filipo's superior power in any absolute sense. It was, above all, a *moral* argument which disclosed the social conditions of economic investment and prosperity. In the patrimonial logic of social capital, persons inspire trust to the extent that they make their relationships visible in acts of solicitude. According to Filipo's argument, John was not an 'individual' – witches usually come closest to this most despised form of personhood (see Englund 1996b) – but a person who displayed more solicitude towards 'Malawians' than towards Lumbe villagers. By the same token, Filipo implicitly drew a distinction between John's and his own moral standing in Lumbe. The argument gained its force because a prominent villager articulated it, but its success was more than a consequence of Filipo's cynical manipulation – he had put his finger on a key aspect of morality. This close association of power with moral personhood will receive more attention in subsequent case studies. The post-war predicaments will also raise the question of new kinds of power relations in the Dedza–Angónia borderland.

4

GENDERED EXILE

From Chitima village's paths to war to Lumbe villagers' exile in Mfuno village, power relations have appeared as critical factors in shaping the social capital by which political support and refuge have been achieved. The patrimonial logic of social capital revolves around a dynamic in which trust is not an individual's propensity but a sentiment that emerges with a perceived capacity to 'care for' (*kusamala*) a wide range of relationships. This dynamic, as seen in the confrontation between Filipo and John described in the previous chapter, inspires contentious moral arguments which separate persons from each other as much as they presume that there are enduring bonds between them. In other words, it is a paradox of the patrimonial logic that people's explicit concern to cultivate personal relationships constantly leads them to create distinctions against one another, sometimes by quietly withdrawing from a relationship, sometimes through a violent confrontation. Distinctions, in any event, serve as the measure of trust.

The dynamic and morality of power relations in Dedza–Angónia borderland villagers' displacement can be probed further by highlighting certain salient social facts, such as age and gender. The social age of persons is a crucial component of their capacity to command the moral authority that legitimate power entails. In a strict sense, social age and authority are so indistinguishable that to regard one as the condition of another is a tautology. Persons 'grow' (*kukula*) by marrying and having children and grandchildren; in this context, personal growth is tantamount to the achievement of authority. Such growth, however, is not reducible to separate moments in the life-cycle, such as marriage. The *chikamwini* pattern of marriage, by which men move to live near their in-laws, keeps men social juniors in their wives' homes for several years, burdened, in the past, by merciless labour obligations towards elders (Mandala 1990: 30–2). Male labour migration enabled young husbands to obtain resources for their own patronage, and the migration of young men to towns and agricultural estates, though clearly less profitable than their fathers' and grandfathers' earlier migrations to South Africa, continues to mitigate the confines of *chikamwini*. Even more, Renamo's war, as has been seen, enticed some youths to break away from the plight of being social juniors.

The fact that persons in subordinate social categories can and do find ways to circumvent existing power relations invites processual analysis, an appreciation of contingency in the dynamic of social relationships. Responding to that challenge, this chapter highlights the experiences of three women and their immediate families during displacement. Although this focus on women permits a closer look at gender in the processes of displacement in the Dedza–Angónia borderland, gender by no means inspires an exclusive interest in women's social position. At issue is the constitution of persons in social relationships, how various domains and positions become gendered.

In Chapter 2, the main *dramatis personae* in Chitima village's path to war were men. Women's invisibility in village politics does not, however, indicate 'subordination' in any obvious sense. On the one hand, both Frelimo and the Catholic Church give recognition to women in their local organisations, and most public discussions, such as during litigation, appear to give equal weight to the views of women and men. On the other hand, women's contribution, through cooking the maize products of the land they cultivate, carries forward the work of procreative substances in the creation of foetuses and, after birth, of persons (Englund 1999). In this most profound realm of reproduction, therefore, the gendered identity of men is predicated on female work and substance.

The effect of such historical contingencies as displacement is to unsettle existing patterns of social life. Even though my approach in this book is to avoid generalisations about displacement until a number of extended-case studies are thoroughly analysed, it must be said that the governmental and humanitarian interventions that shape the experiences of forced migration are, if only implicitly, often gendered (see Indra 1999). The previous chapter showed, for example, how the relief operations of the Red Cross provided Krevor with employment in Dedza town and how, with this income, he was able both to start preparing his second marriage and to prevent Nachisale, his first wife, from moving to a settlement where most of her closest relatives spent their exile. Ironically, and certainly inadvertently, the relief agency was a factor in transforming domestic relations in a setting in which the *chikamwini* marriage usually tied men to their wives' families. More broadly, aid workers' own entrenched ideas of sex roles commonly benefit men as refugee representatives and household heads (Matlou 1999: 136–7). For borderland communities themselves, displacement and repatriation across borders can become issues involving gender, with men, jealous of their economic and political standing, evoking borders to manipulate women's moves (cf. Flynn 1997b).[1]

A sense of time and place has to be retained when discussing such matters. Displacement in the Dedza–Angónia borderland extended into the period of increasing official 'gender awareness' during the 1990s. Refugee women in Mfuno village, for example, were treated to needlework classes by

community workers from Dedza town. Although the difficulties of marketing their products soon made women lose their interest in this form of aid,
the project indicated official concern with women's income-generating
opportunities. A further proof of somewhat enlightened official attitudes
was the acceptance that women could also qualify as household heads in the
management of relief aid. Yet perhaps the most consequential fact in
Dedza–Angónia borderland villagers' displacement was refugees' self-
settled status. The Lumbe villagers of the previous chapter became embroiled
in an unusually abrupt change, even though, as has been seen, their
experiences were not all of a piece. For most refugees, however, pre-existing
ties to Malawi entailed a myriad ways in which exile could make its impact
on personal relationships. For men and women alike, such ties, and the
absence of the restrictions that refugee camps often impose, guaranteed
some scope for negotiation about the move and access to resources (cf.
Colson 1999: 25).

Negotiation, patently, was not always open-ended. Dedza–Angónia borderland villagers' ability to utilise the international border in creating distinctions, even constraints, has already been demonstrated. This chapter's
focus on three women addresses, among others, the question of gender in
the *patri*monial logic of social capital. Were the processes by which they
endured their exile gendered; were they conditioned, for instance, by their
dependence on the patrimony of some indispensable male?

The most obvious link between the three women was, indeed, a man, a
big man at that – Luis. As will be recalled from Chapter 2, Luis was the
pioneering nationalist in the border village of Chitima and the full brother of
Rafaelo, the village headman and a trenchant anti-nationalist. Luis's prominent position in Frelimo left little ambiguity for the three women's political
allegiances, and they suffered, mainly through their daughters, harassment
by Renamo guerrillas. Flight was, therefore, inevitable, an act which the
three women wholeheartedly accepted.

The focus on the three women is instructive precisely because it shows
how little the big man in their lives could actually determine the patterns of
their subsequent exile. Two of the women were Luis's wives, one his cross-
cousin. Luis relied to a considerable extent on these women's pre-existing
ties to the Malawian border villages, particularly Mfuno, when he fled.
Some attempts to settle, as is described in this chapter, were more successful
than others, an indication that the three women were themselves constituted by different sets of relationships. As a matter of fact, they had, whether
before, during or after exile, little to do with one another, with Luis alone
moving between their households. The three women had, moreover, somewhat contrasting personal pasts as Malawians and Mozambicans. Nasoweka,
Luis's second wife, was born in Malawi and moved to Mozambique as a
young unmarried girl; Namadzi, Luis's junior wife, was born in Malawi and

moved to Mozambique as a married woman with two children; and Namanyada, Luis's cross-cousin, was born in Mozambique and had never lived in Malawi before displacement. Skolastika, Luis's first wife, whose exile is not described here, was born in Mozambique and, as a refugee, was shown the site for her house by the headman of Mfuno. The three women's pre-existing ties to Malawian border villages, by contrast, permitted more negotiation over the site of asylum, with their successes and failures giving insight into the question of gender in the dynamic of trust.

HOMES AND ORIGINS
Cross-border relationships across the decades

During her exile, Nasoweka, Luis's second wife, lived in the central area of Mfuno village, away from the border area which was most congested by refugees. Most of her immediate neighbours were Mfuno villagers, and the nearest Chitima villagers were Sofiya and Nalipenga, her mother and sister (see Figure 4.1). Pre-existing ties to Mfuno enabled them to find a relatively tranquil site for their exile. These were the ties which had not been severed when Liwonde, Sofiya's father, had taken them to Chitima in the early 1950s, following the Portuguese ordinance mentioned in Chapter 2. In 1986, Sofiya had lived for several years as a widow in the same household with Nalipenga, herself the unmarried mother of two adolescents. Nasoweka and Luis had two daughters who married men from Chitima during displacement. The houses of these daughters were also located near Nasoweka's in Mfuno.

Luis built a house for Nasoweka near Mary's house, on approximately the same site where she had lived before the move in the early 1950s. Even though Tiyamike, Liwonde's brother and Mary's grandfather, never moved with his family to Mozambique, Mary is regarded as a 'sister' (mchemwali) by Nasoweka and Nalipenga, and as a 'child' (mwana) by Sofiya. The solicitous relationships between these women were never affected by cross-border moves. Through visits, they engaged in mutual support, both before and after independence. For Nasoweka, it was above all with Libentina, Mary's daughter, that she shared her relief aid during displacement. She received support herself, such as relish, and assistance in daily routines. The circle of women in Libentina's neighbourhood also included a number of her sisters. Mary's sisters had died, and she was herself ailing. For Nasoweka, Libentina was clearly the closest person in this neighbourhood, as she had been before displacement.

A son of Amfuno, the founder of Mfuno village, fathered Nasoweka after an adulterous relationship with Sofiya. Despite her apparent illegitimacy, Nasoweka is known by the mfunda-name that derives from her father and, ultimately, Amfuno. Her parents' liaison enables her to trace kin-relationships among a large number of Mfuno villagers, but displacement did not

Figure 4.1 Nasoweka's siblings

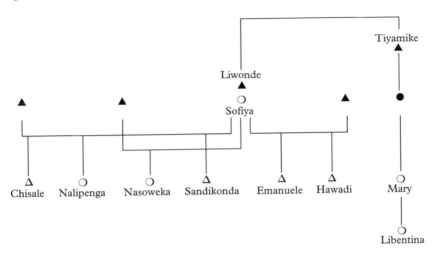

seem to occasion extensive engagement in these relationships. Among her patrilateral kin, she maintained, as before and after displacement, an active relationship only with her father's daughter, born of a marriage with a Mozambican woman. This sister was the only surviving child from that marriage and, like Nasoweka, lived her childhood in Mfuno before moving to Chitima. Displacement had the effect of making her, along with Nasoweka, one of the most reluctant returnees to Chitima after the war. The two women appeared to see little sense in moving back and forth between Mfuno and Chitima villages, preferring to stay in Mfuno. As they themselves explained, it was Rafaelo, the village headman of Chitima, who insisted that they had to live in the country where their gardens were.

For Nasoweka, Sofiya and Nalipenga, 'Mozambican' and 'Malawian' identities were seldom the subjects of spontaneous contemplation during their exile. Although they frequently joined other refugees in their complaints about the inadequacies of food aid, in practice they hardly ever dwelt on the fact that they had fled from Chitima, or spoke of it as their home. Rather than expecting Libentina and Mary to allocate them land in Malawi, moreover, they merely resumed the cultivation of their own land in Mozambique towards the end of their exile.

In this low-key approach, they were sharply unlike Sofiya's sons. For example, Sandikonda, who also spent his exile nearby but who never ceased to juxtapose Malawi with Mozambique, invariably referred to Mozambique as 'our place' (*kwathu*). As will be seen in the next chapter, Hawadi, Sofiya's youngest son, adopted quite the opposite point of view by emphasising that his home was in Malawi. This discrepancy in the assertion of national identities was integral to different persons' management of valued relationships. Other case studies in this and the next chapter show that it did not indicate, for example, women's general aversion to ingrained national identities.

There was nothing natural in the ease with which Nasoweka was able to settle among Mfuno villagers in Malawi. Seen from the perspective of social age, the importance of which I described earlier, Nasoweka's return to the site which her immediate family had left in the early 1950s should have posed more difficulties. She spent her childhood in Malawi, and her adulthood in Mozambique. The fact that her flight was, in effect, a successful return proved that her 'growth' as a person had continued to involve relationships on the Malawian side of the border. The memory of her belonging to Mfuno was shared by those who never moved to Mozambique, a memory they had kept alive for over three decades before the flight.

Malawians or Mozambicans?

Shared memories, as will become clear from other case studies, should not be taken for granted. And yet, despite all her moving from 'home' to 'home', if anything, Nasoweka did not simply reproduce the pre-flight configuration of her valued relationships – she even became entangled in new relationships. Prominent among these was Nazulu, a woman from a distant village in Angónia, who became one of Nasoweka's closest companions, although they had never met before and Nasoweka had never visited Nazulu's village.

Nazulu was, with her old mother, sister, husband and children, among the first refugees to reach Mfuno. They followed their fellow-villagers in their flight to Mfuno. Although some of these villagers, like the Lumbe villagers described in the previous chapter, had pre-existing relationships in Mfuno, Nazulu's immediate family had none. Escorted to the site by the village headman of Mfuno, they settled near Libentina's house, where Nasoweka came to settle a couple of months later.

A neighbourhood of women of approximately the same age emerged between four adjacent houses. Despite their varied experiences of war and the influx of refugees elsewhere in the village, the women seemed to have little interest in comparing their national identities. It was with Nasoweka and Libentina, above all, that Nazulu and her sister began to share the daily tasks of drawing water, collecting firewood, pounding maize and looking after children and grandchildren. They did not begin to address or refer to one another with kin-terms but used mainly *mifunda*-names or even first names. Before the return to Mozambique, Nasoweka recruited Nazulu, her sister and their children to perform piece-work (*ganyu*) in her gardens. Their relationships assumed qualities of solicitude virtually on a par with Nasoweka's active kin-relationships. When Nasoweka fell ill, Nazulu was the one who accompanied Nasoweka's daughter to a healer several kilometres away to collect medicine for her.

When repatriation to Mozambique began, Nazulu and her husband promised Nasoweka and Luis that they would not demolish their house in Mfuno. The idea was that they would use the house when they came to receive food aid in Mfuno, to visit border markets or to assist during 'trouble' (*chobvuta*) – a funeral or illness – in Nasoweka's family. Nasoweka and Luis also promised to visit Nazulu's village frequently. Only a couple of weeks after Nazulu's family's repatriation to Mozambique, however, her husband came to demolish the house and to sell its timbers as firewood. He and Nazulu adopted the arduous habit of walking between their village and Mfuno during the day when food aid was delivered. On the other hand, the only time Nasoweka visited Nazulu's village during the months that followed their repatriation was when she went to express her condolence (*kupepesa*) after the funeral of Nazulu's mother.

Nasoweka is an example of a 'refugee' who was not inclined to assert that the flight had caused much disruption in her life. Her solicitous relationship with Nazulu, however, was one significant transformation that took place in the pattern of her valued relationships. Yet the quality of this relationship did not seem to outlast exile. Even though their relationship appeared to continue in situations of crisis such as funerals, the former neighbours did not visit each other regularly, and did not participate intensely in each other's lives after repatriation to Mozambique. This does not in any way diminish the intense solicitude in their relationship during displacement. Apparently, they did not engage in the relationship with short-term advantage in mind, but with the morality and solicitude of an enduring relationship.

On the eve of repatriation, Nasoweka found that there was little flexibility in the question of national allegiances. Her cultivation of land in Mozambique and continued stay in Malawi would have embarrassed Luis, her husband and the Frelimo chairman. These undercurrents were apparent when Nasoweka was drawn into a debate at a beer party with Rafaelo, the headman. Their debate, which took place soon after the signing of the Rome peace treaty, concerned the security situation in Mozambique. Nasoweka's stories of continuing violence in Angónia irritated Rafaelo, who was keen to see his village rebuilt soon, so that he could resume his headmanship in the permissive post-war situation. Rafaelo wondered whether Nasoweka wanted to return to Mozambique at all. He asked, 'Where is your home?' (*kodi kwanu ndi kuti?*). At first, Nasoweka replied quietly, as if to test the effect of her answer, 'In Malawi' (*ku Malawi*). Confronted by interjections of dismay from Rafaelo and his companions, she declared hastily, 'In Mozambique' (*ku Mozambique*).

Luis, another village leader and Rafaelo's long-standing opponent, was no less determined about the question of national identities. He saw no reason even to ask Nasoweka's opinion when he began building a house for her on the Mozambican side of the border. As such, the relationships that made Nasoweka a Chitima villager and Luis's wife compelled her to leave her neighbourhood in Mfuno. Luis had given her all her land, and his position as the Frelimo chairman made her prominent. Conversely, of course, she constituted Luis's prominence, given the fact that her decision to stay in Malawi would have undermined his authority in the village. Yet during repatriation, big men in the village emphatically imposed the definition of 'home' on her.

A FLIGHT THAT FAILED
Mortified homecomers

While Nasoweka lived relatively quietly throughout her exile, her co-wife, Namadzi, endured more personal disappointment. Apart from the house which Luis built for her and other material support he provided, he was, once again, indifferent to his wife's experience of displacement.

The flight of Namadzi's family was initially an attempt at a return like Nasoweka's own. But it ended in failure. The family, which included Namadzi's parents and some of their sons and daughters and their spouses, were refused the right to return from Chitima in Mozambique and to settle in the village of Edward, Namadzi's father, in the Ntcheu District of Malawi.

Nantuwa, Namadzi's mother, had lived in a virilocal pattern of marriage (*chitengwa*) in Edward's village until 1964, when she, Edward and their children moved to Chitima (see Figure 4.2). All their children – four daughters and two sons – had married by then, but the generosity of Paolo, Nantuwa's mother's brother (*malume*), provided them with so much land that Namadzi, her siblings and their spouses also settled in the Zakariya division of Chitima, only her youngest brother remaining with his wife in Chitima's Machanza division. When the flight began in 1986, the family, led by Edward, did not go to a refugee settlement on the opposite side of the border. Instead, they proceeded to Edward's village about three kilometres towards the interior of Ntcheu District.

But they were shocked to find that they were not welcome. Edward's siblings bluntly told them to go where the other refugees from Chitima had fled. 'They stopped us on the road' (*anatiyimitsa pa njira*), Namadzi described to me their reception. They were told that once they had left the village, they had left it forever. This led to the conclusion that none of the land which they had previously cultivated was available. The assurances by Namadzi's family that they were looking not for land but for a place to stay until the circumstances changed in Mozambique fell on deaf ears. They turned back and settled in the village in the Masasa area in Ntcheu where most members of the Zakariya division spent their displacement; Namadzi's brothers spent their exile in Mfuno, near their wives' families.

A comparison between two funerals during the displacement exposes the extent to which Edward had ceased to be 'rooted' in any particular village.

Figure 4.2 Nantuwa's family

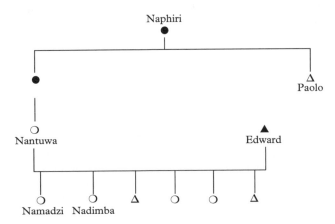

Edward, who died during the displacement, was buried not in his village of origin, which was only about three kilometres away, nor in Chitima, but in the graveyard of the refugee settlement in Masasa.[2] On the other hand, the burial of the widow of Ferdinand, the former headman – Nantuwa's mother's sister – who died almost at the same time, was a striking contrast. Paolo, the Catholic Church leader, and other elders decided that the burial should take place in Chitima. They argued that, in spite of the war, she had to be laid to rest next to her husband in order to placate both her spirit and her husband's. Her prominence as a headman's widow undoubtedly affected the decision. Yet the burial of the deceased in the graveyard of his or her home is usually indispensable to the the proper conduct of all funerals. Moreover, the choice of the burial-place and the erection of a memorial on the grave are also occasions for the bereaved to display their relative prominence. In Edward's case, his burial disclosed, in line with the failure of his return, the extent to which his village of origin had ceased to be his home. On the other hand, particularly because his wife was still alive, his children had little chance of arguing that his burial should take place in Chitima.

The emergence of conflicting memories

The situation of fleeing across the international border and thereafter seeking a return to a village of origin was hardly the same for the co-wives, Namadzi and Nasoweka. In each case, the persons involved gave the situation a distinctive definition, based on their memories of earlier acts and events. In Nasoweka's case, she returned successfully to her village of origin, and the exiled persons and their Malawian relatives shared the perceptions of the situation. In Namadzi's case, they did not. The conflict, with its present traces of past resentments, was cumulative through a long process, the outcome of which was the village's unwillingness to allow the displaced persons to be homecomers entitled to village membership and land. In order to understand this resentment, one has to consider the events that made them leave Edward's village in 1964.

The formal reason for the departure of Edward's family was a new primary school, built on his largest garden. During their childhood, Namadzi and her siblings had spent extensive periods in Chitima with their maternal grandparents. This ensured that their arrival in Chitima was not considered to be a dramatic event. It is crucial to note, however, that Edward's relatives had not done anything to prevent him from moving to Mozambique. No more land had been allocated to him to compensate for the land which he had lost, and apparently the relationships between his family and most of his relatives became dormant. The fact that they ended up in an outright confrontation when he and his family finally attempted to revive them suggests, however, that deeper resentments were involved.

A few years before the building of the primary school, Edward had already taken his family from the village to settle by the main Malawian highway, a couple of kilometres from the village. This was the place where Edward, an ambitious businessman, had a grocery store. Namadzi and her siblings admit that their father had 'many problems' (*zobvuta zambiri*) with his business in the face of continuous demands that he share his wealth with his fellow-villagers. At the same time, his relationships with some of his affines in Chitima, particularly with Paolo, himself a relatively affluent villager, were of a very different quality. More generally, until the mid-1970s, the benefits they derived from male labour migration to South Africa and from the presence of Portuguese entrepreneurs ensured that few Chitima villagers paid particular attention to Edward's prosperity. Edward's children recall that he had welcomed the opportunity of moving to Chitima, particularly because of the prospects for conducting business away from his relatives' immediate presence. In Chitima he found, however, that he could not compete with the Portuguese shops. Instead, he concentrated on farming.

Just as Edward had attempted to narrow the scope of his active kin-relationships, so too Namadzi and her siblings did little to maintain ties to his village. None of them married a member of his village, and, after Namadzi's first husband had died, none of their spouses came even from the vicinity of Edward's village. Moreover, some members of the family started to gain considerable prominence in Chitima. Namadzi herself became the wife of Luis, the leading Frelimo chairman, and her first-born daughter married a man whose paternal grandfather was Achigalu, the founding figure of the Manguluwe division, and whose maternal grandfather was the son of Zakariya. Nadimba, in turn, became not only Frelimo's female leader but also one of the most popular of all Frelimo officials in Chitima.

During the many years before the flight, their ties to Edward's relatives, while dormant, were not severed by an open conflict. When Edward's family fled, their definition of the relationships in that village assumed that some solicitude still prevailed, but Edward's relatives' definition of the situation implied that unacceptable claims to membership in the village were being made. In effect, for Edward's relatives, even exile was not a crisis severe enough to revive dormant relationships. What was built on the morality of enduring solicitude in one memory was sharply contested in another.

THE RISE AND FALL OF CROSS-BORDER COMPASSION
Discovering kinship

The case of Namanyada, Luis's cross-cousin who had never lived in Malawi before the flight in 1986, illuminates yet another facet of cross-border relationships during displacement. She fled with her daughter Malitina and Malitina's five unmarried children, all of whom remained together, living in the same household as before and after their exile.[3] During the displacement, they lived in Mfuno near the family of Namanyada's late senior co-wife and, in particular, near her daughter Rose, with whom Namanyada and Malitina became close in performing acts of mutual assistance (see Figure 4.3; cf. Figures 2.2 and 2.3). Previously, living on opposite sides of the international border, physically nearby yet socially distant, they had had little to do with each other. Fred, Namanyada's husband, was the only link between them.

Despite her past as a border villager, the case of Namanyada is, therefore, an example of a cross-border relationship which emerged only during the displacement. The three women – Nasoweka, Namadzi and Namanyada – were all members of the same border village, but whereas the personal pasts of Nasoweka and Namadzi had included, to varying degrees, significant events and relationships on both sides of the border, Namanyada had always been first and foremost a Chitima villager.

By virtue of her old age, her personal 'growth' had coincided with many transformations in the village. Already during the 1930s, when Chitima villagers were still living by the Mawe river (see Chapter 2), Fred had come from Mfuno to marry her. She wanted to refuse, but Jeremiya, her mother's brother (*malume*), who later detached his group from the rest of Chitima

Figure 4.3 Namanyada, Malitina and Rose

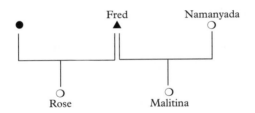

village, insisted on her accepting Fred. As was seen in Chapter 2, when
Jeremiya left the original cluster of Chitima villagers, Namanyada's young
family accompanied him. Thus they came to be situated in the emerging
centre of the village, and, for its part, Namanyada's 'growth' as a mother
and grandmother consolidated the new centre. Closely identified with the
new leaders of Chitima, she remained a stranger to the family of her co-wife.
The death of this woman in the 1950s, and the fact that Namanyada became
Fred's only wife, did nothing to bring her closer to the family on the other
side of the border.

After their flight in 1986, Fred built a house for Namanyada near Rose's
house, but Malitina was put up for a couple of months in Rose's kitchen-
hut, before her husband Zunga came to build a house for her. Zunga was a
Malawian from a village in the Bembeke area and had a senior wife in his
home village. Later he recalled that he had been terrified by the events in
Chitima to such an extent that he was not sure whether he wanted to return
to Malitina at all. He had been tilling the soil of her garden when he noticed
approaching guerrillas only a short distance away. Fully aware of the atrocities elsewhere in Mozambique, he ran to Malitina and Namanyada in the
village, and, in great haste, they fled to Fred's family in Mfuno. When the
threat of violence eased, Zunga came back and built a house and a kitchen
for Malitina. In effect, three new houses were built, all only a few metres
from Rose's house.

Namanyada and Malitina were the recipients of remarkable generosity
from Rose during the displacement. They had not been able to collect many
belongings when they fled, and they subsequently found that the *Machanga*
had stolen everything left behind. Upon their arrival in Mfuno, Rose had
shared some of her clothes with them and had even bought new cooking
utensils for them.

After Fred died in 1988, their relationship became intense in its own
right. Even though Namanyada and Malitina resumed the cultivation of
their nearest gardens in Mozambique only a couple of years after the flight,
they were given additional relish from Rose's vegetable produce throughout
their exile. Rose's family, in turn, received items from their relief aid, such as
cooking oil, sugar and soap. This extensive co-operation in the daily routines
and the mutual support between Namanyada, Malitina and Rose demarcated the three women's households as a place in which there was intense
solicitude. Bibiana, the leader of Catholic women in Chitima, Luis's sister
and Paolo's wife, had long been Namanyada's closest friend, but she spent
her exile in another part of Mfuno. She and Paolo were assisted by a
Catholic Church elder in Mfuno, and it was only after repatriation that
everyday conviviality re-emerged between the households of Namanyada
and Bibiana.

Dispersed by repatriation

For Namanyada, Malitina and Rose, what the displacement brought together, repatriation tore apart. The quality of their relationship changed dramatically after their repatriation in 1993. Tension increased so much that Namanyada and Malitina never bade a proper farewell to Rose. Afterwards, they tried to avoid beer parties when they knew that she was there, and they sat in a different group at functions at which she was present. Neither side could deny that their relationship had deteriorated, but both sides saw different reasons for this situation.

The immediate source of tension lay in Rose's demand for 'gifts' (*mphatso*) when the preparations for the repatriation to Chitima began. She told Namanyada and Malitina that she expected to receive one blanket as well as money from each of the three houses that had been built during the displacement. When Namanyada and Malitina said that they had no spare blankets or money to give, she dismissed these claims as a 'lie' (*bodza*). No further open confrontation ensued, and Namanyada and Malitina simply moved to their new houses in Chitima one day without informing Rose beforehand. By the end of my fieldwork, they had not discussed the issue with her again – or anything else, for that matter. The avoidance of each other that ensued provided a stark contrast to the earlier solicitude.

When Namanyada and Malitina discussed the issue, they raised three points as providing particularly salient justifications for their action. First, they recalled with dismay how Rose's sometimes excessive habit of drinking *kachasu* liquor had often disrupted their domestic tranquillity. Moreover, they said that Rose was frequently insulting when she was drunk. There had been incidents when she had shouted 'refugees, go home' (*malefuchi, pitani kwanu*) at other Chitima villagers, although not at them, as Malitina and Namanyada admitted. Second, there was, as in so many other cases, the issue of land. After the repatriation, Namanyada and Malitina began to question Rose's reputation for hospitality and complained that she had not given them any land to cultivate. Third, they pointed out that they had stayed at their husband's and father's home, respectively. Therefore, Rose had no reason to ask them to 'pay' (*kulipira*) anything. It is significant that Rose had spoken of gifts, whereas Namanyada and Malitina spoke of payments.

Seen from Rose's perspective, there was a measure of despair in her attempt to elicit a formal recognition for her compassion, for the altruistic work she had performed over the years when Namanyada and Malitina had been virtual extensions of her household. She was an unhappy woman, a tragic figure, despite the fine clothes that her frequent brewing of beer for sale enabled her to buy. Many of her children had died young, fathered by different men, and her own dependence on *kachasu* liquor was a frequent topic of gossip, as was her alleged prostitution.

In 1986, Fred's return, together with his Mozambican family, had restored dignity to her household. No longer was her neighbourhood known merely for the drunkards who flocked there searching for beer; prominent Chitima villagers also visited there. In this regard, Rose's demand for gifts envisaged not an end to a relationship but, on the contrary, a new beginning by creating an obligation for her to reciprocate. A payment, by contrast, would have replaced an ongoing exchange with a transaction which had a definite end.

In this case, both sides represented their actions as if they were within an enduring kinship framework. During the displacement, Rose had grown accustomed to address Namanyada as her 'mother' (*mayi*). After the repatriation both sides remembered the relationship as having been one between genuine relatives, but the other side was interpreted as having manipulated the relationship, failing to remain on solid moral ground. For Rose, gifts were a natural gesture signalling a new phase in a relationship which had already involved many exchanges. In the interpretations of Malitina and Namanyada, however, what Rose's demand revealed was that Rose had simply acted out of a desire for a payment and had not received them as kinsfolk at all. When contentious memories began to displace a shared memory of solicitude, the land question and Rose's drinking habits were readily recalled. Her generosity over the years was disregarded.

This tension does not alter the quality of their relationship during the displacement. Rather, the perceptions of fulfilment of kinship morality went unchallenged as long as the circumstances remained the same. The idiom of 'gifts' belonged to the realm of kinship, but repatriation had already begun to reshape Namanyada's and Malitina's relationships. The end of exile heralded the re-emergence of Bibiana's, Namanyada's and Malitina's households as the sites of shared everyday conviviality. United by their efforts to rebuild the village and to open gardens that had been long uncultivated, the women, like many other returnees, were predisposed to forget their exile. The new circumstances appeared to erase the need to display special courtesy towards Rose. Although both parties perceived the relationship in the same terms, their definitions of one another's actions did not dovetail.

GENDER AND THE PATRIMONIAL LOGIC OF SOCIAL CAPITAL

The contrasting ways in which Nasoweka, Namadzi and Namanyada endured their exile were similar only in the extent to which Luis, though closely associated with them, was invisible in its events and relationships. None of the three women depended on this big man in their search for refuge on the other side of the border. For Nasoweka, cross-border relationships with her classificatory sisters and mothers enabled her to experience the flight as a virtual homecoming. Namadzi followed her father to his village, only to find out that they were not welcome. Namanyada resembled more a helpless 'refugee' when her displacement began, without any actual or imagined ties to Malawian villages. However, female solidarity unexpectedly undermined uprootedness when her husband's daughter received her with great courtesy.

The 'female solidarity' in Nasoweka's and Namanyada's cases indicates a contrast between the patrimonial logic of social capital and the small-scale exchange relations that emerge more often among women than among men. Among Dedza–Angónia borderland villagers, as described in Chapter 1, the households of parents and their children are the most usual units of agricultural labour, and every such household has its own granary. Given the uxorilocal norm, village neighbourhoods consist of distinct households of related women, a pattern that has persisted in the face of changing economic fortunes (see Davison 1993; Peters 1997b). However, Nasoweka's and Namanyada's cases show how the boundaries between households are frequently crossed by women's mutual assistance, which ranges from casual help in small routine matters to extensive gift-exchange. As has been noted elsewhere in Malawi, the exchange of food and other items between different households can emerge even among women who are not related by kinship or affinity (see Vaughan 1983). By simultaneously maintaining separate households and engaging in exchange between them, women appear as *persons-in-relationships*, not as individuals. Because it is only adult women who have granaries, the exchange that circulates the contents of those granaries makes women's 'growth' visible (see Englund 1999).

The broad outlines of moral personhood – the need to make apparent the fact that personal growth is predicated on social relationships – are the same for women and men among Dedza–Angónia borderland villagers. The patrimonial logic of social capital, while indicating the same notion of moral personhood, entails a more specific sense in which that morality is displayed. Here the person becomes identified with particular clusters of people in mobilising, for instance, political support. In the case studies of this book, it is invariably men who personify such extensive sets of relationships in political life, from local party politics to the headman's domain. Even outside village politics, it is men who seem to mobilise others. In Namadzi's case, however unsuccessful their flight was, the family chose its direction on the basis of Edward's remembered prosperity in his village of origin. In the previous chapter, it was Evelesita who led a cluster of Lumbe villagers into exile – but her choice of direction was itself motivated by their belonging to the orbit of her affluent son, John.

As I noted in the beginning of this chapter, women are hardly 'subordinated' by the patrimonial logic of social capital, because they *constitute*, through their reproductive and productive work, those clusters and the crucial distinctions between them. The cases of Nasoweka and Namanyada have also demonstrated how the ties between women can be sufficient to secure their welfare during such potential crises as exile. The most critical question of gender affecting power relations in the patrimonial logic of social capital stems, of course, from the access to a cash economy and to the state that men enjoy more than women. Although, as will be seen in the Epilogue, the post-war predicament appears to have deprived almost everyone in the Dedza–Angónia borderland, men's economic and political leadership sometimes imposes effective constraints on women. An example was Nasoweka's 'forced repatriation' by the Frelimo secretary and the village headman, her husband and brother-in-law respectively, from the setting she had come to regard as her home. Such an example points to variations in the nature of power relations among Dedza–Angónia borderland villagers, a problem to be revisited later in this book.

5

MIGRANTS AMONGST REFUGEES

However abrupt and unwanted, displacement in the Dedza–Angónia borderland affected people who had long been accustomed to migrations. Whether because of colonial boundary-making or colonial and postcolonial labour migration, many villagers had been migrants before they became refugees. During the Frelimo–Renamo war, humanitarian aid played a pivotal role in making myriad experiences the one phenomenon of 'displacement' – involuntary rather than voluntary migration. Entitlement to aid codified 'refugees' as a category distinct from 'locals'. As has been seen, however, displacement in the Dedza–Angónia borderland encompassed highly varying personal experiences. Previous migrations, through the ties they had made or broken, could make all the difference. This chapter shifts the focus from 'refugees' to migrants who attempted to settle in the Dedza–Angónia borderland in the context of exile and repatriation. Like the previous shifts of focus between different persons and families, this focus introduces more complexity into the study of displacement.

The focus on migrants amongst refugees also highlights the economic situation in which exile came to be embedded on the Malawian side of the border. By the mid-1970s, more than a decade before displacement in the Dedza–Angónia borderland, male labour migration to South African mines had ended. As was seen in Chapter 1, coupled with the exodus of Portuguese settlers, the end of employment in the South African mines caused an undeniable economic decline, which was exacerbated by the war and the influx of refugees.

Malawi had witnessed economic growth from the 1970s until the early 1980s, growth which did not result in the equitable distribution of wealth (Banda et al. 1998: 72–4; cf. Pryor 1991). Although Malawi's prescription of liberalisation had achieved some macro-economic targets, Structural Adjustment, which was first introduced in Malawi in 1981, had failed to boost the economy by 1990. While a massive return of male labour to smallholder agriculture took place in the absence of clear incentives for them to produce marketable crops, a small elite with large estates often prospered by virtue of direct patronage from Life President Kamuzu Banda and his closest aides. The connection between the end of labour migration to South Africa and the growth of the estate sector appeared obvious when cheap labour started to flow to estates during the 1970s (Christiansen and Kydd 1983).

Farm labourers were also pushed to seek employment by the restrictions the government had imposed on smallholders' crops, particularly the ruling that they could not grow flue-cured, virginia and burley tobacco (Mhone 1992: 17–20; Mkandawire 1992: 180). The government's development strategy further disadvantaged smallholders by granting loans to the large-scale growers of tobacco. For example, the long-term loans which the National Bank of Malawi granted to tobacco growers went from K26,400 in 1973 to K21.6 million in 1982 (Mkandawire 1992: 179). Accordingly, even when understated by official statistics, agricultural wage employment grew faster than the average for all the industries during the period 1968–80 (Kydd and Christiansen 1982: 362).

Labour migration to the South African mines has remained an unparalleled source of wealth among Dedza–Angónia borderland villagers. By a bitter historical irony, villagers have come to remember the era of the apartheid state with nostalgia, while the economic developments in their own independent countries generally evoke dismay. Particularly for young unmarried men, agricultural estates, none of which was established in the Dedza–Angónia borderland, have been the main destinations of labour migration since the late 1970s. Exploitative tenancy agreements, under which the tenants' produce is bought at a fixed price by the estate owners and poor housing conditions are provided, have ensured that employment on the estates has given insufficient compensation for the end of international labour migration.

Until the early 1990s, migration to towns was a secondary option for most youths, and Malawi retained a strongly rural character, with 92 per cent of the population in rural areas in 1977 and 89 per cent in 1987 (Malawi Government 1993: xi). The change of government in 1994 introduced an ideological stance to encourage free economic enterprise by all, and school-leavers, in particular, began to appear in large numbers in the streets of Malawi's urban centres as vendors, often selling goods obtained through cross-border trade and smuggling. Because credit institutions have preferred to support well-established and larger-scale entrepreneurs, no proper accumulation has taken place among vendors and other small-scale entrepreneurs. 'Permanent urbanisation' remains a misnomer for the migration of the majority, with periods of urban residence interspersed with periods of cultivation in villages.

This chapter examines how similar dilemmas of trust and relatedness troubled both migrants and refugees during displacement and repatriation in the Dedza–Angónia borderland. The translocal political and economic forces which made it impossible for migrants to enjoy material security on estates and in towns were, like the translocal forces which bred displacement, integral to varying personal experiences. In the context of exile and repatriation, the arguments between migrants and refugees over homes and origins were often intense, with surprising perspectives emerging into the notion of 'uprootedness'. This chapter continues, therefore, to probe such apparently primordial identifications as nationality and kinship so as to comprehend the processual and often contingent underpinnings of social capital among Dedza–Angónia borderland villagers. The wide fields of potential relationships opened up by cognatic kinship, and the patterns of land acquisition associated with it, emerge as further sources of contingency under tumultuous historical conditions. This chapter also shows the significance of religious associations among migrants and refugees, how leadership in them is predicated on social capital achieved in other realms.

Two very different migrants are at the centre of the extended-case studies in this chapter. Hawadi returned to his village of origin after thirty years of absence, Joji joined his wife's village as a young *mkamwini* husband, a stranger from a far-away district. Though not involved in one another's lives in any direct way, both were linked to the same extended family as Nasoweka, Luis's second wife and the focus of one case study in the previous chapter. Hawadi was the youngest child of Sofiya, Nasoweka's mother (see Figure 4.1). During his long absence from the Dedza–Angónia borderland, Hawadi had developed little interest in party politics, least of all in Mozambique, which he vehemently refused to regard as his home. As will be seen, this already set him apart from many important men in his maternal extended family, most notably Sandikonda, another of Sofiya's sons. Sandikonda had long been a key authority both in the family and in Frelimo in his division of Chitima village.

Joji married Sandikonda's daughter. A young man from Mchinji District in Central Malawi (see Map 1) who worked as a domestic servant in Lilongwe before his marriage, Joji arrived in the Dedza–Angónia borderland with considerable commercial aspirations. These were similar to those of Hawadi, who also wanted to invest his savings in the Dedza–Angónia borderland. The juxtaposition of Hawadi's and Joji's cases, like that of the three women in the previous chapter, discloses the variations in personal experiences which at first glance appear similar in their outlines. Critically important questions of trust and relatedness are addressed when this chapter considers why, despite being migrants arriving at around the same time in the orbit of the same borderland family, Hawadi was ostracised while Joji found his niche.

A PROSPEROUS LAST-BORN
From a reunion to distinctions

Superficially, Hawadi's case is but an addition to the dismal list of failed homecomings in the context of exile and repatriation. In contrast to the other cases of an attempted return, however, Hawadi was initially welcomed by his relatives, after thirty years of absence from the Dedza–Angónia borderland. He was born in 1953, two years after Sofiya had moved from Mfuno to Chitima. He left the area in 1962, at the age of nine, and returned in 1992. If he had a reason during those thirty years to visit Blantyre, Malawi's biggest city, he would stop over at Chitima, but never for longer than a night at a time. He did not participate in the village's events and crises. As a matter of fact, the whole of the 1980s passed without his visiting the area. This absence and neglect, if glaring, was not important in the villagers' arguments at first. Upon his arrival, Hawadi was remembered and welcomed as a relative, a kinsman, long lost but finally at home. Criticisms of him were voiced only *after* almost a year had passed since his return.

This return to Mfuno was the first time since the late 1970s that Hawadi had seen his mother Sofiya and siblings, now refugees. He himself was easily recognised, and he built his house next to Sofiya's in Mfuno. He had arrived on the eve of a new cultivation season; the same season, in fact, when most Chitima villagers restored cultivation in Mozambique almost to its pre-flight level. Because Sofiya felt too weak to participate, Hawadi and Maluwa, the wife he brought with him from Malawi's Mchinji District (see Map 1), started to work in her gardens. During the past few years, the bad security situation had emptied Mfuno of village shops; Hawadi saw an opportunity and opened a small grocery store next to his house. Its supply remained limited to tobacco, biscuits, sweets, sugar, matches, aspirins and, occasionally, soft drinks. With the exception of aspirins, which he bought from Malawi government's Health Officers, Hawadi obtained these items from wholesalers in Dedza town. Maluwa, for her part, began to brew *kachasu* liquor for sale virtually every week.

During the first few months of Hawadi's stay in the Dedza–Angónia borderland, he became the centre of much cordial rapprochement. After the initial reunion, some Mfuno and Chitima villagers, recalling Hawadi's childhood in the area, became little more than nuisances. One neighbour in Mfuno, for example, developed the habit of passing by Hawadi's house during his frequent drinking expeditions, evidently in pursuit of free tobacco and *kachasu* from Hawadi's grocery. Slightly older than Hawadi, he often immersed himself in the memories of their common childhood. In one account that soon became a standardised narrative, he recalled carrying Hawadi on his back to a place far outside the villages, where he had taught Hawadi to herd goats and cattle, to hunt for bush-rats (*mbewa*), and to wrestle with other boys. Hawadi, struggling to conceal his irritation, invariably dismissed such memories as 'lies' (*mabodza*). Yet the neighbour's recollections disclosed a deeper dilemma. The image of Hawadi as a social junior, dependent on others rather than an influential man in his own right, had remained intact during his thirty years of absence.

In everyday activities, however, distinctions in the attitudes of his relatives and neighbours began to emerge. Sofiya and Nalipenga, who was his sister and the unmarried mother of two adolescents, quickly became a part of his household, whereas his other siblings did not receive similar attention, evidently because of their own large families. This was to have important repercussions for the perceptions which his brother Sandikonda and sister Nasoweka, in particular, had of him. Sandikonda, five years senior to Hawadi, was regarded as an authoritative 'guardian' (nkhoswe) in Sofiya's family, although all the major disputes in the family were also heard by her first son Chisale, himself eighteen years senior to Hawadi. Chisale did not live in Mfuno or Chitima, but, during the period of my fieldwork in 1992–3, he was both a Malawi Congress Party chairman and a headman's councillor in his father's village in Ntcheu District.[1]

Hawadi bought new cooking utensils and blankets for Sofiya and Nalipenga, who also received free food and kachasu from him. Although the profit which Hawadi made from his grocery was too modest to sustain the expansion of his business, it was enough to enable him to buy relish, usually fish, which is considered to be a better than average item of diet. Sandikonda and Nasoweka were never, of course, refused food at Hawadi's house, and Sandikonda was always given the best chair when he paid a visit. It seems, however, that after the first few months following Hawadi's return, they were no longer given kachasu and groceries for free, whereas Sofiya and Nalipenga continued to be favoured by getting such items free. Nor did Hawadi supply others with such goods as cooking utensils and blankets.

Diminutive but assertive, and always willing to debate questions of morality, Hawadi was extremely concerned about witchcraft and the image that others had of him. Once, after he had tasted maize beer (masese), he told me a tale of two brothers. One brother is rich and the other is poor. The rich one always helps their old mother with money and other necessities, thereby sacrificing a part of his wealth. The poor one, by contrast, does nothing to help the mother. For this reason, the rich one begins to 'hate' (kudana) the poor one and may even harm him through witchcraft.

Hawadi did not mention any names, but it was evident that he had his relationship with Sandikonda in mind. We had just discussed Sandikonda's habit of begging free tobacco from Hawadi's grocery. In effect, a double anxiety haunted Hawadi. On the one hand, Hawadi as a 'rich brother' could be seen to exclude others, when he almost single-handedly took care of the mother. On the other, he could be seen to begin to 'hate' his 'poor brother', who did nothing to contribute to the mother's welfare. Both dilemmas – exclusion and hate – culminated in the fear of being seen as a witch. Exclusion confined the scope of Hawadi's relationships to his mother and unmarried sister, hate could entail vicious attacks on others.

Hawadi was grappling with particularly grave moral dilemmas. As a businessman, he wanted to set limits to the sharing in his wealth. As a person who had been long absent and who was, in any case, the last-born in the family, he did not want to give the impression of being arrogant and greedy. Most of the time he followed a piecemeal approach to solving these dilemmas. He appeared generous when he felt he had to and refused demands for sharing when he felt he could do so without damaging a relationship. Strikingly, the consequence of his neighbours' and relatives' demands was by no means a dissociation from a wide range of relationships altogether. On the contrary, Hawadi sought to establish relationships outside the immediate circle, first through the local African Church organisation and then in his father's village.

Thirty years of movement

Before describing Hawadi's management of relationships in the Dedza–Angónia borderland in detail, it is instructive to consider the patterns of his moves during the thirty years of his absence from his village of origin. In 1962, Hawadi left Chitima in order to live with his classificatory mother (*mayi*) in the Linthipe area of Dedza District, some twenty-five kilometres from Chitima. This mother was the daughter of Sofiya's mother's sister. The son of Sofiya's mother's sister, Hawadi's classificatory mother's brother (*malume*), was also close to him in Linthipe. The early moves of Amfuno, the founder of Mfuno village mentioned in Chapter 2, had brought these relatives to Linthipe. A number of Amfuno's wives, offspring and followers remained on the sites of his previous settlements, and the largest group outside Mfuno village itself resided in Linthipe.[2]

Hawadi's migration was not part of a wider influx, but he was escorted by Sofiya, who had maintained active ties to her mother's sister's children in Linthipe. Over twenty years earlier, her first son Chisale had moved to live in his father's village in Ntcheu District (see note 1). This spatial distribution of children indicated, and maintained, the spread of Sofiya's valued relationships. However, in the course of time, Hawadi did not simply maintain Sofiya's relationships but managed a configuration of relationships specific to himself.

In 1972, he married an unrelated local woman in Linthipe. He went to work in South Africa in 1973. He spent only one year in South Africa, because his permit was not renewed. He had five children with his wife in Linthipe, of whom only two survived.[3] Soon after his return from South Africa, Hawadi started to work in Kasungu District on a tobacco estate, owned by C. Tamanda Kadzamira, the 'Official Hostess' of Kamuzu Banda's regime. Hawadi became a foreman (*capitao*) and was transferred to Mzimba District in the Northern Region in 1978, after the opening of a new estate there. He married a local woman in the same year and had five children by her. He did not stay long in Mzimba, however, and returned to a tobacco estate in Kasungu. He continued to visit his family in Mzimba irregularly until 1987, when he married Maluwa, a Mozambican woman who had fled from the war to Kasungu's neighbouring Mchinji District.

Many of Maluwa's brothers and matrilateral kin had already left Mozambique before independence and settled in Mchinji. It was to one of her brothers' farms in Mchinji that Maluwa fled, along with a few of her fellow-villagers and relatives. One of her brothers and her mother's younger sister had also settled in the Bunda area in Lilongwe District. These relatives had become Malawian citizens. The brothers in Mchinji were particularly prominent farmers and businessmen who imported goods from Zambia for sale in Malawi.

Hawadi was introduced to Maluwa by her cross-cousin who worked with him on the same estate. Maluwa went to live with Hawadi in Kasungu, although he also built a house on her brother's farm in Mchinji. Hawadi took his livestock – goats and chickens – to this new home in Mchinji and was considering starting his own farm in due course. After he left the estate in 1992, he decided, however, to see whether he could find land in his mother's village. He kept his house and livestock in Mchinji, because he was not confident that his return to Mfuno would be successful.

After almost twenty years as an estate labourer, Hawadi had become frustrated with the unfairness of the labour conditions. He was forced to buy fertiliser on credit, which, in effect, made it much more expensive than buying it for cash. Moreover, his produce was bought at a fixed price by the estate company. Maluwa's brothers greatly influenced Hawadi's decision to quit the estate, because they supplied him with information about conducting business and commercial farming on an independent basis. But Hawadi was not readily incorporated into the enterprises of his brothers-in-law – hence his desire to achieve something similar elsewhere; and hence, too, his arrival in Mfuno with Maluwa and four of their children. Their first-born was left with Maluwa's mother's sister in Bunda in Lilongwe District.

Hawadi's thirty years of absence from the Dedza–Angónia borderland thus included extensive movement, and, superficially, many discontinuities in relationships. For example, each of his major moves has been followed by a divorce in the previous setting and a marriage in the new setting. As will be seen below, his return to the Dedza–Angónia borderland appeared to be no exception in this respect. However, the shifts from one setting to another were more gradual than these observations suggest. For example, Hawadi continued to visit his family in Mzimba even after he had moved back to Kasungu. On the other hand, he left a house and livestock in Mchinji, and a child in Lilongwe, when he moved to Mfuno with Maluwa. These were material extensions of his and Maluwa's persons, and they would have facilitated a withdrawal from the borderland in case of an unsuccessful return. In other words, solicitous relationships certainly withered in the course of Hawadi's moves, but the emergence of subsequent sets of valued

relationships was neither instant nor automatic. His return to the Dedza–
Angónia borderland illuminates the difficulties involved in a particular
setting.

Sofiya's repatriation

Hawadi's difficulties in establishing himself as a moral person in the Dedza–
Angónia borderland, similar to those previously encountered by him in his
problems as an entrepreneur, were first brought into the open by his disagreement with Sandikonda. This disagreement concerned Sofiya's repatriation
to Mozambique at the end of the displacement. While Nasoweka, her
daughter, found it impossible to disobey her husband Luis in the question of
national allegiances, Sofiya felt the impact of the international border through
two other men, her own sons. Although open confrontation was avoided,
Sofiya's repatriation revealed the disparity between the two brothers'
interests. Contrasting national allegiances emerged as the wider context of
the brothers' argument.

Before his return to Mfuno, Hawadi had developed a strong resentment
against Mozambique. He had told his wife Maluwa to refrain from register-
ing in Mchinji as a refugee for relief aid. Nor did they register as refugees in
Mfuno, although all of Hawadi's closest relatives received aid. Hawadi's
fear was that all those who received aid would be returned by force to
Mozambique after the war. In this attitude he had been influenced by
Maluwa's brothers, who had described to him Mozambique's weak currency
and other appalling conditions for conducting business. He was also
convinced that a long time would elapse before there would be peace in
Mozambique.

Hence the disagreement between Hawadi and Sandikonda was, in one
sense, over the question of whether Sofiya's home was in Malawi or
Mozambique. According to Hawadi, Sofiya, and, indeed, all her children,
'were from' (amachokera ku) Malawi, for she only moved to Mozambique
because of her gardens. Sandikonda held a diametrically opposed view.
Although he was not born in Mozambique, Sandikonda would not accept
that he was born in Malawi. Nyasaland, he insisted, was his country of birth,
and he said that the country had changed completely, making Mozambique
the only place where he felt truly at home. An apparent paradox – the
brothers having been born on opposite sides of the international border and
yet each considering the other side to be home – became entangled with the
dispute over Sofiya's repatriation. With his sons, Sandikonda built a house
for her near his own house in Chitima, whereas Hawadi rendered no
assistance in the building of the house. Nalipenga moved to live in the house
when most Chitima villagers left Mfuno, but Sofiya followed her in late July
1993, almost two months later.

Hawadi and Sandikonda apparently never discussed their differences, but both expressed openly their views on the matter. Hawadi maintained that Sofiya was too old and weak to return to Mozambique and that she should be allowed to live her old age at her 'home' in Malawi. It should be noted that the distance between her house in Mfuno and the house in Chitima was less than half a kilometre, and that she was able to walk such distances; she also still performed domestic tasks in her house. For Sandikonda, in turn, it was self-evident that Sofiya was going to return 'home' to Mozambique, and he was clearly becoming impatient with the delay in her repatriation. Sofiya herself, at first, was very reluctant even to consider moving to Chitima. Her reluctance was commonly interpreted as stemming from the benefits she received while she was linked to the household of Hawadi and Maluwa. Nasoweka wryly observed, 'They give her *kachasu* liquor every day' (*amawapatsa kachasu tsiku lili lonse*). After Sandikonda's persistent requests and persuasion, however, she finally agreed to move.

In another sense, therefore, the contest over Sofiya's repatriation and her Malawian/Mozambican identity concerned Hawadi's and Sandikonda's respective authority within the family. Sandikonda's conduct as a guardian (*nkhoswe*) was inseparable from his understanding of the family's proper place in Mozambique, a conviction that was further strengthened by his own position in the Frelimo organisation of Chitima village. While Luis, the Frelimo secretary in the village, could not accept that one of his wives failed to return to Mozambique, Sandikonda similarly feared that the dispute over his mother's repatriation undermined his position in Frelimo. Wary of a confrontation, Hawadi submitted to Sandikonda's persistence and thereby revealed the limits of his own authority, both in the family and in the two border villages.

The tie between Hawadi's and Sofiya's houses remained intense, nevertheless. Most of Sofiya's meals were prepared by Maluwa; she either took the meal herself to Sofiya's house, or it was collected by Nalipenga. Hawadi's fourteen-year-old daughter from his first marriage, who had by chance found her father in Mfuno while on her way to Blantyre, decided to stay. She was accommodated in Sofiya's house in Chitima, a further link between the households.

This daughter, in fact, made Hawadi's family entitled to the returnees' food aid administered by the Mozambican government. When she was introduced to Rafaelo, the headman of Chitima, he suggested that she register for the aid. After a moment's thought, Rafaelo, keen on making the number of his villagers as large as possible, concluded that Hawadi, Maluwa and their children should also be registered, because the daughter really belonged to their family. Since no mention was made of the need to move to Mozambique, Hawadi decided to accept the offer of aid.

Sofiya's repatriation did not alter Hawadi's perceptions of Mozambique. It did alter, to some extent, his perception of the border. When other villagers suggested to him that he might not be able to continue cultivating his mother's gardens if he did not move to Mozambique, he dismissed these ideas by observing that he lived so close to the border that his house was 'very near' (*kufupi kwambiri*) Mozambique. Alternatively, he explained that he and Maluwa were only helping Sofiya. The produce was hers, and the food which she shared with them was a compensation for their work.

Access to land, however, did trouble Hawadi. He was aware that only Nalipenga among Sofiya's children had been given land by their mother. This troubled him, because he thought that, if Luis died before Nasoweka, Luis's family could ask her to stop cultivating Luis's land and to find a place on her mother's land. It is by no means customary among Dedza–Angónia borderland villagers to expel widows or widowers from their spouses' land. Hawadi's speculation was grounded, rather, on two exceptional circumstances; on the one hand, only one child was cultivating land given to her by her mother, although that mother had claims to vast areas of uncultivated land. On the other hand, in Hawadi's view, the fact that Nasoweka and Luis lived in the same village, and that Nasoweka was not living in a virilocal marriage (*chitengwa*), could also contribute to the development he envisaged.

A further reason for Hawadi's reflections on the land question was a dispute which arose between Sandikonda's wife and her sister over the former's attempts to expand her gardens. This unsuccessful attempt made Hawadi speculate that, given the fact that Sandikonda had seven children, even Sandikonda could eventually look for land from Sofiya. Hawadi's worries were probably exaggerated in the light of the vast uncultivated areas to which Sofiya had claims, but they reflected his increasingly bleak perceptions of his prospects in Mfuno and Chitima. These perceptions were also greatly influenced by the mounting pressure to move to Mozambique now that he was receiving aid; even Rafaelo had asked him to build a house in Chitima. By mid-1993, it was evident that Hawadi was, as so many times before in his life, considering a change in his circumstances.

Aspirations and isolation

On the whole, Hawadi's management of relationships did indicate his desire to stay in the area. In addition to wrestling with moral dilemmas posed by his neighbours and matrilateral relatives, he tried to expand the configuration of his active relationships through the African Church and the relatives in his father's village. Whenever Church issues were discussed, he made it known that he had been an African Church elder for eleven years in Kasungu. He began to attend the African Church services soon after he had returned to Mfuno, and it became evident that he had quickly developed ambitious plans.

The congregations of the African Church in the Dedza–Angónia borderland consisted of considerably older persons than those of the Presbyterian and Catholic Churches. Although elders occupied leadership positions in all the churches, youths played an active role in the Presbyterian and Catholic Churches; for example, they were Sunday school teachers and the leaders of their own youth groups. Nothing similar was available to them in the African Church in the Dedza–Angónia borderland. As already mentioned, it was rarely the first Christian church to which a person belonged, but a choice which emerged in specific life-situations, sometimes as a consequence of outright expulsion from another church, more often because of its tolerance of beer-drinking and polygamy. For Church members themselves, their brand of Christianity represented respect for 'the customs of our ancestors' (*miyambo ya makolo athu*). Respect for elders, a crucial aspect of Church members' definition of their valued customs, however, did nothing to provide Hawadi with a ready constituency in the Dedza–Angónia borderland. His status as a social junior was no less striking in the Church than in the family and neighbourhood.

After the rebuilding of Chitima, there were two places of worship for African Church members in the area: a church building at the Bembeke turn-off in Malawi, and a Church elder's house in the Zakariya division in Chitima. Because both were more than a kilometre away from Hawadi's house, he started campaigning for a new church building in the immediate vicinity of his own house. He realised that, because of the small number of African Church members in Mfuno, the church should be built in Chitima. His argument, therefore, was that Mozambicans should also have a proper church building instead of worshipping in a Church elder's house and that it should be erected in the Machanza division. He claimed that most African Church members lived in that division, a claim which contradicted the widely accepted fact that most members lived in the Zakariya division. The Machanza division lay, however, closest to Hawadi's house on the Mozambican side of the border.

Thus, in an apparent contradiction of his notion of 'home' in Malawi, Hawadi's argument emphasised the anticipated benefit for 'Mozambicans'. Yet when he elaborated the argument, 'Malawians' were also drawn in to the debate. He observed that the Malawian members of the African Church in the nearby villages would probably want to attend the services in the proposed place rather than at the Bembeke turn-off. The church, Hawadi concluded, was to be erected 'on the border' (*pa malire*) so that people from both sides of the border would regard it as theirs.

No one seemed to want to back his proposal. Of his close relatives, only Nasoweka belonged to the African Church, but she chose to ignore Hawadi's command that she should not attend the services in the Zakariya division. Nasoweka herself was a leader in the women's group of the Church and clearly identified herself with the prevailing Church organisation in

Chitima. Both Luis and Rafaelo, the most prominent Church members in Chitima, were also unsympathetic to Hawadi's idea, Luis stating bluntly, 'There is only one African Church in this village.' After the other Church elders, most of them strangers to Hawadi, in Zakariya and at the Bembeke turn-off, had also dismissed the proposal, he started to entertain the idea much less actively. It is probable that he had begun to campaign for his cause too soon, before he had established himself as a veritable Church elder. This was a part of his general difficulties in the area after thirty years of absence. The claim that Hawadi had been an elder for eleven years in Kasungu was not, in itself, persuasive in a context in which there was no lack of Church elders and in which credentials had to be earned locally.

By mid-1993, almost a year after his return to Mfuno, Hawadi had started to focus his management of relationships on his father's village, Kanyama, some six kilometres from Mfuno, on the road to Dedza town (see Map 2). None of Hawadi's relatives in Mfuno and Chitima, not even his brother Emanuele, had maintained active ties with the father's family in Kanyama. The father had left Sofiya soon after Hawadi's birth and remarried in the Mua area of Dedza District, several kilometres from Mfuno. The father died there in the 1980s, but five of his sisters, Hawadi's *adzakhali*, and many of their children were still alive in 1993 and living in Kanyama.

In early 1993, Hawadi had already developed a habit of passing through Kanyama when he took supplies for his grocery store from Dedza town. Although the visits were brief, he was well received with meals and courtesy. He also began to hand out some of his supplies during the visits. One of his *adzakhali* and her daughter – a divorcee and Hawadi's cross-cousin – became particularly close to him, sometimes visiting his house in Mfuno. They were also favourably received by Maluwa, whose relationships in the area had been confined mainly to Sofiya and Nalipenga.

Simultaneously with Hawadi's increasing involvement in relationships in Kanyama, however, clouds started to gather over Maluwa's well-being in Mfuno. Some bickering between her and Hawadi had become apparent to the visitors to their grocery store, and later, in September, the friction culminated in violence. Upon his return from a beer party late one evening, Hawadi beat her with his fists and a stick, until she managed to escape. Maluwa fled to Chisale's house in another village about three kilometres away. She demanded that Hawadi should be given a reprimand. On the following morning, she was accompanied to her house by Chisale and Sandikonda, who held a hearing, attended by her and Hawadi. Incidentally, this was a day when Hawadi's cross-cousin from Kanyama called at their house, and, therefore, she also heard the whole case.

During the hearing, Hawadi accused Maluwa of jealousy because he had met his first wife by chance in Dedza town recently. His cross-cousin was not mentioned as a source of jealousy. Hawadi asserted that Maluwa had stopped performing all her domestic chores; an assertion which was disproved by eyewitness testimony, including that of Hawadi's daughter. Maluwa maintained that Hawadi was her husband, and that she did not want a divorce but only a reprimand. This was promptly given by Chisale and Sandikonda, who called Hawadi's behaviour 'shameful' (*chochititsa manyazi*). They also warned him that if he did not change his behaviour, he alone would have to pay the costs of the divorce case.

It is revealing to consider, given the frequent incidence of domestic violence in the area, the extent of moral disapproval that was levelled at Hawadi after this conflict. For several days, he was the subject of much gossip. The general conclusion was to castigate Hawadi as a 'wicked' (*woipa*) and 'mean' (*wankhanza*) person. He was soon publicly humiliated at a beer party by Luis, who remarked that Hawadi treated his wife like a 'slave' (*kapolo*). He was now openly suspected of reviving his relationship with his cross-cousin with marital designs in mind. Nevertheless, villagers noted that the cross-cousin seemed to have stopped visiting him, and he, in turn, did not pass through Kanyama on his visits to Dedza.

Hawadi tried to give up drinking beer as a consequence of the incident, but a month later a crisis erupted again. This time Maluwa fled in the night to Sandikonda's house and told him that, after a row, Hawadi had threatened to kill her, if she tried to sleep in the same house with him. In spite of the efforts of Sandikonda and his wife to prevent her, before dawn she embarked on a journey to her mother's sister in Lilongwe District. Penniless, she expected to make the journey of some seventy kilometres on foot, carrying her youngest child on her back and leaving the other children behind.

Afterwards, Hawadi refused Sandikonda's demand that he should provide money for the transport of Maluwa's remaining children. According to Hawadi, he did not have enough money to do so. In the moral uproar that ensued, his 'wickedness' was again publicised, and many expressed sympathy for Maluwa, primarily because she had been seen to perform her work in a way that made Hawadi's behaviour particularly unjustified. Hawadi had now earned a reputation which made it extremely difficult for him to remarry soon in the area. Moreover, Sandikonda decided to build a hut for Hawadi's daughter near Sofiya's house and forbade her to work for her father. The argument was that Hawadi would now give her all the woman's work in the house, which would be too much for a young girl. Hawadi had to do something bizarre for a man – to cook food for himself. He used piece-workers (*anthu a ganyu*) to fetch water and firewood. Isolated and humiliated, at the end of my fieldwork in 1993 he was entertaining vague hopes of emigration to South Africa.

The public criticism of Hawadi was not simply a consequence of his violence against Maluwa. Nor were his difficulties in settling due to past resentments, as was the case in John's and Edward's failed returns to their villages of origin. Hawadi had not established a set of relationships which would have provided support against, and thereby dissipated, public criticism. His desire to become an African Church elder, for example, was too ambitious in the light of his being a recent arrival. Hawadi's problems – entrepreneurship and domestic violence – were by no means phenomena that invariably led to moral bankruptcy in the Dedza–Angónia borderland. It was a measure of Hawadi's narrow scope of active relationships in the area that no effective counter-opinion emerged in his favour. Conversely, had Hawadi maintained a wider scope of relationships in the area during his absence, his problems might not have ended in a crisis.

When the crisis erupted, therefore, unhappy memories swiftly replaced the focus on common kinship. Sandikonda, for example, remarked on more than one occasion that Hawadi's relatives could have died in the Dedza–Angónia borderland, but he would not have come to their funerals. The memories of shared kinship and shared childhood gave way to the memories of what had *not* been shared during Hawadi's thirty years of absence. The war, more than anything else, came to divide the experiences of Hawadi and his relatives in the Dedza–Angónia borderland. *He* did not know what it was like to live under the terror of the *Machanga*, to flee to Malawi and to live on handouts from relief agencies. Even more, by his refusal to move to Mozambique, Hawadi seemed to belittle such tribulations – the 'home' was, in his view, in Malawi, and the war and exile did not really concern him. The contentious issues raised, once the circumstances so demanded, were copious.

FINDING A NICHE
A stranger's arrival

In contrast to the case of Hawadi, in which ties to the village of origin remained rudimentary during absence, in Joji's case spatial mobility permitted selective management of relationships in different settings. In his case, recently established relationships provided a foundation from which to maintain long-term solicitude, rather than vice versa. The longer Joji stayed in his village of origin, the more likely he was to become embroiled in conflict. At the same time, he remained close to specific persons there even during his absence. Moreover, in contrast to many of the other cases cited above, Joji's case demonstrates the value of relationships which fall outside the scope of kinship and affinity.

Joji, a self-professed Nsenga by ethnic identity, was born in 1968 in the Mchinji District of Malawi. He met Martha, Sandikonda's oldest daughter (see Figure 5.1), when they were both working in Lilongwe. He moved with her to the Dedza–Angónia borderland in 1989. He had no previous ties to the area, and all of Martha's closest relatives were refugees in Mfuno. The

Figure 5.1 Joji and Martha

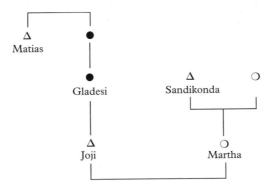

young couple also settled in Mfuno. Joji soon made friends with Thomo, another Nsenga from Mchinji District, who lived at the Bembeke turn-off with his local Malawian wife. Although they had never met before, Joji and Thomo began to address one another as 'brothers' (*achimwene*). Ten years senior to Joji, Thomo was a relatively prominent businessman and had established numerous connections in the Dedza–Angónia borderland. Joji himself wanted to use his savings from Lilongwe as capital for his own business, and he found in Thomo a willing adviser.

Thomo had bought a sewing-machine and was a successful tailor. He suggested that Joji should try trading in clothing and introduced him to Charlie, a young unmarried man living at the Bembeke turn-off. An Nyungwi from the outskirts of Tete town, Charlie had become a refugee in the Dedza–Angónia borderland, where his father had been a teacher before the war. With Charlie, Joji started to collect second-hand clothes from a market in the Linthipe area of Dedza District, some twenty-five kilometres from Mfuno. They then sold these clothes in the villages in the Bembeke area.

By 1993, the close friends, Charlie and Thomo, came to be at the centre of a circle of some thirty active Jehovah's Witnesses, living near the Bembeke turn-off and in the surrounding villages. The circle was largely due to Charlie's fearless efforts to spread the faith. The earlier Jehovah's Witnesses in the Bembeke area had been suppressed during the persecutions in Malawi in the early 1970s.[4] The new converts had in common the fact that most of them were relatively young and that many were engaged in business, as traders, tailors, builders and butchers, in the main. Significantly, however, only one of the six owners of grocery stores in the small trading centre at the Bembeke turn-off had shown any interest in the faith by 1993, and he was fearful of the reactions of the other owners of grocery stores, if he joined them. Indeed, the other grocers were passionate in their condemnation of the sect. Two owners' threats of detaining the Jehovah's

Witnesses in the area were particularly ominous because of their important positions in the local Malawi Congress Party organisation. This hostility, in effect, contributed both to the close-knit nature of the new Witnesses' group and to the suspicion with which the majority in the area viewed them.

Having all but finished secondary school in Mozambique, Charlie engaged in various petty businesses in different towns in Mozambique and Malawi, including Lilongwe, where he was baptised as a Jehovah's Witness. Upon returning to his parents at the Bembeke turn-off in 1988, Charlie started to talk openly about his faith. In 1990, Joji's participation in the meetings and studies of the Jehovah's Witnesses grew out of his friendship and business partnership with Charlie and Thomo. He had arrived in the Dedza–Angónia borderland as a Catholic, and Martha and all her closest relatives were also Catholics. Nevertheless, Joji persuaded Martha to attend the studies, under Charlie's supervision, with him. Joji's relationships with his affines, and indeed with Mfuno and Chitima villagers overall, never became particularly cordial. In the borderland, the congregation of Jehovah's Witnesses was the core of his valued relationships.

Long-term friction, long-term solicitude

The intensification of Joji's involvement in relationships in the Dedza–Angónia borderland must be understood in the light of his difficulties and aspirations in his village of origin. When Joji began living with Martha, he hoped that his stay as a *mkamwini* husband would be short and that they would move to Joji's home in Mchinji, where he expected to have access to vast areas of uncultivated land. His ambition had long been to open a farm of his own. Although Martha never consented to this proposal, it was not in itself the reason why Joji's return home failed.

Being the oldest child in the family, even as a young boy Joji had already started to look for ways to support his mother, Gladesi, who became a widow in 1983. Never remarried, she stayed with Joji's three sisters and three brothers in Mchinji. Two of the sisters married after Joji moved to Martha's home, but he also continued to send remittances to his mother from Mfuno. In May 1993, however, he received the news that Gladesi was seriously ill. Suspecting witchcraft, Joji decided to take her to a healer (*sing'anga*) near Mfuno.

When Joji arrived in his village in Mchinji, he learned that Gladesi had visited hospital. Because she had been too weak to return to her village, on her way back she had stayed in a village where her sister lived. As night was falling, Joji decided to see his mother on the following day, and he fell asleep in a hut which his younger siblings had vacated for him. Later that night, he was awoken by noise in the hut in which he was sleeping. He could hear heavy breathing and somebody moving in the hut. Because he was unable to see the person in the darkness, he asked who it was. Wasting no time, the intruder grabbed Joji's throat and tried to strangle him. Joji fought back and made enough noise to awake his siblings in a nearby hut. By the time they came to the hut with light, the intruder had disappeared.

Joji was thoroughly shaken by the incident, convinced that he had been the victim of a murder attempt. On the following day, he went to see Gladesi, but when they returned together to their home village, they did not go to Gladesi's house. They stayed, instead, at the house of Joji's classificatory brother (Joji's father's elder brother's son) in a different neighbourhood. On the third day after his arrival, Joji took Gladesi and her two youngest children with him to Mfuno.

Joji had no doubt about the identity of the intruder. He was sure that it had been Matias, the brother of his maternal grandmother (see Figure 5.1 above). The friction between Joji and Matias had been long-standing, with Joji attributing its reason to Matias' 'jealousy' (nsanje) because Joji was supporting his mother and siblings. Matias and Gladesi lived in the same neighbourhood, and, according to Joji, virtually the whole village was in uproar, morally outraged, after the night's incident. Matias was accused of trying to kill his grandchild (mdzukulu), but there was no formal hearing of the dispute. Matias simply denied the charges vigorously. However, Joji was now convinced that Matias was also responsible for Gladesi's illness, a conviction that was later confirmed by the sing'anga near Mfuno.

At the time of Gladesi's visit to the area, Sandikonda and his wife had already moved back to Chitima, whereas Joji was still building a house for his family. This was, in fact, the first time that Joji's and Martha's parents met, but Sandikonda and his wife were not favourably impressed. They complained privately that Joji's mother and young siblings 'had run away from hunger' (anathawa njala), and asserted that they had no maize in their granary in Mchinji because of 'laziness' (ulesi). They also blamed laziness, rather than illness, as the reason why Gladesi did not help them in the tasks of preparing new houses which preoccupied Chitima villagers during her visit. Significantly, after Gladesi's visit, which lasted for a couple of weeks, Joji complained only that Martha had been backbiting, although it hardly escaped him that she had merely echoed Sandikonda's and his wife's discontent. Joji was clearly determined to keep up the appearance of harmony with his affines, because, as he often observed, they would understand his difficulties with Martha and would refrain from having a dispute, if he left her.

A trajectory of interests

Joji's relationships to his relatives in Mchinji thus evinced both extreme friction and wholehearted solicitude. By virtue of being Gladesi's eldest son and offering generous assistance to her and her children, Joji was undermining Matias as the guardian (nkhoswe) of the family. As mentioned already, Joji's relationships in the Dedza–Angónia borderland evinced a somewhat similar tendency towards sharply contrasting qualities, his affines remaining socially distant, and the congregation of Jehovah's Witnesses dominated his relationships. Joji's increasing difficulties with Martha coincided with the mounting tension in his village of origin. As a consequence, he sought to bring both sets of solicitous relationships spatially near to him.

Among Mfuno and Chitima villagers, only Joji and Martha began attending the meetings and studies of the Jehovah's Witnesses. Their intent was to accomplish all the studies required for baptism and to have a formal wedding in the local Kingdom Hall, which had recently been built on the Mozambican side of the border near Masasa in Ntcheu. Both Joji and Martha pursued their studies with diligence in 1990–1 under Charlie's tuition, and both completed the first of the four books required for baptism. From 1992, however, Martha grew slack in her attendance at the studies and services. Moreover, to Joji's great irritation, she also began to visit beer parties and even to participate in the drinking. Although their third child was born in early 1993, from late 1992 onwards it was widely perceived that their marriage was falling apart. Joji never quarrelled with his affines but insisted that Martha's parents, in particular, understood his difficulties with her.

Martha confronted Joji on two fronts. She displayed, on the one hand, increasing scepticism about the teachings of the Jehovah's Witnesses, and she annoyed Joji, on the other hand, by her apparent neglect of her duties as his wife. The imminent end of the world promised by the Jehovah's Witnesses had begun to appear implausible to Martha, and she defiantly told Joji that 'I am tired of waiting' (*ndatopa kudikira*). Joji, in turn, complained that she lacked 'respect' (*ulemu*), and that he had to perform many of her chores for himself, such as preparing the bath-water. Moreover, Joji had assumed a habit of paying meticulous attention to his and Martha's appearance. Their house in Chitima was a typically modest, grass-thatched, small building with no extensive furniture, but Joji spent much of his small profit to keep his family well dressed and clean. In a move that was highly exceptional among Dedza–Angónia borderland villagers, Joji started to buy Colgate toothpaste in Dedza town. To his immense irritation, however, Martha took little notice of his instructions when to use it. She would often use it before going to a beer party, where her drinking of beer undermined, in Joji's view, the effect of the toothpaste.

These difficulties with Martha coincided with disturbing news from Mchinji. Although Gladesi and her two youngest children returned to her village in Mchinji with medicine from the *sing'anga* near Mfuno, her illness endured. In August 1993, Joji received the news that she was dead. Convinced that Matias was responsible for her death, and fearing for his own safety, Joji did not attend Gladesi's funeral. It was now clear to him that he could not return to live in his village of origin as long as Matias was there, but he was anxious to take his two young brothers to live with him in the Dedza–Angónia borderland.

But he wanted to leave Martha first and to find another wife. His desire was to marry a Jehovah's Witness; 'a beautiful Witness' (*mboni yokongola*), as he privately specified. Before his mother had died, this quest for a new wife had already led to a three-week absence from the Dedza–Angónia borderland. He had met two male Witnesses in Chitima, employed to grow tomatoes on a piece-work (*ganyu*) basis, from the southern Malawian District of Balaka. They had encouraged Joji to settle in Balaka, where, they said, there was an ample congregation of Jehovah's Witnesses.

Joji did not reveal his destination to Chitima villagers, but, because he had taken all his clothes with him, Martha and her relatives were doubtful whether he would return. But things did not turn out as Joji had planned in Balaka. Later he explained his decision to return to the Dedza–Angónia borderland in terms of business opportunities. In Balaka, it would have been difficult to find goods for resale, and agriculture would have been the only source of income. The congregation of Jehovah's Witnesses that he found there was also smaller than he had expected. Beyond that, he developed painful boils in his throat while he was in Balaka. Despite the fact that his companions in Balaka also developed similar boils, Joji thought that Matias was again responsible. He decided to return to the *sing'anga* near Mfuno village who had helped Gladesi. Although he found relief, Matias in Mchinji became a source of increasing anxiety for him. Gladesi's death only seemed to confirm his worst fears.

After the Balaka trip, Joji resumed living with Martha and privately boasted that he had no need to leave the area in order to find a new wife. He finished building the house for Martha in Chitima, but he remained as marginal a figure in the village as ever. His dislike of beer parties and politics, as well as his faith, were objects of some bewilderment, even ridicule, among most Chitima and Mfuno villagers. Joji, in turn, never lost a chance to criticise the life-style of the youth in these villages. He complained, virtually irrespective of whether anyone listened, that people did not realise that 'time was finished' (*nthawi yatha*), and that there was a need to start studying with the Jehovah's Witnesses. Joji himself continued his studies every Sunday at the Kingdom Hall and was completing the second book in the required reading.

By the end of my fieldwork in 1993, he had arranged with Thomo, his Mchinji 'brother' at the Bembeke turn-off, to move into one of Thomo's houses and to take his two young brothers from Mchinji to this house. He was also confident that he had already found a new wife from a nearby village. The woman was a Catholic, but Joji decided to let her know about his faith only after she started to live with him in order to avoid 'frightening' (*kuchititsa mantha*) her. Even if she was going to refuse his proposal, Joji was determined to leave Martha and to start living near his 'brother'.

Despite their short duration by 1993, Joji's relationships with the Jehovah's Witnesses in the Dedza–Angónia borderland evinced solicitude on a par with some of his long-established relationships in his village of origin. The configuration of valued relationships, though specific to Joji, took shape amid relationships and contingencies far beyond the parameters of that configuration itself. It was not, in other words, simply Joji's own interests and actions that accounted for the social capital with which he could manage his valued relationships. For example, Matias's jealousy, as Joji perceived it, erupted into violence and witchcraft; Martha's loss of interest in the Jehovah's Witnesses was a corollary of her revived closeness with Chitima and Mfuno fellow-villagers. Such unexpected difficulties made Joji discard his earlier interest in opening a farm in Mchinji, and he developed new interests. Joji's perception of Matias's wickedness reinforced his desire to take care of his mother's family; his estrangement from Martha and her relatives accentuated his commitment to the Jehovah's Witnesses. Consequently, the congregation also provided the base for his continued solicitude with relatives in Mchinji without the need to return to Matias's orbit.

CONTINGENCIES OF MIGRATION

The shift of focus in this chapter from refugees to other migrants has added further nuances to this book's perspective on displacement. The fact that refugees were not the only migrants in the Dedza–Angónia borderland made refugees assume the roles of 'hosts' in some situations, with surprising consequences for villagers' own definitions of the 'displaced' and the 'local'. In Hawadi's case, for example, a long-absent returning migrant arrived in a setting where, despite his closest relatives' exile, social relationships revolved around established patterns of authority. After initial rapprochement, he began to feel the effects of long absence on his ability to realise his aspirations in the area. Joji, on the other hand, settled in the area through the local congregation of Jehovah's Witnesses, where the distinctions between refugees and locals were underplayed.

While the two migrants had very different experiences of what being a 'refugee' might mean in the Dedza–Angónia borderland, neither encountered disempowered 'victims'. These extended cases of attempts to settle in the area have sustained, therefore, the overall argument of this study about displacement. It must be understood, to reiterate, as a predicament which was contingent upon highly variable personal trajectories and translocal political and economic factors.

Hawadi and Joji were migrants whose desire for prosperity made them, under the conditions of the postcolonial political economy in Malawi, abandon agricultural estates and urbanisation in favour of combining trading with smallholder cultivation in villages. For neither of them was this desire for prosperity incompatible with a wide field of active relationships. As a matter of fact, both cases demonstrate, like earlier case studies, the indispensable role that relationships play in pursuing such a desire, and Hawadi's failure to establish a set of supportive relationships also annulled his commercial efforts. In understanding Hawadi's trials and tribulations, his poor share of social capital in the area must not be seen as a consequence of a fixed pattern of authority which apparently left little for a returning migrant like him to achieve. On the contrary, Hawadi was not confined to the particular set of relationships in which Sandikonda personified considerable authority, and the ramifying ties of cognatic kinship, for instance, enabled him to revive, from oblivion, relationships in his father's village.

In fact, Hawadi's failure to generate the social capital necessary for attaining his commercial aspirations underlay the very rapprochement that first greeted him in the Dedza–Angónia borderland. It gained momentum from the memories of shared kinship and childhood. Those memories were not, in a strict sense, nostalgic; they evoked an image of Hawadi as a social junior, an image that served his relatives' and neighbours' interests in the present and, in view of his relative affluence, in the future, also. The mismatch of interests, with Hawadi focusing on other sets of relationships, introduced negative nostalgia. Hawadi was now recalled to have neglected his relatives and neighbours for thirty years. His attacks on his wife bespoke the same innate wickedness.

While the previous chapter highlighted the effects of gender on social capital, Hawadi's case makes evident how the notion of social capital must also take into account villagers' own understandings of social age. Hawadi's long absence, in itself, did not prevent him from settling in his area of origin; what was crucial was the way in which he sought to realise his interests without paying due attention to his standing as a social junior.

The extended cases in this book qualify the long absence from a village of origin as the ultimate reason for difficulties experienced in return migration (cf. Ferguson 1999: 123–65). Chapter 3 drew our attention to the effects of the most recent actions a person had committed. Throughout the many years of his residence far away in Malawi, John had maintained close ties to Lumbe, his village of origin. His failure to return was a consequence of his management of relationships *after* the flight of his fellow villagers. More broadly, the earlier pattern of migrating to work in South Africa is another example among Dedza–Angónia borderland villagers of the fact that long-term absences have not necessarily narrowed the scope of a person's relationships in the village of origin. Remittances and gifts were common means by which these relationships were maintained.

Despite the focus on the active management of relationships which their scale affords, the extended cases in this book present contingency as a recurrent theme in the lived experiences of war and exile. Time and again, persons face the limits of their ability to realise their interests. The lonely figure of Hawadi cooking his own food is unparalleled among the many portraits of this book, but even for Joji, whatever his success in settling in a new area, personal interests did not remain the same as events unfolded. He was pushed to modify his interests by other persons' actions which he could not anticipate. After the war and exile, as the next chapter and the Epilogue show, the return to 'normalcy' in the Dedza–Angónia borderland has not made villagers' management of relationships any less prone to sudden reactions to contingencies. The new era has introduced new anxieties, difficulties which seem, for many, to have betrayed the promise of peace.

6

PARADOXES OF REPATRIATION

'Viva Frelimo!', cried Alfredo at the opening of the first village meeting after Chitima's reconstruction in late 1993. 'Viva!', roared the crowd, in a routine that had not been used for some seven years. In point of fact, the times were different now, and not even Alfredo and Luis, the staunchest Frelimo leaders in Chitima, could conduct a village meeting as if it were a party rally. Reconciliation, expressed through such idioms as 'mutual honour' (*kulemekezana*), was their concession to the changing times. War and exile had taught villagers to acknowledge the existence of different interests in village politics. Some used the occasion to turn the spirited Frelimo slogans into jokes. Rafaelo, the village headman, who was widely seen as a Renamo collaborator, listened to Frelimo leaders' slogans and speeches in apparent calm and, to the surprise of many, began his own speech with those slogans. His opening was, however, a parody which the crowd greeted with uncontrolled laughter.

The peace treaty between Frelimo and Renamo was signed in Rome in October 1992 (see Introduction). In a country where the capacity of the central government was in doubt, some observers were inspired to see the success of the treaty as a 'people's peace' (see Wilson 1994b). To be sure, the will to abandon the war, in both rural and urban areas, had become overwhelming after persistent insecurity and impoverishment. Whatever the balance of power between Frelimo and Renamo, many Mozambicans seemed to think that the war between the two movements had to end. In the Epilogue, I discuss the post-war realities after a few years had passed since the repatriation of the Chitima villagers. Here the focus is on the immediate aftermath of repatriation in the Dedza–Angónia borderland. 'People's peace', seen from the perspective of Chitima village politics, appears as a process that carries past contests with it into new political and economic conditions.

This chapter picks up the extended-case study of Chitima village politics, personified by the full brothers Rafaelo and Luis. While Chapter 2 showed the village's path to war through nationalism and postcolonial discontent, this chapter explores the effect of the new pluralism on the antagonisms and allegiances that village leaders brought with them to the post-war situation.

For Chitima villagers, one of the most striking transformations was Rafaelo's resumption of his headmanship. The introduction of the headman and the Frelimo secretary as equally legitimate authorities was, for the post-war government, a means to seek reconciliation and wider popular partici-pation. In a particular setting, however, the two poles of authority were not simply 'recognised' (cf. West 1998; West and Kloeck-Jenson 1999). The various minor offices they encompassed came to be further loci of contest, sometimes subverting and sometimes supporting the authorities personified by Rafaelo and Luis.

These observations contribute to a growing theme in the critical litera-ture on displacement – whether repatriation is to be understood as a simple 'return home' (see e.g. Crisp 1986; Harrell-Bond 1989; Allen and Morsink 1994; Allen 1996; Black and Koser 1999). When Chitima villagers encoun-tered rampant poverty and inadequate aid after their repatriation, the homecoming bore little resemblance to an arrival in a haven of peace and prosperity (cf. Rogge 1994: 40). These dire material conditions loomed large in villagers' post-war arguments and shaped the familiar antagonisms in unexpected ways.

More broadly, the study of repatriation, like the study of displacement itself, must be wary of the entrenched spatial metaphors which inform much official discourse on refugees (Hammond 1999). If refugees are 'uprooted', then this discourse represents repatriation as a return to the natural state of socio-cultural life, the best possible end to exile. But lost in such a discourse is the hard physical and symbolic work many returnees have to perform in order to create conditions which would define a 'home' for them. This chapter shows how, in contrast to their own expectations, Chitima villagers found little to which to 'return'; the flight from the war had left conflicts unresolved, the houses open for Renamo's destruction and many gardens taken over by weeds. As before, villagers had to cope with contingency and uncertainty, and so too must the analysis of their predicament. Against the studies of repatriation which increasingly serve the institutionalised patterns of returnees' aid (see Preston 1999), the extended-case method, with its eye for detail and complexity, unsettles the apparent fixity of the phenomenon.

To be sure, the post-war situation has its own potential for triggering conflict. In Zimbabwe, the will to commemorate war victims and heroes introduced war memorials, which, against the best intentions of the state, raised contentious questions about who actually belonged to the nation (Kriger 1995; Werbner 1998). In more localised contexts in Zimbabwe, the ceremonies of healing were important aspects of reconciliation but also had the potential of being manipulated for further conflict and division (cf. Reynolds 1990; Ranger 1992; Schmidt 1997). The existential and cosmo-logical weight of wartime atrocities was certainly heavy; improperly buried persons could come to haunt their surviving relatives as vengeful spirits (Lan 1985: 35; Werbner 1991: 186–7); land polluted with violence and bloodshed had to be cleansed through ritual (Ranger 1992: 704).

In the Dedza–Angónia borderland, the post-war predicament had a somewhat different content. Because no one was killed during the war in Chitima, the spirits of the dead did not haunt Chitima villagers more than local Malawians (see Englund 1998). Healers (*asing'anga*), and the notion of healing (*kuchiritsa*) overall, did not appear in Chitima villagers' discourses on the post-war situation. Nor were they interested to debate the credentials of national politicians. Here they were unlike Malawians in the Dedza–Angónia borderland, who, during the repatriation of refugees, grappled with the concept of multiparty democracy by arguing about the misdeeds and virtues of *Ngwazi* Kamuzu Banda (see Englund 1996a).

Multipartyism – especially the rumour that about twenty new political parties had been established in Mozambique – also interested Chitima villagers. For many middle-aged and elderly Chitima villagers, multipartyism was potentially another source of war, because they feared that all the numerous parties would not be able 'to agree' with one another (*kugwirizana*) (cf. de Brito 1994; Harrison 1996). Despite being fed national news by hearsay and the Mozambican and Malawian radios, however, Chitima villagers were considerably less preoccupied with their distant national leaders than with the familiar figures of village politics.

Chitima villagers came, for their small part, to support the heartening statistics of repatriation to Mozambique. Like most refugees in Dedza and Ntcheu Districts, they had already departed before the United Nations and other aid agencies began implementing their repatriation programmes (see Bonga and Wilson 1993: 7; cf. Wilson with Nunes 1994; Koser 1997). By early 1994, no refugee settlements remained in Malawi. The determination to return appeared to be strong when the vast majority of refugees had no time to wait for the transport arranged by the UNHCR – in the end, only 22 per cent of refugees used such transport (UNHCR 1995: 6). Of the UNHCR's Mozambique repatriation budget of US$108 million, only 20 per cent was used on transport and repatriation, while a reintegration programme in Mozambique came to absorb 80 per cent (Dolan 1999: 86). Food aid for returnees had begun to be delivered in Angónia before the repatriation, but many Chitima villagers believed that the government would provide more material assistance and 'development' (*chitukuko*) only when it was clear that the village had indeed returned. Aid was received simultaneously on both sides of the border for several months, although practically all the refugees had left Mfuno village by October 1993.

As during the war and exile, the villagers' management of relationships was embedded in politico-economic conditions beyond their control. The post-war conditions had assumed a clearer pattern of neo-liberal laissez-faire a few years after repatriation, as the Epilogue will show. This chapter explores how the conflicts, and indeed paradoxes, of repatriation emerged by describing and analysing, first, the formal distribution of political offices after the rebuilding of the village. The chapter then shows how the antagonism between the village headman and the Frelimo secretary appeared to continue despite the new conditions. These conditions, particularly through villagers' expectations of aid and 'development', soon began to make the antagonism obsolete, and Rafaelo and Luis joined one another for visits to the district capital to lobby for the improvements which the villagers wanted. Villagers' discontent was not, however, a simple reflection of their dismal material conditions. The specific ways in which discontent was expressed were manipulated, to an important degree, by certain prominent villagers, who had their own vested interests in the deepening popular discontent. The chapter shows, finally, how these interests, rather than indicating a coherent 'strategy', themselves underwent transformations as events unfolded during repatriation.

THE DISTRIBUTION OF OFFICES

In Chitima village, reconstruction was in full swing by May 1993. Chitima villagers shared a widespread concern over the success of the peace treaty and the achievement of public security in Mozambique. Following the confident decision by Rafaelo, the headman, to start building an iron-roofed brick house for his senior wife Deliya, others prominent in local politics followed his lead. But the more cautious attitude of Luis, the Frelimo secretary, was consistent with most villagers' view that Renamo, rather than Frelimo, was the threat to the peace process. Luis thought that building an extravagant house in Mozambique was, at this stage, unwise. He sold the iron sheets of his senior wife Skolastika's house instead of bringing them back to Mozambique.

Many other Chitima villagers also built temporary houses, following the lead of Luis rather than Rafaelo. Their intention was to defer the building of new and bigger houses until after a year or two of careful watching over the state of the peace in Mozambique. But residence in Mozambique was widely believed to be a local requirement for the cultivation of gardens.

For Chitima villagers, as mentioned, the most marked change introduced by the post-war state policies was Rafaelo's reinstatement as the village headman. Already during displacement, he had been recognised as a 'headman' (mfumu) by relief agencies and Malawian authorities, who consulted him and Luis as representatives of refugees. In practice, the opportunities to exert authority as a Chitima leader during displacement were very limited. Refugees from different villages were usually treated as one group, and all the public events in Malawian villages were conducted under the supervision of Malawian headmen and party officials. It was only upon his repatriation to Mozambique that Rafaelo's position became clear.

No formal ceremony marked Rafaelo's reinstatement as the village headman. The Frelimo officials in Villa Ulongwe had sent a message that the end of the war had prompted the government to 'return' (*kubweretsa*) the office. Rafaelo simply resumed his position, unchallenged. Luis and the other Frelimo officials were, by contrast, re-elected to their positions. The first Frelimo meeting took place in July 1993 in Mtimbo village, about four kilometres from Chitima along the border to the south-east (see Map 2). Here lived Betha, who had been the Frelimo *secretário* for the frontier area since independence. He held, therefore, a higher position in the party organisation than Luis. At the meeting in July, which was convened to elect the principal Frelimo officials at the area and village levels, Betha was re-elected as the area *secretário*, and Luis as the *secretário* for Chitima village. Luis was re-elected unopposed, and, when he tried to decline, in the expected show of modesty, by referring to his old age, long and tumultuous applause forced him to accept the office. At the same meeting, Alfredo, Nadimba and Sadlek were re-elected, also unopposed, as his 'vice-chairmen'. Thus the highest rung of the party organisation assumed exactly the same composition as before the war.

In Chitima village itself, there was one major meeting which gathered together almost the whole adult population. Intense squabbles preceded this meeting, as is described below. When the meeting did finally take place in late August, it sought to distribute the offices in Chitima village politics once and for all. A large gathering of Chitima villagers turned up, and Rafaelo and Luis were seen to sit next to one another and to conduct the meeting in an apparent consensus. As mentioned before, Alfredo opened the meeting with the 'viva Frelimo!' slogan, thereby suggesting that Frelimo had convened the meeting. All the speeches in the meeting, however, had a pointedly conciliatory tone. They urged the villagers to give up backbiting, to live in peace and not to divide the members of Chitima into Mozambicans and Malawians, because, it was said, all who lived in Chitima were Mozambicans. Both Luis and Rafaelo urged people 'not to despise one another' (*osanyozana*), but to 'honour one another' (*kulemekezana*). Their words were echoed in the speeches by the rest of Chitima's political leaders.

The main issue of the meeting was the selection of the village headman's councillors (*nyakwawa*) and the Frelimo chairmen for each division of the village. Each of the five divisions received three chairmen, three 'chairmen for the youth' (*macheriman a yufi*), one female Frelimo official and three headman's councillors. All the offices, except Frelimo's female *macheriman*, came to be occupied by men. As noted in Chapter 2, the use of 'chairman' as a title is complicated by the fact that it is widely used even by persons who have no formal position in the party organisation. On the other hand, there were persons who were not formally reinstated after the repatriation, but who, nevertheless, were widely considered to be venerable chairmen.

During this distribution of offices, most nominees showed rather more reluctance than the display of mere modesty entailed. Persistent persuasion, even threats, by Rafaelo and Luis, who dragged the mortified candidates forward to be accepted or criticised by a vociferous crowd of women, were needed to elicit a positive response from the candidates. There were no fixed material benefits that would flow from the offices of chairmen and councillors on this rung of the authority structure. After the repatriation, when such events as beer parties, girls' initiations or weddings took place in the village, it was usually only Rafaelo who, as the village headman, received formal gifts.[1] Many nominees admitted afterwards that their reluctance was due to the uncertain security situation in Mozambique. They feared that they would be targeted first, if hostilities erupted again.

On the whole, the nomination of three chairmen and three councillors for each division ensured that virtually all the prominent male elders in Chitima became involved in the formal authority structure. This was reinforced by the fact that there were also chairmen who were not formally reinstated, even though they were widely considered to have important positions. 'Chairmen for the youth' did not necessarily involve youths but married men, some of whom were even middle-aged. Many of them were *akamwini* husbands from other villages in Mozambique or Malawi. In many cases, they had not occupied positions in Frelimo before.

Several of the village headman's councillors, on the other hand, had earlier been Frelimo chairmen. This was not surprising, given the fact that Frelimo was officially the ultimate authority in Chitima before the war. Although Stefano, Andrea and Pitala, who, according to a popular view in Chitima, had helped Rafaelo to bring the *Machanga* to the village (see Chapter 2), were nominated as councillors, this position was also assumed by persons who were not perceived to have sympathised with Rafaelo or the *Machanga*. Rather, the councillorship passed, in many cases, to those who were remembered as having occupied the position before independence, even if these persons had subsequently become Frelimo members.

The local organisation of the Catholic and African Churches added, of course, even more offices to this constellation of local politics. During displacement, 'refugees' had formed a Catholic *limana* grouping of their own in Mfuno, excluding those Chitima villagers who had been both willing and able to associate themselves with the groupings of Mfuno village. Upon the repatriation to Chitima, however, new *limana* groups were established in every division. While many of their offices were occupied by women, Paolo retained his position as the leading Catholic Church elder in Chitima. Chitima Catholics continued to attend Church services in Mfuno village until the building of their own Church was completed in 1995. As mentioned in Hawadi's case in the previous chapter, the African Church also retained the same organisation as it had had before and during the displacement.

Soon after the meeting in August, Luis began to arrange Frelimo meetings in the divisions of Chitima. Once again, his objective was to nominate people to positions of authority, this time youths to act as 'soldiers' (*asilikari*) in their village divisions. Their duties overlapped with those of the chairmen and councillors in that they were all supposed to maintain discipline, but the 'soldiers' were also assigned the task of 'capturing' (*kugwira*) the culprits who failed to appear in the village court. Fifteen young, mainly unmarried, men from Zakariya, twelve from Maphiri, nine from Manguluwe, seven from Machanza and seven from Mtunda were selected. Luis gave them vague promises that they would at some point be sent to Villa Ulongwe to learn tactics of self-defence and arrest. No weaponry was provided for these 'soldiers'.

Youngsters had also been nominated to look after discipline in different village divisions before the war, but many thought that the numbers of the nominees had now more than doubled. This increase in the numbers of the villagers associated with Frelimo indicated, on the one hand, Luis's desire to counter the effects of the headmanship as another official pole of authority in the village. On the other hand, Luis was also concerned about the emergent interest in multipartyism, which stemmed, in 1993, mainly from the political debates in Malawi. Moreover, some youths had demonstrated their interest in becoming 'soldiers' by joining or otherwise supporting the *Machanga*. Perhaps the memory of this earlier enticement also prompted Luis to expand the pool of youths incorporated into Frelimo.

These formal distributions of office hardly clarified Chitima's political constellations. No local or central authority explained how the numerous chairmen and councillors were differentiated by their duties and scope of authority. Since the court (*bwalo*) was the headman's principal arena in Chitima, most of his councillors heard and prepared its cases. However, many chairmen also participated actively in the court proceedings. In any case, the chairmen's and councillors' formal orbit consisted of exactly the same tasks of keeping discipline and announcing the messages of the headman or the party *secretário* in their village divisions. Moreover, the implication, of course, was that there was a considerable overlap between the scope of authority of Luis and Rafaelo.

The irony of these post-war circumstances is clear. As Chapter 2 demonstrated, a distinction was the precondition for the growth of Luis and Rafaelo in prominence. After the war, however, they found themselves back at square one – state policies declared them to be commensurate and equally legitimate authorities. The rest of this chapter examines how state policies, once again, were given a localised flavour by the processes of trust and moral personhood among Dedza–Angónia borderland villagers.

FROM RIVALRIES TO COMMON INTERESTS
Antagonism continued

The wide range of offices, their overlapping duties and scope of authority imply that the actual configurations of authority are constantly remade, not defined by the formal distribution of offices. The trust that any particular chairman or councillor inspires is a consequence of managing particular relationships. By continuing, particularly in this section, to approach local politics through Luis, Rafaelo and the relationships they personify, I do not seek to underplay the range of relationships which constitute authority in Chitima village. On the contrary, this chapter shows how, for Chitima villagers themselves, Luis and Rafaelo have personified quandaries of compelling importance and have, as such, served as useful templates for pinpointing the sources and consequences of ongoing arguments. This chapter examines how the popular perception of Luis's and Rafaelo's rivalry came to be replaced by widespread appreciation of their common interests. The difficulties surrounding the returnees' aid were an important prerequisite for this shift of understandings to take place.

After the repatriation, as mentioned above, squabbles and intense backbiting preceded the formal distribution of offices in the first village-wide meeting. The meeting in late August was convened after six weeks of disagreements and open mistrust between Rafaelo and Luis. Rafaelo convened his court at exactly the same time as Luis tried to hold a Frelimo meeting. On every occasion, Luis found the court proceedings already under way when he arrived at the scene and was forced to cancel his meeting. After several humiliating cancellations, Luis proposed new spatial arrangements so that the headman's court and the chairman's meetings could be summoned irrespective of each another.

Significantly, this proposal was not successful. The objections by several chairmen, councillors and elderly women gained momentum from the perceived antagonism between Luis and Rafaelo. It was argued that the spatial division of the party's and the headman's orbits would have been tantamount to establishing 'two villages' (*midzi iwiri*). After a delegation of chairmen and councillors had discussed the matter with Rafaelo, it emerged that he was prepared to accept the Frelimo meeting, if the headman's councillors were also selected at the same meeting. Rafaelo was anxious to ensure, in effect, that his headmanship was recognised as as an office equal in authority to Luis's chairmanship. The first village-wide meeting would be the most suitable occasion to demonstrate this new division of authority.

Immediately after the repatriation, many Chitima villagers thought not only that the antagonism between Rafaelo and Luis endured, but that the change of state policies had further polarised the two brothers. Luis's conduct, in particular, nourished this understanding. He appeared jealous of the village court from which he, like Rafaelo after independence, had been excluded. On the eve of the repatriation, Rafaelo's closest councillors, Stefano and Pitala, had informed Luis that the court was in the domain of the village headman. They had explained to him that it dealt with issues within the village, and that it had to be kept separate from the affairs of party politics. The councillors had observed that a case is brought to the attention of the 'government' (boma) only when it is not settled in the headman's court. Luis, accepting this definition, refrained from attending the court proceedings. But he took a keen interest in its decisions and soon found in them his major weapon for discrediting Rafaelo.

Luis echoed a popular view by observing that Rafaelo's court rulings were unreasonably harsh. In one divorce case, for example, Rafaelo had ordered a man to pay an exceptionally heavy fine of 410 kwacha (US$94). Luis started to keep a private record of Rafaelo's rulings and fines in the court – a practice of note-taking which he called 'putting into a file' (kulowetsa mufaili). His intent was to show this 'file' to government officials in Villa Ulongwe as evidence of Rafaelo's mismanagement of the headman's duties. Another source of irritation for Luis was the fact that Rafaelo led the court proceedings in close co-operation with Stefano, their sister's son. In private conversations, Luis disseminated the view that it was unacceptable for persons of 'the same family' (banja limodzi) to dominate at the court. Luis also stated, even in public meetings, that Frelimo would not order villagers to pay fines, because they were poor. Instead, the offenders would be given useful tasks, such as digging latrines for the elderly. Many villagers recalled, however, that Luis had imposed fines when he ran the court after independence.

Luis's rhetoric built on widespread discontent with Rafaelo. Although this discontent apparently led to Rafaelo reducing the fines at the court, he usually ignored the criticism. Unlike Luis, Rafaelo seldom mentioned any names when he engaged in backbiting, but chose to speak more broadly about the government or Frelimo. It was only after Rafaelo's misbehaviour at his own house that the extent of his unpopularity was dramatically revealed. In early October, he drank kachasu liquor excessively, and upon his return to his senior wife Deliya's house, he beat her badly with a stick. Deliya fled, in horror, first to her sister Namanyada, and from there to her cross-cousin Luis. Luis exhibited deep dismay at the violent assault on a weak old woman. As in Hawadi's case, described in the previous chapter, the intensity of the moral uproar in the village was a measure of how dismayed many villagers were with the culprit's overall moral standing. A number of Frelimo chairmen asked Alfredo and Luis to bring Rafaelo to the court. Although Luis gave a vague promise of calling together the elders of Chitima in order to 'teach' (kuphunzitsa) Rafaelo, nothing happened. These events took place, as is described below, when a certain alliance had emerged between Rafaelo, Luis and Alfredo. Popular discontent with Rafaelo was left to simmer because of the leaders' inertia.

The discontent with Rafaelo erupted unexpectedly. A week after he had beaten Deliya, Rafaelo appeared at a beer party in the Zakariya division. The regular headman's portion of beer had already been sent to him, and he had consumed this, and apparently also some *kachasu*, at his house. Upon his arrival at the beer party, he demanded loudly a whole bucket of beer, because, he declared, 'I am the headman' (*ndine mfumu*), and Chitima villagers are 'my people' (*anthu anga*). The response that he had already received the headman's portion of the beer was to no avail. Instead, Rafaelo started to hurl obscene remarks at the woman who had brewed the beer. He was thereupon pulled aside by four young men of the Zakariya division, beaten and left alone to cry for help from passers-by. Even though no weapons were used, the fists of the young men had caused such injuries that Rafaelo had to go to hospital on the following day. No dispute ensued, however, because Rafaelo admitted that he had been in the wrong when he demanded more free beer.

Many Chitima villagers were clearly pleased about the incident and considered it a just reward for Rafaelo's earlier misbehaviour with Deliya. But even before his attack on Deliya, many Chitima villagers had commented, in private conversations, on his 'lack of love' (*kusowa chikondi*) for his subjects at large. The incident at the beer party reflected, therefore, Rafaelo's broader difficulties in reviving his authority after his collaboration with the *Machanga* and his conduct of the court. It is virtually unheard of for a village headman to be beaten by his own villagers.

Although three of the young men were Frelimo 'soldiers' (*asilikari*) nominated by Luis, the assault was not orchestrated. Nor did it subvert Rafaelo's position permanently, because even Deliya, who had at first declared that she was not 'the headman's wife' (*mkazi wa mfumu*), accepted him again after a short period of time. But it did give Luis a new opportunity to manage the popular perceptions of *his* authority. Only days after Rafaelo's humiliation, Luis generously distributed among Chitima's chairmen a bucket of beer, which he had received as a gift from a beer party. This was not what he usually did on such occasions. Given the growing discontent with both Luis and Rafaelo, few would have been convinced by Luis's direct criticism of Rafaelo. Instead, by distributing beer, and with Rafaelo's arrogance fresh in mind, Luis attempted to inspire trust and to produce a sharp contrast between the perceptions of Rafaelo's morality and his own.

Antagonism discontinued

Post-war state policies had created conditions under which the antagonism between Rafaelo and Luis was becoming obsolete as a constitutive fact of Chitima village politics. The overlapping scope of their authority entailed similar popular expectations. In contrast to their subordinate councillors and chairmen, it was increasingly difficult for Rafaelo and Luis to make their authorities appear distinct. Gluckman's concept of 'inter-hierarchical positions' elucidates the reason for this difficulty. Rafaelo and Luis had both become 'the lowest member(s) of the superior hierarchy and the highest member(s) of the subordinate hierarchy' (1968: 71). The sometimes disparate agendas of the two 'hierarchies' often met in the persons of Rafaelo and Luis.

This contradiction, and the limits of Rafaelo's and Luis's antagonism, emerged in relation to Chitima villagers' expectations of 'development' (chitukuko). As has already been shown for Portuguese settlers before independence and as is discussed further in the Epilogue, 'development' embraces a moral condition among Dedza–Angónia borderland villagers, a condition in which enhanced material security is inseparable from a sense of enduring relatedness. During the repatriation, villagers received no outside assistance in the reconstruction of the village. Relief aid for returnees began in Mozambique in late June, but villagers retained their ration-cards, which entitled them to the fortnightly food deliveries in Malawi. This overlap of aid continued for no less than almost six months, until the delivery point was finally closed in Malawi in December.

The food items of the aid were provided by the World Food Programme on both sides of the border. The items in the returnees' and refugees' aid were largely the same: maize flour, cooking oil, beans and, at first, blankets.[2] Because the overlap of aid coincided with the season when most Chitima villagers had completed the first full harvest after the war, there was an abundant supply of maize flour in Chitima village. The relief maize flour in Mozambique was considered, however, to be of poor quality, and in many cases it was fed to domestic animals or sold to Malawians. On the whole, Chitima villagers were interested in the returnees' aid less because of food than because of the rumours that chemical fertiliser, buckets and watering-cans would also be delivered. Apart from blankets, however, no non-food items were received.

Considerable inconvenience accompanied the reception of the returnees' aid. The greatest was the fact that it was delivered in Mtimbo village. Villagers from the farthest corner of the Mtunda division had to travel about eight kilometres to reach Mtimbo. Those who could afford the fare made the journey by bus, and some, mainly from Malawi, came on bicycles. The effect was to create a system of conveying the aid to the recipient's home for a charge of K1.50. The inconvenience was compounded, furthermore, by persistent delays and logistical errors in the delivery of the aid. Villagers were often called to assemble in Mtimbo only to find that the aid had not yet arrived, and at worst a person had to wait for four days before it was his or her turn to receive the aid items. The aid was also meant to be delivered every four weeks, but in practice the interval was at least six weeks.

Popular opinion among Chitima villagers demanded, immediately after the first aid delivery exercise in Mozambique, that the delivery point be removed from Mtimbo to Chitima. This opinion was reinforced by the fact that Mtimbo was a considerably smaller village than Chitima. Luis, Rafaelo and Alfredo announced that, according to the correct procedure, a census had to be conducted first in order to convince the authorities that Chitima indeed needed a delivery point of its own. In early September, the task of conducting the census was delegated to Luis's eldest son, who wrote down the 'head' (*mutu*) of each 'family' (*banja*) and the number of persons in the family. The definition of the 'family' was, in this context, the narrowest possible, corresponding to a 'household'.

Luis and Rafaelo ordered that each household was to give twenty tambala during the census. Although most households complied, the ruling proved to be fatal. Luis's son had disclosed to a few villagers that 585 households had been registered in the census. Because five households earned one kwacha (one kwacha being 100 tambala), practically the whole village was soon of the opinion that a considerable fortune had emerged.

Although Rafaelo and Luis were not seen to spend more time together than before, the money that was collected during the census made Rafaelo, Luis and Alfredo, in the popular opinion, a clique with shared interests – the three men were seen to monopolise the revenue. Although it is not clear how the three men divided the money between themselves, at least none of Rafaelo's councillors seemed to benefit from the census money.

Alfredo was not a mere cipher in this developing alliance between Rafaelo and Luis. Given the tension that had prevailed between Rafaelo and Luis for several years, it would have been extremely difficult, in personal terms, for the two leaders to co-operate. On the eve of the repatriation, Alfredo had developed a highly respectful attitude to Rafaelo, who, in turn, received him with courtesy at his house. Yet in the view of some Frelimo chairmen in Chitima, Alfredo's identification with Luis was uncritical. As is analysed below, however, Alfredo's prominence largely required this identification, which had emerged in the broader context of Alfredo's relationships.

The response of the three men to the popular criticism was that money was needed for transport to Villa Ulongwe, where the census information was to be given to government officials. This explanation was refuted by many villagers, because the three men could have travelled to Villa Ulongwe and back by bus for a dozen kwacha. Moreover, the most critical villagers observed that if the journey had been made on bicycles, the costs would have been even smaller.

Ignoring these criticisms, the three men made the journey together by bus and, upon their return to Chitima, gave vivid descriptions of their findings in the district capital. A government official, for example, took them to see warehouses, where they saw huge amounts of relief maize waiting to be delivered to the countryside. They had also noted that white people were in abundance in the town. Some of them, Alfredo described at a beer party, looked as dazzling as shining stars (*nyenyezi*). Most of the white persons could only be seen as they passed by in their cars, with usually two white persons in each car.

Rafaelo, Luis and Alfredo were among the first Chitima villagers who visited the town after the war. Their reports on relief maize and white people suggested that 'development' was just round the corner. But no assurances had been obtained on the main issue of the visit, the removal of the delivery point of the aid from Mtimbo to Chitima. It was evident that a contest ensued between Chitima and Mtimbo leaders over the issue, with both sides travelling to Villa Ulongwe to lobby. Betha from Mtimbo village was clearly in a better position than the Chitima leaders, because he was the Frelimo chairman for the frontier area.[3] Popular discontent with Luis, Alfredo and Rafaelo increased after their first visit to Villa Ulongwe, and did not lessen, as they had expected. The demand for 'development' also became more pronounced as not even a single new borehole had accompanied the repatriation. Feeling pressure, Luis, Alfredo and Rafaelo embarked on a second journey to Villa Ulongwe in early October.

They deliberately timed their second visit to coincide with the first anniversary celebrations of the Rome peace treaty. The three men were the only Chitima villagers who attended the celebrations in Villa Ulongwe. When they returned two days later than expected, the village was rife with rumours about what had happened during their second outing to the town. Their weary faces, bearing indisputable signs of hangovers, spurred much gossip, now with the conclusion that the three men had engaged in excessive drinking and had even spent money extravagantly on bottled beer rather than on the cheaper local brands.

The three men attempted, none the less, to inspire trust by assuring villagers that they had demanded development for Chitima from government officials. Their demands included the sinking of boreholes; the return of the Portuguese to re-establish their farms and shops; a medical doctor; a school and teachers; a separate building and a supervisor for the disabled; the elimination of mosquitoes in the area; and the disinfection of drinking water. Few villagers were able to take such a report seriously. Luis was confronted at a beer party by a group of women who asked for 'seeds' (*mbewu*) so that they could start to cultivate. Seeds contrasted with empty words, but the women also played upon the imagery of fertility; *mbewu* is a common euphemism for semen. Unable to provide seeds, Luis appeared impotent in a highly subversive image.

The issue of the collected money continued to haunt the three men. Luis and Rafaelo were observed to buy expensive new clothes for their wives, and Alfredo had three new chickens and two new rabbits. When they were confronted with these criticisms, Luis replied that he got money from the sale of the iron sheets of Skolastika's house, and Alfredo said that he had recently had a beer party at his house. Moreover, at the risk of causing more offence, they asked why it was possible for Church elders to collect money, while their similar act as village leaders was condemned. In any case, the events and popular discontent had unexpectedly bound the three men in a moral alliance. In this alliance, Rafaelo's and Luis's antagonism gave way to concerted efforts to counter the emerging criticism that their leadership was incompetent. As was described above, it was at this point that Rafaelo misbehaved and was beaten, but he was not subjected to a reprimand by Luis and Alfredo.

The 'alliance', or the 'agreement' (*chigwirizano*), between Rafaelo and Luis was, however, more a villagers' tentative understanding of their shared interests than the pattern by which they managed their relationships. These arguments and events did not suddenly conflate their constitutive sets of relationships. As mentioned, Luis redistributed beer among Chitima's Frelimo chairmen soon after Rafaelo's misbehaviour. Moreover, it was during this period that Luis initiated the rumour of his joining the government in Maputo. Maputo is the ultimate symbol and source of the government, and the fact that Luis could suggest in all seriousness that he was going to join the government there indicated his unique position in Chitima. For example, with an air of self-importance, he used his imminent transfer to Maputo as a reason when he referred some Malawians who asked for land in Chitima to his subordinate chairmen and the village headman. Luis had never been renowned for modesty, but the post-war challenges to his authority seemed to make him ever more assertive. Other Frelimo leaders in the village became 'boys' (*anyamata*) to him, with the consequence, as will be seen in the Epilogue, that he alienated himself from Frelimo's village organisation.

Making a more positive gesture, soon after the second visit to Villa Ulongwe, Luis launched a project which promised pensions to Frelimo 'veterans' (*akuluakulu*) in Chitima. He announced that Frelimo was going to pay a monthly pension to all those who had supported the party and the nationalist cause from the beginning. He wrote down a list of over sixty Chitima villagers, but it was clear that current concerns had informed his recollections of past activism. It was not surprising that Rafaelo's name was not on the list, but it was remarkable that Sandikonda and Sadlek, prominent chairmen in Chitima, were likewise excluded. By contrast, included were such pointedly sceptical Frelimo 'veterans' as Paolo, Andrea and Pitala, all former Renamo collaborators. Also on the list were Alfredo and Luis's three wives and their siblings, except for Thereza, Sandikonda's wife and the sister of Luis's first wife. Luis did not claim that the list was complete, and he added more names, if he heard 'acceptable' complaints about exclusions. By the end of my fieldwork in 1993, Luis had not taken the list to Villa Ulongwe.

THE EMERGENCE OF A CRITICAL DISCOURSE
The roots of authority in autonomy

Rafaelo, Luis and Alfredo were not pushed into an 'alliance' simply by the new state policies. Also crucial was the way in which other villagers attempted to manage their relationships in the new circumstances. The contradictory positions of the three leaders, and the 'alliance' they fostered, was an *emergent* rather than an imposed condition. Just as the earlier interventions by Frelimo and Renamo had resulted in many local variations in Mozambique, so too the post-war reforms came to be embedded in existing relationships. In Chitima village, Sadlek, the Frelimo chairman in the Mtunda division, personified central aspects of this popular criticism against Rafaelo, Luis and Alfredo. His management of relationships provides one perspective on the field of village politics which influenced the squabbles and alliances of the three men.

Sadlek's leading position in the Mtunda division must be understood in the light of the process by which the division itself was formed. Mtunda is spatially the most isolated division in Chitima, and its nearest Chitima divisions, Machanza and Manguluwe, lie some two kilometres away (see Map 3). The closest neighbours, in fact, are members of Mtunda village on the opposite side of the border.

The name of the division reflects its closer historical links to Mtunda village in Malawi than to any other division in Chitima or Mfuno. Mtunda village was established very early in the twentieth century by newcomers from Dowa District further north in central Malawi. The Mtunda division, in turn, came into being by seceding from Mtunda village in the early 1950s. The division's founders, the families of Nasokera and her sister, had joined Mtunda village in the 1930s (see Figure 6.1). This had taken place after the death of Nasokera's parents, who had originally fled from a dispute in Mua area towards Lake Malawi to the Bembeke area. It is not clear how many siblings Nasokera and her sister left behind in the Bembeke area when they moved to Mtunda village. The children and grandchildren of Nasokera and her sister have not maintained active ties to their relatives in Bembeke.

All the land that Nasokera and her sister cultivated was in present-day Mozambique. The emergence of the Mtunda division took place, therefore, at the same time and for the same reason as the emergence of the Machanza division. The Portuguese ordinance, which made cultivation in Mozambique conditional on residence there, forced the families of Nasokera and her sister to move away from Mtunda village. In the case of the Mtunda division, the founders, fewer than two dozen persons, moved as one family group and left no clusters of that family in Mtunda village.

Filimoni, Nasokera's husband, came from Ntcheu District, whereas Nasokera's sister appears to have had children by several men. Filimoni had been given the councillor's position by the leaders of Chitima in the early

Figure 6.1 Sadlek and the founders of Mtunda division

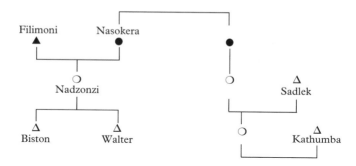

1950s. Sadlek came to fill that position when Filimoni died in the late 1960s. Born in the late 1930s in the Chongoni area some eight kilometres to the north-west in Dedza District, Sadlek married in the Mtunda division in the 1950s. The fact that an office of authority passed to the sister's daughter's husband of Filimoni's wife – a *mkamwini* living in an uxorilocal marriage – indicated the smallness of the division and its lack of men of suitable age. Nadzonzi's two brothers were assumed to have died as labour migrants in South Africa, whereas the brothers of Sadlek's wife were many years junior to Sadlek. In the 1970s, a few households moved from Mtunda village to the Mtunda division in order to cultivate in Mozambique. However, the family into which Sadlek married was still regarded as the core of the division.

Whatever his background as a humble *mkamwini* husband, Sadlek became one of the most important men in Chitima. He was not involved in the first wave of Mozambican nationalism in the area; he joined Frelimo only at the time of independence. As a consequence, the transition from councillorship to chairmanship was smooth in Mtunda, with no change of incumbent. Although he appears to have become a proud supporter of Frelimo, Sadlek's prominence in Chitima as a whole has largely been a function of his unchallenged seniority in Mtunda.

Another factor contributing to Sadlek's rise in prominence in Chitima has been, somewhat paradoxically, the close association of the division with Mtunda village on the Malawian side of the border. This has made Mtunda division relatively autonomous from the rest of Chitima village. The authority that first Rafaelo as the headman and then Luis as the Frelimo secretary granted to Sadlek, especially in the village court, has been a means to curtail this autonomy and to tie the division to Chitima. Yet, at the same time, Sadlek's important role in the village court has fostered a perception of his prominence in the entire village. Many members of the Mtunda division have long used the term 'headman' (*mfumu*) when they refer to Sadlek. For them, the distinction between the authorities of the headman and the party has rarely been clear-cut.

Displacement enhanced Mtunda members' understanding of themselves as one political unit and, as a corollary, the respect for Sadlek's authority. Exiles in Mtunda village, the division members were more closely linked to Mtunda village in the daily conduct of their affairs than to Mfuno village, where they received relief aid. Because there were no refugees from elsewhere in Mozambique in Mtunda village, the 'refugees' in Mtunda villagers' discourse were usually the members of Mtunda division, primarily the founding family of the division. Especially in the settlement of disputes, the leaders of Mtunda village granted Sadlek authority to judge cases that involved 'his' people from the Mtunda division. Even though the founders of the division had moved to Chitima from Malawi, Sadlek willingly participated in the definition of the Mtunda division as 'refugees'. In effect, by virtue of the Mtunda leaders' attitude, Sadlek was able to exert more power as a village leader than Luis and Rafaelo had managed to do during the displacement.

In the first Chitima-wide meeting after the repatriation, the selection of the councillors for the Mtunda division adopted the suggestions by Sadlek. The nominees were Biston and Walter, who were classificatory children (*ana*) of Sadlek, and Kathumba, who was the husband of Sadlek's daughter, a *mkamwini* and Sadlek's son-in-law (*mpongozi*), from a nearby Malawian village (see Figure 6.1 above). These men had not occupied positions in village politics before and had no close links to the leaders of the other divisions in Chitima. A number of subordinate chairmen and 'soldiers' were also selected for the Mtunda division. Most of these chairmen had been in the same positions before displacement, but it appears that their involvement in village-wide politics had always been negligible.

Disentangling relationships

The distinction between the authorities of the party and the headman, which accompanied the repatriation to Mozambique, did not correspond with the existing relationships within the Mtunda division. In contrast to many prominent villagers in the other divisions, Sadlek's prominence had required little allegiance to either Rafaelo or Luis. Indeed, Sadlek's prominence was predicated on the extent to which he was able to appear as an authority distinct from these leaders of Chitima village.

After the repatriation, such apparent independence seemed increasingly difficult to attain. At first, Sadlek opposed the idea that councillors should be nominated for the Mtunda division. Subsequently, his 'children' and son-in-law were nominated to these offices. Sadlek's involvement in expressing the popular discontent with Rafaelo and Luis, therefore, was integral to his prominence in the context of the new state policies. But Sadlek did not follow a consistent 'strategy'. In the course of the unfolding events after the repatriation, his management of relationships had different phases.

On the eve of the repatriation and immediately afterwards, Sadlek clearly sought to associate himself with Rafaelo. He visited Rafaelo's house frequently, even offered some assistance in the building of the house, and they were seen attending beer parties together. Once shortly after the repatriation, both Rafaelo and Luis unexpectedly appeared at the same beer party, but they were promptly shown to separate houses by the owner of the beer. Luis was accompanied by several Frelimo chairmen, whereas Sadlek accompanied Rafaelo to the other house. During this period, Sadlek was also widely cited as the source of the rumour that Luis was looking for ways of killing Rafaelo by witchcraft. Luis was greatly irritated by this, and he accused Sadlek of wanting to 'destroy' (*kuononga*) the village. The nub of the problem, Luis asserted, lay in Sadlek's desire to have 'two chairs' (*mipando iwiri*), the positions of both the chairman and the councillor.

Significantly, Luis heard about this rumour from Stefano, his and Rafaelo's sister's son. Stefano was clearly predisposed to endorse Luis's view that Sadlek was going to destroy the village. The intensification of Sadlek's association with Rafaelo undermined Stefano's own authority, because this was itself predicated on his close association with Rafaelo. Sadlek's position in the newly established headman's court blurred further Stefano's position as Rafaelo's right hand.

Sadlek's association with Rafaelo was bound to make his Frelimo chairmanship appear in a new light and, as a concomitant, increase his detachment from Luis's orbit. In other words, in the context of the new state policies, Sadlek's management of relationships underplayed the necessary disjunction between the two sources of authority. Already during the preparations for the repatriation, Sadlek had argued in private conversations that the mistrust between Rafaelo and Luis heralded a bleak future for Chitima. His observation struck a chord with the uncertainty among Chitima villagers. But it received new content as the events unfolded.

The commencement of aid deliveries in Mtimbo village caused the greatest inconvenience in the Mtunda division, the most distant division from Mtimbo. The arrangement of transport became necessary for most Mtunda members, and these inconveniences caused the popular discourse described above. For the first time, Rafaelo, Luis and Alfredo were defined as one clique mismanaging the affairs of the village. Sadlek's criticism of the three men intensified as his association with Rafaelo lapsed. Sadlek continued to attend court cases, but towards the end of my fieldwork in 1993, his relations to the three men had assumed, outside the formal contexts of village politics, a pattern of outright avoidance.

Sadlek's views on the post-war circumstances were revealed particularly clearly during a beer party in late August 1993. In the presence of a few friends from Chitima and Malawi, a prominent village chairman of the Malawi Congress Party engaged Sadlek in a discussion about the current political developments in Mozambique. His questions were prompted by Sadlek's complaints that Luis and Rafaelo were damaging the prospects for peace in the village by their continuing mistrust of one another. In Sadlek's view, a distinction had to be drawn between the party (*chipani*) and the government (*boma*) in Mozambique. The government, he claimed, was constituted by the parties of Frelimo and Renamo.

The Malawian chairman then asked him whom he represented in Chitima, the party or the government. Sadlek replied that he represented the government, which amused his listeners, because Sadlek was thereby understood to imply that he could support both Frelimo and Renamo. The Malawian chairman noted, however, that Sadlek was a Frelimo chairman, and concluded that he was really behind Luis rather than Rafaelo. Sadlek protested and declared that he supported both of them, because, he asked rhetorically, 'Are they not brothers?' (*sachimwene amenewa*). The attending consumers of beer were overtaken by laughter at this point. It was clear, none the less, that Sadlek had offered his remark in all seriousness. He was predisposed to deny that there was any discrepancy between the two sources of authority.

This exchange took place at Sandikonda's house, and Sadlek's interlocutor was Chisale, Sandikonda's elder brother. The exchange occurred when Sadlek had openly detached himself from both Rafaelo and Luis. Sandikonda had now become his closest companion and co-critic of Chitima's leaders. A Frelimo chairman for the Machanza and Manguluwe divisions, Sandikonda had long been a close friend of Sadlek. After the repatriation, their friendship intensified in tandem with Sadlek's decreasing association with Rafaelo. In spite of the distance between the Machanza and Mtunda divisions, Sandikonda and Sadlek soon visited one another virtually every day. They shared meals at one another's houses, reciprocated in buying beer and *kachasu* liquor, and Sadlek provided Sandikonda with a whole year's supply of pepper (*tsobola*), a rare crop in the Dedza–Angónia borderland. The conduct of Rafaelo, Luis and Alfredo was repeatedly reviewed in their deliberations, and their bleak judgements were communicated to other villagers.

Like Sadlek himself, Sandikonda was motivated to encourage popular discontent by the particular set of relationships that constituted him as a person. His orbit was, formally, identical to Alfredo's. Alfredo was also a chairman for both the Machanza and Manguluwe divisions, in his case by virtue of both matrilateral and patrilateral links. Both Sandikonda and Alfredo were also Liwonde's grandchildren and saw themselves as 'brothers' (*achimwene*) (see Figure 6.2; cf. Figure 4.1). There was often confusion between them about the representation of Liwonde's descendants in litigation,

Figure 6.2 Alfredo's and Sandikonda's pedigree and conjugal bonds

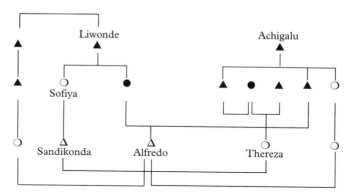

weddings and funerals. Alfredo was only two years senior to Sandikonda, who guarded, together with his elder brother Chisale, Sofiya's children against Alfredo's authority. Both had also married in the Manguluwe division, although Thereza, Sandikonda's wife, lived in the Machanza division. Hence Sandikonda's prominence was largely conditioned by the extent to which he was able to disentangle his relationships from Alfredo's. Given Alfredo's close association with Luis, Sandikonda's submission to Luis would have entailed submission to Alfredo as well.

When the delivery of aid for the returnees was commenced in Mozambique, Sadlek and Sandikonda became the most articulate and fearless critics of Rafaelo, Luis and Alfredo. They expounded their views to other villagers at beer parties, during chance meetings in the village and gardens, and during the endless hours which Chitima villagers spent in waiting for aid in Mtimbo village. The extraction of villagers' money by Rafaelo, Luis and Alfredo, their spending that money in Villa Ulongwe and the hardships involved in receiving aid in Mtimbo were the key issues that Sadlek and Sandikonda raised to discredit the three leaders. In addition, Sadlek and Sandikonda asserted that Luis and Alfredo did not have valid Frelimo membership cards, as they themselves had. They also evoked memories of past misconduct. Before the war, Sadlek and Sandikonda reminded fellow-villagers, Luis collected money from those who attended his feasts, although he had received free beef from the Portuguese. Rafaelo's collaboration with the *Machanga* was raised again to reinforce the unfavourable perception of his present conduct.

Sadlek and Sandikonda were the most prominent Chitima villagers to voice this criticism. As such, their criticism was bound to contrast two different kinds of leadership, that of Rafaelo, Luis and Alfredo, on the one hand, and their own, on the other. The subversive intentions of Sadlek and Sandikonda led to a clandestine visit to Betha in Mtimbo village. They not only attempted to solicit a promise of an aid delivery point in Chitima, preferably in the Mtunda division, but also tried to convince Betha of the need for the realignment of Frelimo leadership in Chitima. None of these propositions received Betha's support, and they did not approach him again.

Sadlek and Sandikonda never publicly announced to their fellow-villagers their willingness to replace Luis and Alfredo as the highest Frelimo leaders in Chitima. The headman is virtually never ousted from office before his death. Nor did the criticism by Sadlek and Sandikonda inspire collective efforts to realign the Frelimo leadership. This must be understood in the light of Luis's and Alfredo's own efforts to counter the popular discourse; the criticism, in other words, did not strip them of all agency. As has been described, Luis, in particular, attempted to correct the emerging perception of himself by launching a rumour of his transfer to Maputo, by redistributing beer and by promising 'pensions' to Frelimo veterans.

Sadlek and Sandikonda provide one perspective on the post-war arguments about authority in Chitima. The emerging critical discourse was neither their own invention nor a means to overpower the three leaders in any definite manner. Nevertheless, as prominent villagers, Sadlek and Sandikonda launched, by their criticism, an influential formulation of the growing discontent. In the context of the new state policies and unfolding local events, Sandikonda and Sadlek, far from being power-hungry individuals engaged in perpetual attempts to undermine other prominent villagers, were compelled by the relationships which constituted them as village authorities to shift their allegiances. At any given moment, moral alliances, however impermanent and indeterminate, were integral to a person's political aspirations.

Sadlek's position as the Mtunda leader motivated him, at first, to introduce a contrast to Luis by his close association with Rafaelo, and later, as events unfolded, to join Sandikonda in defining the three men as a united clique with shared interests. Sandikonda, in turn, was motivated, primarily, by the specific configuration of his relationships in which Alfredo's prominence undermined his own. These motivations were inseparable from the views Sadlek and Sandikonda held about the party, the government and, indeed, about the appropriate moral order of their village. As during the *Machanga* war, the relationships of Dedza–Angónia borderland villagers themselves were the very media through which the party and the new state policies were perceived and *lived*.

TRUST AND THE POST-WAR TRANSFORMATIONS

The paradoxes of repatriation in the Dedza–Angónia borderland highlight the ambiguity of 'return', already noted in other contexts in previous chapters. The war ended with an accord, but the effects of displacement and material devastation, or the tensions that had preceded the war, could not be undone at will. Chitima villagers 'returned', therefore, to a setting that both was and was not familiar. The same old characters resumed the positions of leadership in the village; Chitima's status as a distinct 'Mozambican' village was reasserted in village meetings. It was villagers' expectations of aid and 'development' from the government that eventually led to unease at 'home'. The Epilogue shows how this unease, some years after the repatriation, pushed Chitima villagers into novel reflections about their relations to the central government.

To unravel the paradoxes of repatriation, this chapter began with the proposition that the post-war reconciliation and re-establishment of authority must be understood as ongoing arguments. The subsequent analysis has traced different phases in these arguments among Chitima villagers, from the perceived antagonism between Rafaelo and Luis to the definition of their common interests by critical villagers. This definition was not simply a consequence of new state policies; it emerged in the course of the processes by which village leaders sought to appear as moral persons who inspire trust.

The involvement of Sadlek and Sandikonda in formulating the critical discourse is best understood within the patrimonial logic of social capital. Sadlek's involvement arose from his leadership in one village division and from the distinct nature of that division. Sandikonda's involvement disentangled him from the formally identical, but potentially superior, authority of Alfredo. By their criticism, Sandikonda and Sadlek sought to dissolve their identification with Luis, Rafaelo and Alfredo as Chitima leaders. Yet the distinctions drawn in the patrimonial logic of social capital entailed a connection; the negative qualities of the three leaders made the two critics' positive qualities visible.

The patrimonial logic of social capital, with the strong moral discourse that renders it open to empirical study, provides insight into villagers' own means of monitoring the abuse of power. As contended in the Introduction, even though persons are motivated by specific interests, expediency and instrumentalism provide poor explanations of their conduct. Profound moral considerations are often at stake, interwoven with ideas of personal propriety.

The extended cases in previous chapters have shown how villagers' critical debates often revolve around contradictory perspectives of the past. Unfavourable popular opinion, for example, prevented John from returning to Lumbe village (Chapter 3), and Namadzi and her siblings from spending their exile in their father's village (Chapter 4). In these cases, the memories of 'home' were challenged by the memories of departure from the village of origin. The analysis of Dedza–Angónia borderland villagers' moral arguments has shown, however, that departure has merely served to pin down the sources of estrangement in the present. Far from being a matter of expediency and instrumentalism, the conflict of memories and definitions arises from the fact that persons are constituted by multiple relationships, many of which entail sharply different standpoints, and undermine any one person's attempts to control the unfolding events.

As in the study of post-war Zimbabwe (cf. Werbner 1998), the instability of social memory has also highlighted key aspects of Chitima villagers' arguments about authority after the war. Luis's conduct before the war, and Rafaelo's during it, amplified their critics' discourse on the post-war management of the village. But the post-war social memory was not uniform, nor free of ambiguity. On the one hand, Luis could retrieve at least some of his sovereignty as the Frelimo leader by associating himself with Maputo and Frelimo 'pensions'. On the other hand, the regaining of the official legitimacy of the headmanship justified the war for Rafaelo.

Some villagers' collaboration with the guerrilla movement's practices of extraction and coercion is, however, a poignant reminder of another logic of value and power in the history of the Dedza–Angónia borderland. It has compromised the popular constraints on power embedded in the patrimonial logic of social capital. The three leaders' alleged mismanagement of their subjects' money after the war appeared to extend predatory practices to the new Mozambique. The Epilogue discusses more evidence of such a scenario, but the knowledge needed for understanding the external and internal factors in the war and displacement among Dedza–Angónia borderland villagers has already begun to emerge. The analytical distinction between the external and the internal is necessary, as is argued more fully in the next chapter, in order to understand the disparate power relations which have moulded Dedza–Angónia borderland villagers' lives. The external–internal distinction is inappropriate when it becomes identified with specific institutions, so that, for example, the state, Frelimo and Renamo come to represent the 'external' and the village headmanship the 'internal'. By appreciating the external–internal distinction as historically variable power relations, analysis throws complexity, and the limits of any one 'logic', into starker relief.

VALUE, POWER AND 'SOCIAL CAPITAL'

After a plethora of extended cases, the conventions of analytical ethnography demand a demonstration of what conclusions they provide when all are considered together. The reader expects to find solace in a synthesis, consolation in the conclusion that underneath the diversity is a small set of governing first principles. As was contended in the Introduction, however, extended cases do not give unmediated access to facts, as if description and analysis were separate moments in ethnographic writing. Description *is* analysis, because the ethnographer's attention is necessarily selective. Analytical ethnography attempts to make the assumptions that guide such selections explicit, and in this book the emphasis on diversity and variation has been an open reaction against certain other available assumptions in the study of war and exile. The assumed clashes between 'tradition' and 'modernity', or 'peasantry' and 'the state', not to mention the invariable 'refugee experience', produce illusory similarities among phenomena which encompass a variety of personal trajectories and historical conjunctures. As such, the assumptions of diversity and variation are geared to a better understanding, despite the fact that analysis will always remain selective and partial. By the same token, the contribution of the extended-case method would be compromised if the scales of generalisations blinded its eye for detail.

As was also contended in the Introduction, the social world of Dedza–Angónia borderland villagers has been moulded by events and translocal movements which render comparison with other histories possible. This book has deployed a specific analytical vocabulary to identify a pattern in diversity and to allow comparison. A key concept in that vocabulary – 'social capital' – has been revised rather than simply applied in the course of analysis. The conclusion to this book, in other words, is best seen in the alternative perspective it can provide into the issues which have preoccupied the discussion about social capital.

Once cleansed of its economism, 'social capital' can be made to address central issues in understanding the nature and emergence of value in social life. The study of historical processes from war to peace presents particularly apposite instances for a further elaboration of the following issues; the dynamic rather than static character of social capital, its association with situations of conflict, and its embeddedness in variable historical conditions (cf. Woolcock 1998: 159). The aim is not to rescue a concept which, with its imprecision and lack of historical and political nuance, might rather be consigned to oblivion (cf. Fine 1999). The aim is to redefine the discussion about social value by exposing the limits of a current analytical construction.

The extended cases in this book have highlighted trust as the content of social capital by which persons have achieved support in local politics and refuge during displacement. Two revisions to the current discussion about social capital have proved to be particularly pertinent. First, the circular nature of much of the discussion has been avoided by refraining from representing trust as a 'cause' of instances which, in point of fact, have trust as their corollary. Instead, by applying processual analysis, the extended cases have focused on trust as an emergent property of social life, always a fragile achievement amid the risks of historical conjunctures. Second, this has also meant that conflict – the overt evaporation of trust – has been as important to understand as success in social life. Further issues have arisen to specify the content of social capital and its varying conditions; Dedza–Angónia borderland villagers' understanding of moral personhood, and the unstable correspondence between power and authority.

The occasional separation between power and authority provides a standpoint for this chapter's reflections on the dynamic of social capital among Dedza–Angónia borderland villagers. In the extended cases, authority has been predicated on a specific form of moral personhood, consolidated through 'growth' (*kukula*) in social age. Growth is made visible in acts which demonstrate the person's capacity to 'care for' (*kusamala*) others, who, in turn, constitute the person's growth by being his or her subjects. Once conflated with authority, power thus appears as a particular capacity to act – personal capacities are consequences of combining with the capacities of other persons.[1]

Three observations clarify the contours of relational personhood. First, despite the close association between the extended-case method and the analysis of social networks in some studies (e.g. Mitchell 1969), this book has advisedly refrained from using 'network' in its analytical vocabulary. Even though network analysis has greatly contributed to a dynamic view of social life, the very imagery of a 'network' situates persons apart from the relationships which constitute them. It evokes, like individualistic notions, a centre, the self as an agent who places himself or herself more or less strategically in a network of relationships. Second, the patron–client paradigm also fails to convey the underpinnings of authority among Dedza–Angónia borderland villagers (see e.g. Barnes 1986; Platteau 1995). Persons may relate to one another as patrons and clients in certain situations, but when the paradigm comes to highlight all local politics, the moral and existential aspects of authority are easily obscured by a focus on dyadic contracts. Third, as has been seen, authority does not accrue by the simple aritmethic of accumulating followers, but, rather, by making distinctions against other clusters of relationships. The conflicts and arguments which make those distinctions visible dissipate any lingering assumptions about 'communalism', as if it were a necessary contrast to the individualistic notions of personhood.

This processual view of authority, conducive to discerning the dynamic of social life, is given further nuances by the separation of power from authority at certain junctures in the history of the Dedza–Angónia borderland. If understood as a person's potential for exercising coercion and control, power has sometimes required negligible authority – public moral approval – among Dedza–Angónia borderland villagers. From coercive colonialism to gruesome guerrillas, some villagers have at different historical moments found opportunities to engage in the exploitation of their fellow-villagers. Analysis is, therefore, challenged to expand the scope of power from particular conflict situations to its structural and institutionalised aspects (cf. Lukes 1974; Gledhill 1994; Wolf 1998). This chapter considers such a challenge in the framework of understanding external and internal factors in war and displacement as endured by villagers. That is also the framework in which generalisations can be drawn from the extended cases.

DIVERSITY IN WAR AND DISPLACEMENT

First, however, it is useful to recapitulate some of the observations made in the various case studies. The Dedza–Angónia borderland has been characterised by two particularly salient historical conditions. On the one hand, the nature of the borderland has been that of a frontier area. On the other hand, the Portuguese administration and Frelimo never implemented their resettlement policies in the area.

The Dedza–Angónia borderland has long been a frontier where villagers have innovatively absorbed diverse influences (cf. Kopytoff 1987). The sources of these influences have ranged, for example, from the nineteenth-century Ngoni migrations and the incorporation of Chichewa-speaking peoples to widespread labour migration in the twentieth century; from the spread of Catholicism in the early years of the twentieth century to the often disparate encounters with the Portuguese administrators and entrepreneurs; from the rise of nationalism in Malawi to Renamo's arrival in the mid-1980s. Villagers' active engagement in, and disengagement from, such influences suggest that the Dedza–Angónia borderland, in one sense, is anything but a periphery. Situated on the frontiers of two countries, it has been a veritable centre in its own right.

In another sense, peripheral conditions have been the lot of Dedza–Angónia borderland villagers. Both before and after independence, villagers' ties to the central government, particularly in Mozambique, have been weak. Primary schools have been the most important institutions set up by the central government on the Mozambican side of the border, whereas villagers on both sides of the border have often used markets and health services in Malawi. Above all, the specificity of the Dedza–Angónia borderland experiences is underscored by the fact that, due to the high population density, Frelimo never implemented its unpopular resettlement policies.

Nevertheless, as has been argued throughout this book, it would be a hasty conclusion to assert that, in Dedza–Angónia borderland villagers' world, the state has been 'soft' (cf. Scott 1988), or has faced a 'decline' (cf. Young 1994), or that the Dedza–Angónia borderland belongs to that category in which, according to Bayart, 'one only talks of the State out of diplomatic convention' (1993: 263). The state has long been integral to Dedza–Angónia borderland villagers' relationships – this in spite of the weak grip of the central government. The state, or the government (*boma*), is a central idiom and force in village politics. As a source of legitimate authority, however, *boma* appears to be rapidly losing its attractions under the post-war conditions, as the Epilogue makes clear.[2]

The shifting association of *boma* with power and authority provides in itself sufficient reason for regarding the external–interal divide as a matter of variable power relations. The familiar dualisms in some studies of the Mozambican war and of politics in Africa more generally thus give way to a subtler understanding of historical conditions. In the Dedza–Angónia borderland, the local project has not been to evade capture by 'the state's hegemonic drive' (Chabal 1994: 84) but, on the contrary, to make the state congruent with villagers' views of authority. In this sense, the interest in 'good governance' that has accompanied the use of 'social capital' as an analytical tool in the World Bank (1997), for example, would benefit from recognising how authority emerges and is maintained in specific settings. Rather than requiring supervision from donor agencies, Dedza–Angónia borderland villagers have, in their arguments and aspirations, demonstrated a formidable capacity to challenge and revise the abuse of power. By viewing the external–internal divide as historically variable power relations, analysis can comprehend the conditions in which such challenges are feasible.

During the period from the dawn of independence until the war, the fact that the one-party state did not occupy the entire space of authority among Dedza–Angónia borderland villagers was a crucial precondition for the close correspondence between power and authority. Nationalism aroused widespread interest among villagers, and the area avoided some of Frelimo's policies which fuelled discontent elsewhere. Certain post-independence policies and events, however, inadvertently circumscribed Frelimo's authority. The deposing of headmen and the exodus of Portuguese settlers were the most significant unintended consequences of the villagers' nationalist cause. The end of labour migration to South Africa and the lack of consumer goods undoubtedly contributed to some villagers' early interest in Renamo.

In Chitima village, Rafaelo, the headman, had personified all along a counter-nationalist configuration of authority. His disengagement from the nationalist cause and Frelimo was a precondition of making his authority visible. At the same time, the Frelimo–Renamo war was not simply an occasion to settle disputes and rivalries within, for example, 'lineages'. On the one hand, the very configuration of contrasting authorities in Chitima was itself an outcome of processes that had begun under colonialism. On the other hand, primordial, or 'structural', lineage rivalries are also an implausible notion because of the circumstances into which the local supporters of Frelimo and Renamo were thrust. The unintended consequences of this engagement shaped their antagonisms and allegiances in unprecedented ways. The post-war circumstances, in turn, created conditions under which certain prominent villagers could make earlier antagonisms appear obsolete.

The examples from other local studies of the war, discussed in the Introduction, disclosed that, despite Frelimo's apparent zeal for profound transformations, the war came to be enmeshed in great local complexities. The relations between party and non-party authorities, including various 'traditional' leaders, could assume so many forms. In Chitima village, the antagonism between the chairman and the headman was a creation of the processes by which authority had emerged, not a 'natural' consequence of their positions. It follows that, even within Angónia District, the focus on Chitima village does not disclose the range of the war's local manifestations. Chapter 3 suggested a very different pattern for a village in a Renamo-controlled area which was never entirely deserted. Some exiles in Malawi even continued to supply their relatives in Lumbe village with items from the refugees' relief aid. As the pattern of flight and exile among Evelesita's group suggested, however, the war had a highly variable impact even on the members of the same village. This indicates, again, how little the rebel movement, with its transnational network of sponsors, could determine the actual patterns of villagers' aspirations and experiences during the war.

The extended cases in this book have also directed attention to refugees and their local hosts as persons whose relationships had histories beyond the immediate challenges of an unprecedented crisis. The management of kinship and national identities, no less than that of the international border itself, has involved complex processes, plots far more intricate than mere 'victims' could weave. The case studies have touched upon three issues, in particular, which have wider comparative significance in the study of refugee crises: the definition of 'refugee'; the management and impact of relief aid; and the patterns of repatriation.

The evidence in this book shows how it would be misleading to define a 'refugee' as a person who seeks asylum across international boundaries (cf. Zetter 1991). Such a definition, informing the policies of aid agencies and the Malawian and Mozambican governments, is virtually meaningless in understanding Dedza–Angónia borderland villagers' experiences and actions during their displacement. The concept of 'refugee' (*lefuchi*) carried connotations of strangerhood, as the villagers themselves understood it. As such, it did enjoy a common currency in the villagers' arguments. But a cross-border flight, or even the entitlement to relief aid, did not determine its application. Above all, as a concept connoting the quality of being a stranger, *lefuchi* was a person who fell outside the scope of solicitude. Dedza–Angónia borderland villagers usually applied kinship terminology to those displaced persons whom they assisted during their displacement.

The complexities in Dedza–Angónia borderland villagers' definitions of 'refugees' indicate the diversity of experiences during their displacement. The case studies showed not only how the usage of definitions like 'hosts' and 'refugees' could be in conflict, but also how they could change in the course of time. For example, the case of Namanyada and Rose described in Chapter 4 situated the shifting definitions, and their ultimate conflict, in the transformations in Namanyada's configuration of active relationships after the flight and the repatriation. Moreover, this book has also shown how the concept of 'refugee' could be deployed by displaced persons themselves to delineate fields of valued relationships. In Chapter 3, the assertions of Ben and Nachisale of their status as 'refugees' were also expressions of their allegiance to fellow-villagers in another settlement and – ultimately – to their village of origin in Mozambique.

A corollary of these complexities in the definitions of 'refugees' is the fact that the entitlement to relief aid, as such, did not define – or stigmatise – a person as a 'refugee'. Most 'refugees' spent their exile in settings in which they already had relationships. The logic of definitions, therefore, was not determined by the fact of exile alone. The 'self-settled' status of the displaced persons in the Dedza–Angónia borderland was another important precondition in this respect. Clearly, the loss of autonomy that often characterises the predicament of refugees in camps was not always found among them (see Harrell-Bond 1986: 300–2). But their access to relief aid did become an important issue in the management of relationships. The sharing of aid has appeared repeatedly in the case studies as a corollary of solicitous relationships between 'refugees' and 'hosts'. Even though such gestures can also be signs of inequality and relative superiority (cf. McGregor 1994), there is no reason to suppose that Mozambicans inevitably were 'clients' and Malawians 'patrons'. Access to aid precisely *enabled* Mozambicans to engage in the negotiation of relationships with Malawians. Moreover, the case studies have shown that the engagement of Malawians in these relationships as moral persons often entailed corresponding gestures, particularly the sharing of relish. And, as the previous chapter showed, the arguments about returnees' aid became occasions to express profound popular discontent and criticism after the war. In this case, also, aid played a pivotal role in villagers' arguments about authority.

This book also provides evidence going beyond the simple distinction between 'repatriation' and 'integration' as the solutions to displacement (cf. Kibreab 1989). Such a dualism dissipates the need to understand the specific conditions under which these solutions appear compelling in the displaced persons' own views. Conversely, despite a history of cross-border relations, Dedza–Angónia borderland villagers do not invariably consider the international boundary fluid and negotiable. In Chapter 5, the disagreement between Hawadi and Sandikonda, ostensibly over their mother's repatriation to Mozambique, showed how the allegiances to Malawi and Mozambique were major themes in the brothers' argument about authority. More broadly, because persons are constituted by relationships, flight, exile and repatriation are all experiences which can reveal the contradictory claims and interests that their relationships entail. In the Dedza–Angónia borderland, 'repatriation', 'integration' and an ambiguous condition between the two – such as in Nasoweka's case described in Chapter 4 – were all potentially successful ends to exile. Humanitarian assistance must cultivate such diversity of circumstances, not remove it as an unwanted obstacle.

EXTERNAL AND INTERNAL RELATIONS OF POWER

For analytical ethnography, as mentioned before, diversity presents the challenge of permitting generalisation and comparison without losing sight of varying conjunctures. If the dynamic of power and authority provides one response to such a challenge, 'power' must denote not only personal capacity to act but also conditions in which it does not require the moral underpinnings of authority. A useful conceptual framework is given in Bhaskar's (1993: 60, 153) distinction between $power_1$ and $power_2$. For Bhaskar, $power_1$ is the transformative capacity in all agency, whereas $power_2$ refers to the relations of domination, exploitation and control. $Power_2$ relations are potentially reversible, or constrained, by the generalised agency of $power_1$.

At its simplest, the distinction could be equated with internal and external power relations. The dynamic of power relations in the Dedza–Angónia borderland, however, is best seen as a continuous movement between the two. Under certain conditions, moreover, the domination and exploitation implied by $power_2$ have not been 'external', but have directly contributed to the formation of power relations among Dedza–Angónia borderland villagers themselves. For example, the Portuguese administration and – later – Renamo empowered Rafaelo, the headman of Chitima, with capacities to exploit his subjects in an unprecedented way. Furthermore, the paradoxical development by which he was reinstated in the headmanship by the Frelimo government was another instance of a blurred distinction between the external and internal sources of power.

Such blurred distinctions, though important in shaping events and experiences, have not instigated irrevocable transformations in the Dedza–Angónia borderland. As has been seen, despite its hereditary nature, the headmanship is subject to checks by the populace at large, from the selection of a suitable candidate to the expressions of popular criticism against the incumbent (cf. Gulbrandsen 1995). Villagers' identifications with Portuguese settlers, Frelimo and Renamo respectively have been ways of managing relationships in the Dedza–Angónia borderland. But equally important, these identifications have sometimes introduced irreversible positions of power. Another way of expressing the nature of irreversible power is to contrast *neo*patrimonialism with patrimonialism. As described in the Introduction, the former is an instrumental and extractive form of the latter, a form of power which is irreversible by the moral arguments about authority in the patrimonial logic of social capital.

There was bitter irony in the Chitima villagers' perception of the immediate post-war transformation. Luis and Rafaelo, the long-standing rivals in village politics, drank the money of their 'subjects' during the first anniversary celebrations of the Rome peace treaty. The analyst, however, must resist the temptation to see irrevocable inversions at issue. The incident, in itself, was hardly a condensed representation of 'new Mozambique'. As leaders who were not simply installed by the state but who held their positions because of their relationships with their 'subjects', the two men's powers were conditioned by their moral standing among the Chitima villagers. At a certain point after the repatriation, this was seriously in doubt. The idea that they collected money during the village census and their inability to meet villagers' grievances contributed to the popular view of these leaders as a clique with shared interests. The problem was whether they personified any relationships at all in the light of their failure to deliver 'development'. Confronted with mounting criticism, they attempted to make their constitutive relationships apparent. One example of such efforts to regain authority was Luis's project of writing down the names of the villagers who he thought were eligible for pensions in Frelimo.

Luis and Rafaelo were thus constrained by the power$_1$ of their 'subjects'. The involvement of Sadlek and Sandikonda, themselves Frelimo chairmen, in expressing the criticism attested to the fact that the post-war contest took place within the same field of local politics – no contradiction between the external and the internal was at issue. In other words, because Frelimo was integral to the definition of authority among Chitima villagers, the logic by which morally legitimate authority was managed encompassed even Frelimo chairmen. The chairmanship often entails, of course, the capacity to act upon other villagers. But it is only under specific conditions that authority becomes exploitation and irreversible by power$_1$. In the recent history of the Dedza–Angónia borderland, such conditions have been created by the Portuguese colonial administration and Renamo rather than by Frelimo.

The sense of moral personhood underlying the conditions of political prominence likewise illuminates the conditions of economic success and, in particular, the notion of interests. The various concepts of 'moral economy', 'good-faith economy' and the 'economy of affection' have attempted to conceptualise economic success and interests in non-market economies, although with doubtful effects. Bourdieu, for instance, argues that, in a 'good-faith economy', agents 'satisfy interest in a (disinterested) manner designed to show that they are not satisfying interest' (1977: 194). Such an economy 'is forced to devote as much time to concealing the reality of economic acts as it expends in carrying them out' (1977: 172). This suggests that a successful act conceals its interest, but, in reality, beneath the 'misrecognition' (e.g. 1977: 176) of those acts, self-interested calculation informs social life.[3]

In a somewhat similar vein, Hyden's 'economy of affection' values the display of moral sentiments, but only at the cost of 'obscuring the naked exercise of power' (Hyden and Williams 1994: 71). Scott's (1976, 1985) concept of moral economy, in turn, is intended to probe the encroachment of the market economy in South-East Asia. In this period of transition, wealthy farmers and landlords are argued to be in an 'ideological vacuum' (1985: 184). The continuing need for casual labour, among other things, ensures that wealthy farmers 'are *not yet* able to dispense entirely with the precapitalist normative context of village life' (1985: 185; emphasis added).

Scott's view resonates with a long tradition in the social sciences, one that foresees determinate transformations in 'developing' countries and regards money as a 'solvent' of social relationships (Turner 1957: 229; cf. e.g. Richards 1939: 153). Rather than envisaging a similar path for all societies, or essentially the same interests behind variable smokescreens as in the 'good-faith economy' and the 'economy of affection', this book underlines the need for understanding the divergent moral meanings which money may have (cf. Parry and Bloch 1989). During the colonial period, the Portuguese entrepreneurs along the Dedza–Angónia borderland established with the villagers a particular moral economy in which money played a crucial role. Their command of vast areas of land did not provoke resentment, because they engaged in relationships with the villagers.

In Chapter 5, the cases of Joji and Hawadi also underscored the importance of relationships for contemporary local entrepreneurs. Both Joji and Hawadi were very ambitious to increase their material wealth by commercial agriculture and trading. These ambitions, however, were not incompatible with their desire to manage wide configurations of relationships. In contrast to earlier interpretations of the Jehovah's Witnesses' social and economic strategies in South–Central Africa (see Long 1968; Poewe 1981), Joji's participation in the sect did not indicate a quest to narrow the scope of his valued relationships. On the contrary, the congregation of Jehovah's Witnesses delineated the scope of his active relationships in his wife's home area and, moreover, enabled him to maintain his valued relationships in his own village of origin without the need to return there. On the other hand, Hawadi sought to manage relationships in the African Church and his father's village of origin in the course of his return to the Dedza–Angónia borderland.

John's failure to return to his village, analysed in Chapter 3, and Hawadi's humiliation in his own area of origin also demonstrated how the aspirations of relatively wealthy entrepreneurs were severely constrained by their failure to engender a wide scope of active relationships. In the Dedza–Angónia borderland, therefore, economic success usually entails the reversibility of power$_1$. Inequalities in wealth exist among villagers, but specific conditions are required to translate these inequalities into relations of domination and exploitation. Land, for example, is distributed within families, and the extensive renting, let alone selling, of land is unknown. Arguments, conflicts and the fears of witchcraft indicate the reversibility of power, making outright exploitation virtually inconceivable. Dedza–Angónia borderland villagers are *interested* when they engage in economic activities, but nothing guarantees that different persons attribute a similar normative content to these interests. The failure of John's aspirations, for example, did not indicate a generalised resentment against commercial farming. It indicated a particular conflict of perspectives, a result of John's management of relationships during the displacement.

In this analysis, conflict is intrinsic to social capital, and shared moral sentiments do not imply moral consensus. Moreover, it is important to remember the extent to which villagers' moral arguments have taken place under conditions that have themselves been moulded by the irreversible exploitation of power$_2$. The war, with its origins in the geopolitics of the Cold War, is a powerful reminder of this, but even Malawi, a haven for those fleeing political violence, has kept villagers under the shadow of exploitation. Chapter 5 highlighted arguments which arose among persons whose economic aspirations seemed doomed to failure in a setting where both migration within Malawi and smallholder cultivation brought few rewards. The Epilogue returns to the villagers' economic problems during the era of political pluralism. The notions of reversible and irreversible power direct attention to these historically variable conditions. There is nothing primordial and intrinsically immutable in Dedza–Angónia borderland villagers' moral sentiments. Far from being 'resisted', exclusive economic and political rewards, under specific conditions, may be willingly pursued by villagers themselves.

EPILOGUE: BORDERLAND REVISITED

'We live like the wild animals of the bush' (*timakhala ngati nyama za tchile*), Luis remarked during my first conversation with him in 1996.[1] Lack of 'development' (*chitukuko*), so searing in Chitima villagers' experience at the end of my first fieldwork in 1993, still dominated local discussions about politics. For good reason, as Luis pointed out; not much except the houses and the fields seemed to be in Mozambique – health services and markets continued to link villagers to Malawi. Their post-war discontent deepened amid increasing doubts about the Mozambican state. Luis's imagery of wild animals in the bush captured this uncertainty by erasing all signs of human intervention from the Mozambican landscape. It was as if the state thought that the Chitima villagers had never returned from their exile.

When Luis made his remark, there were only the two of us, sharing *nsima* at the house of Namadzi, his youngest wife. In public, his pride in being a pioneering Frelimo activist in the area – indeed in being a 'Mozambican' – was unflagging. After President Joaquim Chissano's visit to Angónia during the 1994 electoral campaign, the party had presented Luis with a mountain-bike, the only one of its kind in the Dedza–Angónia borderland, and a large radio-cassette player. Displaying these gifts, he seemed to be impervious to other villagers' envy, a prototypical male elder, 'ripe' (*okhwima*) in his capacity to undermine, possibly through occult forces, any challenge to his person. He had retired from the daily politics of Chitima but retained the privilege of going to the most important Frelimo meetings. These were the meetings in the district and provincial capitals where 'the boys could not go' (*anyamata sangapite*). The 'boys', such as Sadlek and Sandikonda, them-selves grandfathers and Frelimo activists since independence, had been left with the thankless task of representing Frelimo to increasingly discontented Chitima villagers.

I begin this Epilogue with Luis, not only to give a sense of his personal fortunes in post-war Mozambique, but also to indicate the underlying issues. Apart from his prestigious gifts, Luis was also entitled to a 'pension' from the state. He duly collected it in Villa Ulongwe, the district capital, every month. No one else from his list of Frelimo veterans, mentioned in Chapter 6, had been successful in this bid for pensions. According to Sadlek and Sandikonda, and even to Alfredo, Luis's former ally, the list had been instrumental in Luis's success in convincing the authorities about his prominence in Frelimo. After the repatriation, he had swelled the numbers of his Frelimo subjects by handing out free membership cards to children. A mountain-bike, a radio-cassette player and a monthly pension later, he had withdrawn from party politics in the village. Private benefit appeared to have superseded public service.

Serious qualms did haunt Luis; hence the discontent he privately shared with me. For him, the real dilemma was whether he, or any other local Frelimo official, could actually mediate between the villagers and the state in the quest for development. This Epilogue discloses local Frelimo activists' contrasting actions under the post-war circumstances. Overall, an awareness of the state's, or the 'government's' (*boma*), detachment from the villagers had increased, an awareness that ran counter to the earlier importance of *boma* in Dedza–Angónia borderland villagers' social relationships.

Luis seemed to have achieved irreversible power in the sense that was defined in the previous chapter – he no longer owed his prominence and wealth to other villagers. However, the limits of such power became apparent especially in family disputes in which relationships continued to be indispensable. Beyond that, this Epilogue discusses the themes in Dedza–Angónia borderland villagers' moral arguments under the dismal post-war circumstances. These arguments are usefully contrasted with the discussions about liberalism in post-war Mozambique, particularly with the liberal notions of freedom and the self.

ISSUES: MARKETS, DEVELOPMENT AND LIBERALISM

Dependence on Malawi has been a postcolonial, and not simply a post-war, condition among Chitima villagers. After the exodus of the Portuguese settlers, villagers' opportunities to market their produce and to purchase even basic commodities on the Mozambican side of the border have been negligible. Frelimo's efforts at 'socialism' provide only a partial explanation, for a law already legitimised private traders, even in rural areas, in 1979 (Minter 1994: 269). Nevertheless, most private enterprises remained seriously under-capitalised, and rural smallholders' links to markets were tenuous in many districts. The goods shortage in the countryside was thus a consequence of the government's investment in large-scale public enterprises, a predicament that was exacerbated, but not caused, by the war (O'Laughlin 1992: 32; Harrison 1998).

Peripheries such as the Angónia frontier have also had particular problems with markets. The illuminating example given by Abrahamsson and Nilsson (1995: 244) took place during the 1983 drought. Some districts in Tete Province, such as Changara, were severely stricken by drought, and famine was imminent. Smallholders in Angónia, by contrast, continued to harvest a surplus of maize, which they took to Malawi in order to get cash to purchase consumer goods there. Their produce was bought, in fact, by international aid agencies which returned the maize from Malawi to Tete by air. The starving people of Changara did eventually get relief – through maize harvested in the same province but bought for them in a different country.

After the war, looted shops and destroyed roads added more problems to an already difficult situation. But the first two or three seasons after the repatriation yielded good harvests, the overall maize production in Mozambique increasing steadily (Agência de informação de Moçambique 1996b: 15). When he addressed the deputies of the Parliamentary Agriculture and Local Government Commission in September 1996, Pedro Sixpence, the deputy chairman of the Tete Business Association, confirmed this trend on behalf of the farmers in Tete Province (Agência de informação de Moçambique 1996b: 16). He was not satisfied, however. Not only had just a tiny proportion of local surplus been marketed within Mozambique, he said, but in some remote northern districts not a single shop had been reopened after the war. Desperate to sell their produce and to buy consumer goods, villagers were walking en masse to Malawi and Zambia. With the roads in a deplorable state, transport by any other means was firmly beyond their reach.

Mozambique, the long-standing pet of international donors (see e.g. Hanlon 1991; Plank 1993), had not suddenly been left to face national rebuilding and rehabilitation on its own. On the contrary, as Hanlon (1996) has continued to show in his forceful way, the donors' grip on Mozambique was as tight as ever. After the war, the reason why 'development' seemed to reach local settings, particularly in rural areas, only in a trickle, if at all, were the macroeconomic targets which the International Monetary Fund (IMF) and the World Bank imposed on the government. Until the 1990s, the two Bretton Woods institutions were in an implicit conflict, with the IMF controlling government spending and deficits, while the World Bank sought growth through Structural Adjustment and improved supply. In Mozambique, the pendulum swung in the IMF's favour in 1990, after which 'stabilisation' – seen in the obsession with curbing inflation and credit and money supply – was the key concept of economic policies. Such measures of restraint, far from increasing productivity, did little to lift the country from the post-war depression.

At the same time, the enrichment of some people seemed to know no restraint whatsoever. The government launched a campaign of privatisation, but critics noted some state officials' propensity to be the first to assert themselves as private entrepreneurs (see e.g. West 1997: 692). Another scenario, replete with analogies from Mozambique's history, saw private companies taking over the tasks of an increasingly irrelevant government (see Pitcher 1996). In the immediate post-war period, such scenarios, hardly promising for rural smallholders, were compounded by confusion in land administration, different categories of returnees and locals being on a potential collision course not only among themselves but also with foreign investors (see Myers 1994; West and Myers 1996). Whatever the actual form such scenarios would take in the future, the ideological thrust of post-war Mozambique seemed clear. Its ideas of the proper political and economic order drew upon a long legacy of liberalism, whereas its specific economic reforms were best taken to represent late twentieth-century neo-liberalism. A virtual inversion of Frelimo's immediate post-independence concerns ensued, an ideology of a restrained state, of rights and individual freedoms (cf. Hall and Young 1997: 217–34).

The Frelimo leadership's commitment to predatory neoliberalism should not be exaggerated, particularly in view of Renamo's, its elected rival's, much higher stake in the resolutely anti-socialist ideology. At issue are, rather, global shifts in political and economic dispositions, arrangements which, like the remedies imposed by the IMF and the World Bank, destitute Mozambique ignores at its own peril. The package includes notions of the self and freedom which may legitimise avenues to accumulation among the new rich but which are at variance with the sense of moral personhood this book has identified among Dedza–Angónia borderland villagers (see also Ferguson 1995).

In political analysis, for example, the assumptions of liberalism often lead to spurious conclusions. Multipartyism is being promoted as an integral part of liberalisation, but autonomous, freely choosing subjects were not necessarily in abundance during Mozambique's 1994 elections (cf. de Brito 1994; Harrison 1996). Rather than indicating popular support, the vote often followed from a reading of the existing pattern of authority in an area, and, of course, from the wish to seal the end of the war through the ballot box. On the other hand, decentralisation, another facet of political liberalism, is not simply a more 'Africanised' solution to the problem of democracy (as argued by Abrahamsson and Nilsson 1995: 175–7). This book has already demonstrated how the legitimacy of local elites is historically variable, not an unproblematic condition of stable 'communities' (see also Alexander 1997).

Historical variation has highlighted local autonomy amid transnational, even global, political and economic transformations. Privatisation, multi-partyism and decentralisation should not, therefore, be seen as sources of determinacy that suddenly obviate all local variations. Moreover, the creation of wealth through markets, as argued in the previous chapter, is compatible with relational personhood. The question is the way in which the new liberal disposition, like the revolutionary and counter-revolutionary agendas before it, actually reached the Dedza–Angónia borderland. During my revisit, it was apparent that Chitima villagers were prey to a neo-liberalism that left them, and many rural smallholders like them, marginalised in their poverty. No less than during the war and displacement, their arguments and dilemmas provided perspectives into transformations on a global scale. These perspectives were also an opportunity to question the notions of value, personhood and morality in liberalism, despite its apparent opposition to ideology and 'theory'. Towards the end of the Epilogue, therefore, some recent anthropological advocates of liberalism are on trial together with the agencies more directly responsible for marginalisation in the Dedza–Angónia borderland.

MARGINALISATION: POVERTY AND RESISTANCE

When Dedza–Angónia borderland villagers reflected on their condition a few years after political and economic liberalisation in both Malawi and Mozambique, they often took that precious commodity, chemical fertiliser, as an indicator of much else. In both countries, fertiliser was no longer subsidised by the governments, and getting credit to purchase it had involved a rise of interest rates from 18 per cent in 1992 to 55 per cent in 1996. Very few villagers dared to take credit at such interest rates, and, as a consequence, applied very small amounts of chemical fertiliser, the amounts measured now by plates rather than by bags. The 'objective' need for chemical fertiliser, especially on the Mozambican side of the border, was sometimes ambiguous (see Englund 1996c), but for Dedza–Angónia border-land villagers themselves, its importance was beyond dispute. Introduced by Portuguese settlers, and thus associated with the times of plenty (see Chapter 2), the use of chemical fertiliser represented the essence of successful farming.

Dedza–Angónia borderland villagers' difficulties in obtaining chemical fertiliser raised questions about the very integrity of the states to which they supposedly belonged – their complaints were *moral* arguments about marginal-isation. Both governments' responses were certain to appear inadequate. The removal of subsidies signified liberalisation, with villagers being asked to 'shop around' for the best prices. In practice, chemical fertiliser was still available in large quantities, mainly in the possession of the Agricultural Development and Marketing Corporation (Admarc) on the Malawian side of the border, but the prices were exorbitant. Few villagers had the oppor-tunity to 'shop around' in other areas and to find transport for the heavy bags of fertiliser. Similarly, the Mozambican government's wish to see villagers themselves collecting fertiliser from distant markets in order to resell it for profit in villages failed because of their lack of initial capital for transport. Agricultural officers, visible only on the Malawian side of the border, preached soil conservation and the use of dung (*manyowa*) as alternatives to chemical fertiliser. Even though many villagers used dung, they had come to regard it as a pitiable sign of poverty.[2]

Under such circumstances, illegal and semi-legal measures were taken. Villagers on both sides of the border relied on corruption (*katangale*) among the employees of Admarc. The employees could cut holes in bags and sell the released fertiliser in small quantities for their own benefit. Some diverted whole bags and sold them, for example, for 250 kwacha, when the official price was over 300 kwacha. Such practices required trust, but few villagers saw them as intrinsically problematic. Rather, they were measures between poor villagers and badly paid officials to 'help one another' (*kuthandizana*). Seen from the perspective of those who condemn corruption as the antithesis of 'good governance', the irony is clear. For Dedza–Angónia borderland villagers, it was the apparently corrupt local officials who had 'social capital'. By contrast, the central governments, with their policies of political and economic reform, were rapidly losing it.

Katangale became one of the key idioms in Malawi under President Bakili Muluzi, with virtually every sphere of public life becoming open to accusations and counter-accusations of corruption. Dedza–Angónia borderland villagers deplored *katangale* among the national elites but associated related practices with different moral qualities when the perpetrators were known to be poor. Although in its translation as 'corruption' *katangale* was officially free from ambiguity, there had long been uncertainty about the practices that properly belonged to the scope of *katangale*. The term itself appears to have had negative connotations even before 'corruption' became a central issue during the transition to the new regime. The practices to which it referred brought exclusive advantages by illegal or dishonest means. Outright exploitation was often seen to be entailed by *ziphuphu* – bribes usually given in money – which were required by authorities to secure a place in a secondary school or formal employment in towns.

In their discontent with the state, Chitima villagers also adopted more public forms of protest than *katangale*. During my revisit, they proudly refused to pay taxes (*msonkho*). The origin of the dispute lay in the aid distributed to returnees after the repatriation. Chapter 6 described the villagers' difficulties in receiving this aid, and in 1996–7, there was a widespread consensus that aid had been received both for a longer period and in larger quantities elsewhere in Angónia. This was an early indication of the state's disregard of the frontier area, further exacerbated by the lack of development. Chitima villagers paid their taxes, three kwacha for every adult male, during the first year after the repatriation. Thereafter, the tax revolt, led by such prominent Frelimo figures as Sadlek and Sandikonda, was a means of demonstrating that, if the Mozambican state did not provide development, it should not expect anything from the villagers in return.

Not everyone in the village supported the protest. Fearful of their own prospects, primary school teachers viewed it as an unfortunate project of uneducated villagers, pointing out that three kwacha amounted to less than a man's average weekly consumption of beer. The primary school itself, following the Mozambican curriculum, belonged to the rare signs of

Mozambican 'development' in Chitima. Its six teachers worked with some 300 children between standards one and five. There was no school building; only the children of standard one learnt indoors, the newly built Catholic church providing shelter. The church was the most imposing building in the village, complete with an iron roof and brick walls which were white-washed inside. Chitima villagers were, however, quick to remark that the diocese in Villa Ulongwe, and not the government, had provided materials for the church. Apart from the teachers' salaries and an inadequate supply of learning materials, the central government's contribution to the village after the returnees' aid consisted of an immunisation campaign for children of under seven years and the drilling of one borehole. Four other sites for boreholes had been selected, but, several months later, no villager knew whether the work would commence again.

Frelimo leaders, who urged the villagers to refuse to pay taxes, praised President Muluzi for encouraging private entrepreneurship in Malawi. They ignored similar complaints on the opposite side of the border about the price of fertiliser and the lack of credit and capital. For Dedza–Angónia borderland villagers, a local example of improved opportunities for business was a new market-place at the nearby Bembeke turn-off. It operated two days a week and was virtually equal in its supply to the long-established market in Lizulu. However, its limits as a source for the creation of wealth for local villagers were becoming increasingly clear. The market was being taken over by itinerant traders, who made their living in different markets in Dedza, Ntcheu and Lilongwe Districts on different days.

Moreover, the most trusted commodity produced by Dedza–Angónia borderland villagers, tomatoes, lost its value as the market was overwhelmed at the beginning of the rainy season, after the cultivation season in *madimba* gardens. Traders and middlemen from Malawian towns found the produce conveniently in one place, and extended negotiations in the privacy of the farmers' homes were no longer needed. The locals who seemed to benefit the most were women who sold beer during the market days. Even their business was hampered by the need for more capital to expand beyond arranging a standard beer party in a village. A beer house had become necessary to attract customers, a requirement that itself entailed a novel transaction in the Dedza–Angónia borderland – the buying or renting of land.

Despite the actual problems of conducting business in Malawi, Chitima villagers viewed the Bembeke market as an emblem of the Malawi government's commitment to entrepreneurship. Prominent Frelimo officials in the village expressed such a sentiment in their criticism of the Mozambican government, but few went as far as Alfredo, Luis's former right-hand man, in denouncing Frelimo altogether.

He had been disheartened by the exclusive gifts which party bosses had showered on Luis after President Chissano's visit, even though it had been Alfredo who had done the arduous work of announcing the visit in the different divisions of the village. Luis had received not only a mountain-bike and a radio-cassette player, Alfredo claimed, but also suits and shirts. He, like the other Frelimo activists in the village, had received only a T-shirt carrying Chissano's portrait and a woman's campaign wrapper cloth. Through such a discrepancy between gifts, Alfredo realised that his position in the party was much weaker than he had assumed. Troubled by his need to support the families of his two wives despite the deepening economic crisis, he made no secret of his verdict: 'We shall not vote for them again!' (sitidzawavoteranso).

Alfredo's discontent with the government, and with Luis himself, brought him closer to Sadlek and Sandikonda than before, but he maintained a detached indifference to their continuing interest in party politics. For Alfredo and other respectable elders, support for Renamo was not an option, despite the fact that Angónia had elected a Renamo candidate to parliament. Most Chitima villagers were of the opinion that they did not have a representative in parliament. This opinion was a consequence not so much of their discontent as of genuine ignorance about district-level elections results.

In Chitima village, in any event, the Frelimo establishment forced Renamo supporters to adopt a low profile. As the representatives of the state, Frelimo officials insisted on procedures which, in fact, indicated their own unease with multipartyism. Holding a local Renamo meeting required a permit from the government in Villa Ulongwe, they said. A document with Renamo's letterhead was not acceptable. In their own meetings and casual conversations, Frelimo officials also cultivated the memory of the war. Renamo, they suggested, was looking for ways to return to its old 'habit' (khalidwe) of causing 'confusion' (chisokonezo). The imagery of guerrillas' nocturnal visits lived on in the perception that Renamo had its meetings not 'in the open' (poyera), but inside its supporters' houses. However much Frelimo officials themselves were responsible for such a practice, the imagery evoked a clandestine organisation, an organisation bent on undermining the established order.

By the end of my revisit in 1997, the first public Renamo meeting was yet to take place in Chitima. Its local supporters divided into two categories: activists who maintained links to Renamo officials in other villages, and former collaborators who had supported the guerrillas and were widely suspected of voting for Renamo in 1994. The former category consisted of a handful of young men, mainly in the Mtunda division. Rafaelo, the head-man, was the best-known figure in the latter category. Visiting Renamo officials still came to see him at his house, a practice that embarrassed Rafaelo, keen to appear detached from party politics. Other former collaborators had their own subtle ways of expressing discontent with post-war Mozambique. Stefano, Rafaelo's ally and sister's son, publicised his view that no improvement had taken place in Villa Ulongwe since the end of the Portuguese rule. Such a view subverted Frelimo's authority – far beyond the immediate post-war failures and without any obvious allegiance with the ostensibly illegitimate Renamo.

Alfredo needed much less circumspection in his criticism of Frelimo – no one would have suspected him of Renamo sympathies. His unequivocal condemnation, nevertheless, was different from the criticisms of Sadlek and Sandikonda, who still maintained a loyal, if at times ambiguous, allegiance to Frelimo. After Luis's retirement from village politics, Sadlek had become the leading *de facto* Frelimo official in Chitima. In mid-1997, often together with Sandikonda, he conducted public meetings in every division of the village in preparation for the national census and to warn against 'illicit' Renamo meetings. In words that resonated with the events in 1950–1, he announced that the current season was to be the last for those who lived in Malawi but cultivated in Mozambique. They had to stop cultivating or move to Mozambique altogether. In the national census, which was scheduled to take place in August 1997, Frelimo officials and the headman's councillors had to ensure, he urged, that no Malawians were included. Such speeches gave a grossly exaggerated impression of an influx by land-hungry Malawians. In fact, very little immigration took place, apart from the obligations that kinship and marriage entailed, if only because the idea of Mozambique as the land of war still prevailed among Malawians. For Frelimo's village officials, however, the issue of immigration provided an opportunity to define the national order after the war.

NEW CONDITIONS, NEW DISTINCTIONS

A few years after the repatriation and general elections, Frelimo thus continued to constitute authority in the village; and the international border was still asserted to create distinctions between 'Malawians' and 'Mozambicans' – all this despite widespread post-war discontent. Yet, as before, power was not associated with Frelimo simply as a non-local force; Frelimo itself was constituted in the social relationships of Chitima villagers. Hence the critical discourse of Sadlek and Sandikonda, and many subordinate officials, was precisely an argument about the conditions of Frelimo's authority. By articulating the discontent, by their fury at the lack of development and by their refusal to pay taxes, they set moral standards for the state. In their midst they also had an embodiment of the post-war state's dubious priorities: Luis, already an affluent elder before his gifts and monthly 'pension', arrogant towards other Frelimo officials and apparently indifferent towards villagers' poverty.

In his private condemnation of the post-war state, Luis seemed to have a different approach from that of Sadlek and Sandikonda, who still believed in their capacity to influence state policies. For them, Luis's withdrawal was a simple consequence of desire for private gain, made all the easier by the trying times after the repatriation. Supercilious he certainly was, calling other local Frelimo veterans 'boys' and often even failing to appear at funerals. But beneath his withdrawal was his conviction that the state was not interested in the development of Chitima village. On a closer inspection, building on the extended-case studies in previous chapters, Luis's new position and concerns continued to be moulded by the relationships which constituted him as a Chitima villager. The repercussions of a land dispute threw the continuing interface between Frelimo and kin-relationships, and Luis's place in them, into starker relief.

The dispute was over Sofiya's land, and its immediate protagonists were her granddaughter Mary and her son Sandikonda. Nasoweka, Luis's second wife and Mary's mother (see Figure 4.1 above), had received land from Luis, and Sandikonda got land from his wife's family. Mary had married during the displacement and cultivated only a small piece of land with Nasoweka before the repatriation. Afterwards, Sofiya gave gardens to Mary and her younger sister, who had also married during the displacement. Martha, Sandikonda's eldest daughter, had already been allocated a garden on Sofiya's land before the repatriation, because Martha's mother's access to land was clearly more circumscribed than Sofiya's.[3] The dispute arose when Sandikonda appeared to use Martha, his daughter, as an excuse to ease his own family's land shortage and encroach on the land of his mother, Sofiya.

Sandikonda's attempt took place during Martha's absence from the Dedza–Angónia borderland, an absence that indicated Martha's own problems in Chitima village. As described in Chapter 5, she had first married Joji, a stranger who became a Jehovah's Witness in the Dedza–Angónia borderland. After the end of my fieldwork in 1993, as anticipated, they had divorced, and Joji remarried in another village on the Malawian side of the border. By 1997, he had completed his studies at the Kingdom Hall and was able to supervise others. His new wife had also discarded Catholicism and was studying with the Jehovah's Witnesses. Joji claimed that he had found 'peace in the family' (*mtendere wa banja*), though not 'peace in wealth' (*mtendere wa chuma*). He had virtually given up trading and lived on cultivation.

Martha, in turn, found a new husband in the Zakariya division of Chitima, but her moral condition seemed to deteriorate rapidly. This man allegedly introduced her to marijuana (*chamba*) and was himself a womaniser. In late 1995, Martha, high on *chamba* and armed with paraffin and matches, burnt the houses of his two lovers. She was captured and locked in his house for the night. She managed to escape, however, and fled to Lilongwe, where almost a year later, she gave birth to another man's child, who died in early infancy and to whose funeral only Sandikonda from the Dedza–Angónia borderland went to mourn.

I have given these details of a personal tragedy because they affected the dispute. When Sandikonda began to expand Martha's garden before the rains in 1996, Mary complained that he had no reason to do so, because Martha had left the village. Sandikonda spent two weeks, however, working intensively on the land and stopped when he had reached Mary's garden, pre-empting her own plans to expand her garden. Sandikonda refrained from planting on this land, after Sofiya had appealed for unity in the family, but he privately stressed that he had not toiled for nothing. He found it extraordinary that Mary, a 'child' (*mwana*), was preventing him from opening new land. In February 1997, two events changed the matters in his favour: Sofiya died, and Martha returned for Sofiya's funeral. Because she was not taken to a court to answer for the burnt houses, she decided to stay.

Even though resolved in principle, the dispute lived on in its repercussions. Wider fields of relationships, including those that constituted Frelimo in Chitima, soon became entangled with the conflict between Mary and her mother's brother Sandikonda. He was, together with Alfredo, the guardian (*nkhoswe*) of Sofiya's children and grandchildren. It did not take long for Mary, the barren senior wife of a polygynist, to be in a situation in which she needed her guardians.

In March 1997, Mary faced a new crisis in her stormy marriage. She had prepared *nsima* porridge as a gift for her friend who was having a beer party. Mary's husband, already drunk after a visit to the party, arrived just as she was leaving with her gift. He was infuriated when he realised that Mary had prepared food only for her friend, and, after some bitter words had been exchanged, he beat her and kicked her badly. Mary, now frantic with anger herself, left her gift behind and proceeded to the house of her husband's junior wife, determined to beat her as revenge. She was, however, unable to find her.

'It is their own business' (*zawo zimenezo*), Sandikonda and Alfredo dismissed Nasoweka's appeal for assistance in her daughter's marital crisis. They had already conveyed their attitude on the same day when Mary was beaten. On her way to her co-wife's house, she had walked through the crowded beer party, attended by Sandikonda and Alfredo. Conspicuous from the blood running down her face, she wanted everyone to know what had happened. As she walked across the compound, causing commotion in her wake, Sandikonda and Alfredo, her *ankhoswe*, chose to look the other way.

Sandikonda's inertia was understandable in the light of Mary's insolence towards him during the land dispute, but he and Alfredo also had a bone to pick with Luis, Mary's father. As mentioned, they, together with Sadlek, portrayed Luis as a traitor, content with private gain when the post-war state needed to be confronted by Frelimo leaders themselves. Sandikonda and Alfredo explicitly referred to Luis in their private reflections on their refusal to help Mary, calling him 'proud' (*onyada*) and 'conceited' (*odzikonda*). They saw no reason to help the daughter of a man who had detached himself from his fellow-villagers.

The 'cross-cutting ties' (Colson 1962: 108) in family and village politics thus continued to impinge upon Luis's relationships despite his apparent retirement. For all his wealth and prominence, he was unable to mobilise moral support in times of a family crisis. Before the post-war discontent, he would have had few difficulties in this regard, Alfredo being a particularly loyal ally. Alfredo's closeness to Sandikonda – and his position as a guardian in Sofiya's family – indicated transformations in social capital after the repatriation. From Alfredo's point of view, Luis's privileges and concomitant arrogance had resulted in a condition which, devoid of relatedness, indicated further the party–state's moral decline. The refusal of Alfredo and Sandikonda to act as Mary's guardians paralleled their refusal to pay taxes. Just as the state did not deserve villagers' money as taxes, so too Alfredo and Sandikonda were under no obligation to assist Luis's immediate family.

In Alfredo's relationships, distinction emerged through association with Sandikonda and Sadlek against Luis. This entailed support for their out-spoken criticism of Luis, tolerance towards their activism in Frelimo and careful negotiation of authority as Sandikonda's co-guardian in the family. Alfredo and Sandikonda had, jokingly, begun to address one another as *amalume* (mother's brothers) rather than as *achimwene* (brothers). The practice seemed an implicit recognition of the problem of authority that lay underneath their revived closeness.

RELATIONAL VALUE AND LIBERALISM

Revisiting the village prompts more thoughts on the subject-matter of this book: relations – personal, national, transnational and global. War and displacement have been highlighted as profoundly *historical* phenomena through the analyses of personal relationships as sources of value, and, because relationships are embedded in historical contingencies, of the indeterminacy of value. The phenomena are historical in the sense of allowing considerable local variation within transnational and global politico-economic transformations. After the war and the displacement in the Dedza–Angónia borderland, Chitima villagers confronted their marginalisation with defiance that hoped to force the state into a relationship. The state was asked to provide development in return for taxes.

In his critique of perspectives that stress the marginalisation and exclusion of rural Africa vis-à-vis the centres of power, Mahmood Mamdani (1996) offers a useful reminder. This apparent marginalisation, he says, is nothing but a mode of ruling, a late colonial legacy that postcolonial African governments of very different hues have upheld. Under the pretence of appreciating native culture, the colonial state forged notions of customary law in order to maintain indirect rule, coercion becoming vested in selected 'native authorities'. In much of postcolonial Africa, Mamdani argues, power has remained despotic. Conservative states have maintained a mode of rule akin to the decentralised despotism of late colonialism, whereas radical states have tended to develop centralised despotisms. In rural areas, the net result of both has been a mixture of marginalisation and intervention. Intervention has continued to take the form of extra-economic coercion, facilitated by the grossly inflated powers of local state functionaries – chiefs and party cadres.

Marginalisation, despite some Chitima villagers' hopes to the contrary, is thus more than an accident – it indicates a relation between the state and the rural folk, a form of state power, devoid of substantial democracy. The scale of this study, however, brings more historical nuance to Mamdani's generalisations. In the Dedza–Angónia borderland, the 'clenched fist' (Mamdani 1996: 23) of chiefs' power has often been kept in check by the moral underpinnings of reversible power. This book has highlighted the historical conditions of such popular challenges, and the conceptual tools by which the shifts in power relations can be apprehended. Villagers' engagement with external forces has been inseparable from the dynamics of internal relationships. Sometimes, most notably in their collaboration with Renamo guerrillas, this engagement has gone awfully wrong, the nature of power shifting from reversible to irreversible.

It is in the light of these historical variations that the post-war marginalisation must be discussed. Two observations clarify the issue of state power. First, until the political and economic transformations in the early 1990s, the area was in the intersection of two contrasting regimes: a 'conservative' state in Malawi and a 'radical' state in Mozambique. The contrast, through the comparable positions of chiefs and party cadres on the two sides of the border, was scarcely discernible in the villages. The case of Chitima village has shown how the Frelimo secretary assumed many of the headman's duties, and the logic of his popular support, after independence. The Mozambican side of the border gave little contrast to the oppressive state in Malawi when it became embroiled in the war. Second, after the regimes on both sides of the border embraced economic and political liberalism, the immediate consequence was a crisis. Local leaders found it increasingly difficult to associate their authority with resources that would benefit communities at large.

The crisis in the Dedza–Angónia borderland may appear to indicate the failure of particular policies, such as those imposed by the IMF, not a wholesale inadequacy of liberalism. By drawing on this book's understanding of relations, it is possible to see how the liberal disposition may promise even less for Dedza–Angónia borderland villagers than the neo-patrimonialism and centralised socialism of the past regimes. In contemporary Africa, liberalism generates critical discourses about abuses of power, and in some spheres – from middle-class gender relations to the urban-based mass media – these discourses are clearly emancipatory. If there is a unifying 'theory' in the current liberalism in Africa, however, it is a theory of the self (see Williams 1993). Distinct from other selves, the self in liberalism makes choices unhindered by others. Freedom, in the African context, is an attribute of individuals and groups in a 'civil society'.[4]

The removal of subsidies on fertiliser was an early example of such freedom in the world of Dedza–Angónia borderland villagers. They were asked to enter the market as freely choosing individuals, to 'shop around' in order to adjust the price of fertiliser to its proper level. Their difficulties were not simply practical in nature; they indicated more fundamental fallacies of liberalism. *Inequality* may be the long and the short of it, but this study also provides a more analytical attack on liberalism. The targets must, in their analytical grasp, be on a par with the attack. Here two recent anthropological expositions serve to elucidate the world-view of late twentieth-century liberalism.

Anthony Cohen (1994) and Nigel Rapport (1997) have produced intellectually closely related critiques of the social scientific practice which, they feel, has a tendency to undermine the individual. Both regard individuality rather than individualism as their subject-matter, and Cohen (1994: 171–6) offers a seething discussion of politics which promote conformity under the guise of individualism. Both anthropologists elevate individuality to a supreme value and give it an irrevocable moral content. Rapport, in particular, for all his evocations of humanism and postmodern irony, fails to conceal missionary zeal, an intellectual crusade that culminates in the attempt to convince the reader of the 'morally exportable' (1997: 186) liberal beliefs.

The two anthropologists celebrate the individual self as the locus of consciousness and experience. Because agency and creativity emanate from the individual, they go on to reason, distortion accompanies any social scientific account that subsumes the individual under the generalising notion of 'society' or 'culture'. Herein lies the interface of theory and liberalism. Just as theory must give space to individual experience and creativity, so too must liberalism as a moral and political disposition restrain society and the state so that individuality may flourish. Not surprisingly, in this conventional approach, the contrast to liberalism can only be totalitarianism (e.g. Rapport 1997: 190–3).

The deepening sense of impoverishment among Dedza–Angónia borderland villagers lays bare the political and economic consequences of liberalism for a marginalised, effectively disenfranchised population. Yet, again, in case this is seen as an isolated failure of a noble disposition, the analytical critique of liberalism must be pushed to its conclusion. Liberalism fails precisely because *it renders relations invisible* – from personal relationships to transnational and global relations. In the preoccupation with 'rights', accordingly, it makes little difference whether the emphasis is on individual or collective rights. The proponents of collective rights often admit as much, viewing them as complementary to individual rights (see e.g. Taylor 1994; Thompson 1997; Kymlicka 1995). *Relations*, I contend, remain external to the subjects thus defined.

Liberalism betrays an inclination towards subjects at the expense of the relationships that constitute those subjects. Its advocates legitimise this inclination by evoking the obsolete individual–society dichotomy, making other ways of apprehending social relationships unthinkable. In this book, the focus has been on persons-in-relationships. The dichotomy of individual and society has not arisen, because this book has been no more a study of societies than of individuals.

In the post-war Dedza–Angónia borderland, the denial of relations made liberalism particularly catastrophic. Several years of war and displacement had produced a need for rebuilding and rehabilitation which villagers struggled to meet on their own. Their yearning for a relationship did not simply envisage clientelism – at stake was their belonging to a nation-state. After all the effort Chitima villagers had expended to assert their village as Mozambican, the state seemed to have suddenly lost interest in them. Discontent loomed large when Chitima villagers began to question what their predicaments of war and displacement were *for*. No amount of liberal morality provided consolation here; theirs was a morality that began from relatedness. The purpose of this book has not been to romanticise that morality but to show how it has been constituted within myriad, shifting, non-local forces, and how at some times it has pitted villagers against one another, and at other times it has fostered solicitude. The purpose, in short, has been to historicise morality.

Because of the varying conditions of relationships, history has appeared as a source of indeterminacy. But, as discussed in Chapter 7, shifting power relations occasionally replace indeterminacy with determinacy. The analytic result is a sense of an ongoing process, of shifts and tensions that the appropriate scale of analysis enables us to discern. A different scale would easily mistake persistent violence and coercion for historical determinism. For example, in one formidable survey of the Mozambican past, the Frelimo–Renamo war becomes a virtual footnote to a long-term pattern which 'modern Mozambican society finds itself unconsciously repeating' (Newitt 1995: 576).

The histories that have moulded the Dedza–Angónia borderland permit no such conclusion. Villagers' participation in Renamo's violence required specific conditions, conditions which bespoke exclusion and marginal-isation. This was also a source for my disquiet at the end of my revisit. If liberalism promotes neglect and marginalisation in the name of freedom, it may also promote the historical conditions of political violence.

APPENDIX

Chart I Genealogical relations among Chitima and Mfuno villagers

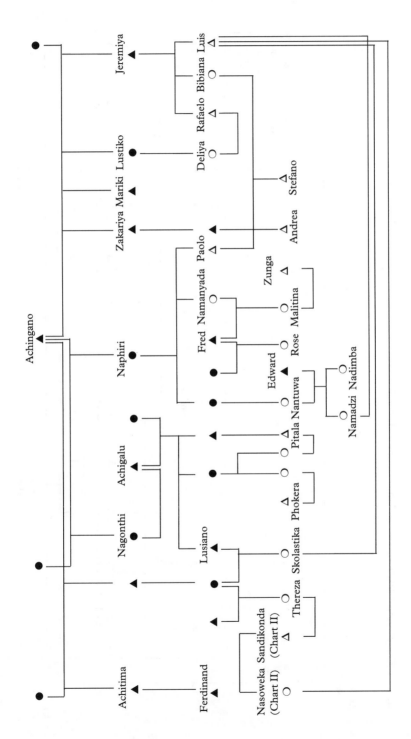

Chart II Genealogical relations among Chitima and Mfuno villagers

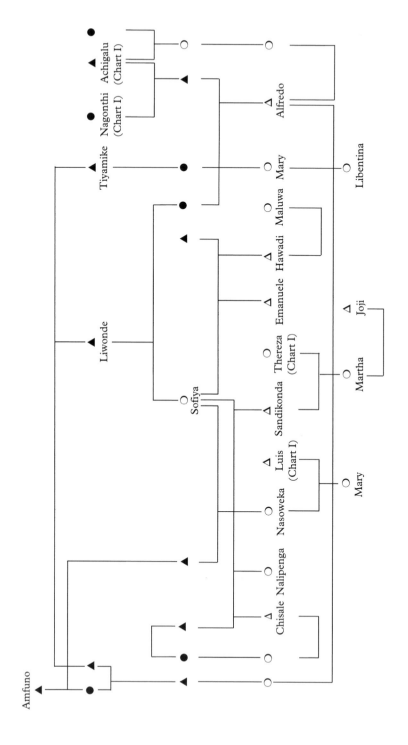

NOTES

INTRODUCTION

1. Frelimo and Renamo are acronyms which are now widely used as proper names. The origin of Frelimo is in *Frente de Libertação de Moçambique*, Mozambique Liberation Front. Renamo derives from *Resistencia Nacional Mocambicana*, Mozambican National Resistance, but during the early years of the war it was known by its English acronym, MNR.

2. Indicating the complex pattern of armed movements and groups in Zambézia, Gimo Phiri's role in the war did not stop with this merger. He left Renamo, with around 500 troops, in 1987, and fought against both Renamo and Frelimo until 1989, when he entered a broad military alliance with Frelimo against Renamo (Wilson 1992b: 2; Borges Coelho and Vines 1995: 33). After the war, Phiri appeared in Malawi in 1996, boasting that he had 3,000 armed men in Zambézia and threatening to wage war on the government, if his troops were not incorporated into the demobilisation programme with Renamo and Frelimo soldiers (Agencia de informação de Moçambique 1996a). I will discuss further the war in Zambézia later in this Introduction.

3. It is important to note, however, that Frelimo soldiers on the ground also consulted healers and spirit mediums during the war (see Wilson 1992a: 548–51). Local studies of the war, discussed later in this Introduction, reveal more clearly how grand ideological schemes were accommodated in practice.

4. The fact that the name *Machanga* derives from the last name of Renamo's first leader André Matsangáissa, and the stories surrounding his death, are documented by Vines (1991: 74–5), Finnegan (1992: 66) and Wilson (1992a: 543).

5. For example, internal conflicts among the two sets of refugees are hardly touched upon by Malkki's study – collective, usually anonymous, 'panels' articulate camp and town refugees' contrasting perspectives. This is ironic, because it is Malkki (e.g. 1997) who has emphasised the salience of personal histories in refugees' variable experiences. Moreover, Malkki (1995b: 198–9) mentions in passing that kin ties and trading networks linked camp and town and that double residency was not uncommon – practices that were bound to blur the distinction in everyday life.

6. The irony is particularly clear when the discourse on social capital presents itself as criticism of neoclassical economics, akin to current institutional development economics (Fox 1997: 964; cf. Nabli and Nugent 1989; Harriss et al. 1995).

7. It would not be difficult to find other examples of differences within this school of social anthropologists. For example, while the unit of study in rural research was, again in contrast to the tenets of Radcliffe-Brownian structural functionalism, usually a local community rather than a lineage (cf. Gluckman 1950: 167; Barnes 1954), some studies still identified the dynamics of social processes with kin-based social structural cleavages (see e.g. Mitchell 1956; Marwick 1965).

CHAPTER 1 BORDERS DRAWN, BORDERS CROSSED

1. The claim that slave raiding accounted for *mfecane* has been challenged on chronological grounds (Eldredge 1992; Omer-Cooper 1993). A more profound question is whether there is enough evidence to speak of 'revolution', or whether merely a transformation in scale took place (cf. Kuper 1993: 470–1).

2. In Malawi, the current hierarchy of 'Traditional Authorities' presents few modifications to the late colonial order of 'Native Authorities'. The current order, from bottom to top, is Village Headman, Group Village Headman, Sub-Traditional Authority, Traditional Authority and Paramount Chief. In Mozambique, chiefs and headmen are also grouped according to a formal hierarchy, particular villages and their headmen belonging to more encompassing chieftaincies.

3. Also known as *nyau*. On *gule wamkulu* in Mua, see Linden with Linden (1974), and in the Dedza–Angónia borderland, see Englund (1996a). More generally, see e.g. Schoffeleers (1968: 330–40, 1992: 34–41); Yoshida (1992); Kaspin (1993); Birch de Aguilar (1995).

4. For an account of the Portuguese ambitions during the 'scramble for Africa', see Newitt (1995: 317–55). From the perspective of Malawi, the Mozambican frontier has always received more attention than the Zambian and Tanzanian frontiers. Demarcation work took place on the Zambian frontier only in 1967, although it had already been defined in 1891 by an agreement between the British Foreign Office and the British South Africa Company (Chitsamba 1971: 32–5). The Malawi–Tanzania frontier, in turn, remains defined by the 1890 Anglo-German Treaty.

5. See, however, White (1985: 325) for a note on the continuance of forced labour in Mozambique after 1930.

6. Letter from the District Commissioner, Blantyre, to the Provincial Commissioner, Blantyre, 5 February 1930. Letter from the Provincial Commissioner, Blantyre, to the Chief Secretary, Zomba, 11 April 1932.

7. For example, letter from the District Commissioner, Mlanje, to the Provincial Commissioner, Blantyre, 7 October 1932. Letter from the District Commissioner, Liwonde, to the Provincial Commissioner, Melokotera, 27 April 1935. Letter from the District Commissioner, Zomba, to the Provincial Commissioner, Blantyre, 8 August 1940. These documents report raids by Portuguese soldiers into Malawi in pursuit of tax-evaders.

8. For example, letter from the District Commissioner, Mlanje, to K. Ommanney Shelford, Chisambo, 20 April 1951. Letter from the District Commissioner, Mlanje, to the Administrador, Milange, 24 April 1951.

9. 'Complaint of Chief Philip Gomani to the Government', attached to the letter from the District Commissioner, Ncheu, to the Provincial Commissioner, Lilongwe, 22 March 1947.

10. Apart from the plane crash, labour shortages on Malawian estates are also commonly seen as reasons for the government's change of policy (see Kydd and Christiansen 1982; Hirschmann and Vaughan 1983: 87; White 1987: 232). In the run-up to the 1993 referendum and the 1994 elections, leaders of the Malawi Congress Party explained the demise as a protest against the Aids tests to which Malawian labourers were subjected in South Africa (see also Chirwa 1998). Nevertheless, the opposition groups aroused much interest precisely because they were expected to 'open' (*kutsegula*) the South African labour market, if elected to power.

11. Ngoni appear in some historical accounts as willing collaborators of the colonial regime. In 1917, they allied with the Portuguese to suppress the Barue rebellion

in the Zambezi valley (Isaacman 1976: 156–77). Many of the foremen in the Zambézian plantations, on the other hand, were Ngoni (Vail and White 1980: 354–5). Such observations, suggesting widespread collaboration with colonial authorities, underline the importance of considering the specific conditions which contributed to the articulation of the nationalist cause in the Dedza–Angónia borderland.

12. Letter from the Government Agent, Nsanje, to the Secretary to the Prime Minister, Zomba, 3 February 1966. Letter from the Secretary to the Prime Minister, Zomba, to all Government Agents and Assistant Government Agents in charge of sub-districts, 1 March 1966.

13. Letter from the Regional Health Inspector, Lilongwe, to the Secretary for Health and Community Development, Blantyre, 26 June 1971.

14. The estimated one and a half million refugees who fled Mozambique settled in the following countries: Malawi (1,000,000 refugees), South Africa (150,000), Zimbabwe (150,000), Tanzania (100,000), Zambia (75,000) and Swaziland (50,000). Added to its population of some nine million, the one million refugees in Malawi represented the world's third largest refugee concentration (Wilson with Nunes 1994: 199). According to the UNHCR (1993) in Tete, the second largest contingent of refugees in Malawi – 150,000 persons – were from the Mutarara District of Tete. Outside Tete, only the Morrumbala District of Zambézia had more than 100,000 refugees in Malawi. The figures released by the Food Aid Relief and Rehabilitation Unit of the Malawi Government in Lilongwe showed in September 1990 that the largest number of refugees lived in the southern District of Nsanje (247,741 persons). Dedza (170,825) and Ntcheu (151,883) Districts hosted the second and third largest numbers of refugees.

15. All the names for villages and persons are pseudonyms in the case studies.

16. In late 1992, US$1 was approximately 4.3 Malawian kwacha. The value of kwacha has plummeted after 1993, and in early 1997, around the period described in the Epilogue, US$1 was approximately 15 Malawian kwacha. All the monetary figures given in chapters other than the Epilogue refer to the situation during the 1992–3 fieldwork.

17. The rains did not fail completely even in 1991–2, when many areas in Southern Africa witnessed severe drought. According to the Development Officer's records, in October–May 1991–2 the area received 784.3 mm of rain, the same months in 1990–1 854.1 mm and in 1992–3 917.0 mm.

18. In 1987, the population density on the Malawian side of the border, including the refugees, was 128 persons per square kilometre (Malawi Government 1993: 73–6). This was more than the density for Dedza District (114), Central Region (87) and the whole country (85).

19. These figures are based on my own census in 1992. By that time, most of these under-five-year olds had been born during displacement. Thus displacement hardly reduced fertility.

20. These figures are also based on my own census. 'Refugees' consist of those who were entitled to the food aid of the World Food Programme. Roughly 20 per cent of the refugee population in the sample originated from elsewhere than Chitima, as was the case also with the total population. It may be assumed, of course, that this 20 per cent had characteristics that made it different from the Chitima population. According to my own observations and the Relief Clerk's records, the differences concerned, however, the experiences of the war, not the general population characteristics.

21. For the purposes of this census, 'household' denoted the inhabitants of a house,

or a set of houses, fed by the same granary. I grouped those refugees who did not have granaries into households according to the units by which they received relief aid. Overall, studying investment in livestock presented few difficulties, because there was little borrowing or renting of livestock between households. A somewhat more difficult task was to define a 'female-headed' household. In the end, I did not include those households where the husband was absent, if he supported his wife regularly through remittances or otherwise. In other words, only the households without a husband altogether were included.

22. As Mair (1951: 103) and Barnes (1959: 226) observed, persons holding the same *mfunda* (pl. *mifunda*) do not have the characteristics attributed to a clan. In Barnes' words, 'there are no clan heads, no clan exogamy, no clan taboos, no beliefs in a common origin from a legendary ancestor, no clan totems, and no correlation between clan and territory' (1959: 226). There are several *mifunda* in the area, and the discovery of the same *mfunda* between persons previously unknown to one another often prompts good-humoured assertions of common kinship. However, a common *mfunda* requires exceptional circumstances, such as living in a foreign country, to be taken seriously as an indicator of *ubale*.

23. In such a case, the child can call both the father and the mother's husband a 'father' (*bambo*). It is, however, commonly perceived that a man can easily 'hate' (*kudana*) other children than his own in his wife's household. In any case, marriage usually implies support for all the children in the household. Conversely, the termination of marriage is indicated by lack of support. Usually, no continued support is expected from the father after a payment to the woman's guardian (*nkhoswe*) in recognition of divorce. In principle, therefore, Dedza–Angónia borderland villagers recognise the 'social father' as the child's 'father *de jure*'. Yet they do not necessarily view him as the child's genitor, whose *mfunda* the child bears.

24. The usage of the terms *mfumu* and *nyakwawa* is sometimes confusing. There is no ordinary term which would distinguish a chief from a village headman; both can be labelled *mfumu*. Moreover, even within the same village, the village headman is sometimes called *nyakwawa*. Such usage is, however, considered colloquial, and the village headman is most often addressed and referred to as *mfumu*. It should be noted that a woman may also be a *mfumu*, but I never heard of a female councillor (*nyakwawa*).

CHAPTER 2 THE PATHS TO WAR

1. The partially overlapping charts of key genealogical relations in the two villages are given in the Appendix.

2. The name Maphiri is the plural of Achingano's and his descendants' 'clan-name' Phiri. It is, like the other names for persons and villages in this book, a pseudonym.

3. As will be seen below, Andrea became after independence a dissatisfied Frelimo member and began to support Renamo. After displacement, he again became a councillor for the Zakariya division.

4. These stories were most often told by Luis's rivals in the Frelimo organisation. Within Chitima village, these included especially Sadlek and Sandikonda, whose dissatisfaction with Luis after the return from exile is described in Chapter 6. The cross-checks of these stories, however, confirmed that Luis and Rafaelo alike were subject to considerable patronage from Leonardo.

5. Such a gesture occurred less commonly among Malawians. One reason may have been the fact that the possession of a Malawi Congress Party membership

card was compulsory for all Malawians. A Frelimo membership card, complete with the photograph of its holder, was a rarer item among Dedza–Angónia borderland villagers. On the other hand, the 1992–3 fieldwork coincided with a period when the legitimacy of the Malawi Congress Party was much more contested than that of Frelimo (see Englund 1996a). In the referendum in Malawi in June 1993, 58 per cent voted for the transition to the multiparty system of government in the villages of the Bembeke area closest to Mfuno.

6. See Ranger (1986) and Alexander (1995: 8–9) on the use of the terms 'guerrillas' and 'bandits' in political arguments.
7. Villagers do not recall that Jeremiya had attempted to mediate in the tension between Rafaelo and Luis. On the other hand, Jeremiya never became an active Frelimo supporter either.

CHAPTER 3 REFUGEES FROM AFAR

1. Patrick's wife and children later fled with her relatives to Lizulu.
2. Apart from Mastala and Lukelesia, only Krevor, Augushtu and Augushtu's eldest son left Mfuno during displacement. Krevor became a watchman for the Red Cross in Dedza town in 1987, whereas Augushtu and his son joined Augushtu's brother in his business in Villa Ulongwe in 1990. The husbands of Yelena and Julieta, like Patrick, were killed by Renamo shortly before the flight. The women remarried with men from Chitima village during their stay in Mfuno.
3. John's close friend, a Chitima villager, helped him to protect his newly built houses in Lumbe against witchcraft. This friend had married in a nearby village in Malawi in 1969. He returned to Chitima in 1993, but his village division was Mtunda, the most distant division from Mfuno. It was only towards the end of displacement that John had begun to establish active ties to Chitima villagers from the divisions closest to Mfuno. This was largely a concomitant of his involvement with a woman from Chitima.
4. In 1992–3, there were seven teachers in the refugees' primary school in Mfuno. All of them were qualified primary school teachers and refugees themselves.
5. Nachisale's young daughter also remained in Mfuno until September to receive fortnightly food rations. These rations continued to be delivered after the majority of refugees had moved to Mozambique. Even after September, the families in Evelesita's group retained their ration-cards and continued to send youths to collect their food aid.
6. The expression *mudzaona*, when uttered in the heat of the moment, is the most usual idiom of curse in Chichewa (see also Yoshida 1992: 256). I use the word sorcery rather than witchcraft in this context merely to indicate that persons may have access to occult powers even without being witches themselves. The sorcery–witchcraft distinction, as such, is problematic (see Englund 1996b).

CHAPTER 4 GENDERED EXILE

1. For a perspective on a patrilineal definition of citizenship and the anomalies created by women's cross-border trade in Zimbabwe, see Cheater (1998).
2. The Malawian villages which received an influx of refugees allocated a part of their graveyards for refugees to bury their dead. If refugees were able to claim pedigree among Malawian families, their dead could be buried where those families laid their dead to rest. Otherwise, such as in Edward's case, refugees were buried at the fringes of graveyards to show that they were strangers.
3. Of Namanyada's four other surviving children, a daughter lived with her family in Blantyre, two sons married in Chitima and one son married in Mfuno.

CHAPTER 5 MIGRANTS AMONGST REFUGEES

1. Chisale had moved to live with his paternal grandmother in a village in Ntcheu District about three kilometres from Mfuno in 1941. Although Chisale had little everyday involvement in the affairs of Sofiya's family, he was a very authoritative figure by virtue of his prominence as a successful labour migrant and as both a headman's councillor and the Malawi Congress Party chairman in his father's village. Chisale's authority, qualified by his absence from his mother's village, ensured Sandikonda some independence as an *nkhoswe*, and the two brothers seldom clashed. Sofiya's other son, Emanuele, who had the same father as Hawadi, originally married in Chitima but separated from his wife during exile. He married a woman from a distant village in Angónia and left with her for her village after exile.
2. This is still considered to be an 'Ngoni' enclave in a 'Chewa' area. It was here, as was mentioned in Chapter 2, that Luis's early companion Phokera also fled with his family in the 1960s.
3. The daughter, who was born in 1978 when the marriage had already ended, joined him in Chitima in 1993.
4. The persecution of Jehovah's Witnesses during Kamuzu Banda's regime is documented by Africa Watch (1990: 63–7). See Wilson (1994a) for an account of Jehovah's Witnesses as refugees and returnees around the Mulanje area in southern Malawi and northern Mozambique.

CHAPTER 6 PARADOXES OF REPATRIATION

1. Luis had been the recipient of these gifts during the years between independence and the war. After the repatriation to Chitima, some villagers continued to give gifts to him. In effect, they had to give a double number of gifts, because Luis insisted that a gift had also to be given to the village headman during such events. Thus, as is discussed below, Luis acknowledged the office of the village headman. Yet, at least initially after the repatriation, he sought to discredit Rafaelo as its incumbent.
2. The quantities were also approximately the same, but because the returnees' aid was expected to be delivered once a month, it was given in larger portions than the refugees' fortnightly rations.
3. In fact, no aid was ever delivered in Chitima and no returnees' aid was given after May 1994.

CHAPTER 7 VALUE, POWER AND 'SOCIAL CAPITAL'

1. The ethnography of personhood among Dedza–Angónia borderland villagers has remarkable parallels with certain currents in Western philosophy which have countered individualistic notions of the person (on Spinoza and Deleuze, see Armstrong 1997: 50).
2. In Malawi and Mozambique, the state, the government, the party and the nation were largely coterminous in the rhetoric of the one-party state (cf. Cahen 1993: 56). Dedza–Angónia borderland villagers' initial perception of Renamo as another 'party' (*chipani*), however, and, as described in the previous chapter, Sadlek's exchange with Chisale on post-war Mozambique, disclose that villagers were able to distinguish the concepts of *chipani* and *boma* even before the more recent turn to multipartyism.
3. To the extent that Bourdieu's agents are groups rather than individuals (e.g. 1977: 38–43), his account does not necessarily carry the assumption of disengaged subjects and 'individual' selves.

EPILOGUE: BORDERLAND REVISITED

1. From September 1996 to July 1997, I was engaged in fieldwork in Malawian urban centres, mainly in Lilongwe. During this period, I visited the Dedza–Angónia borderland several times, sometimes for weekends, sometimes for several weeks. Many friends from the area also visited me in Lilongwe. In 1994, the presidential and parliamentary elections had taken place in both Malawi and Mozambique. In Malawi, Bakili Muluzi and the United Democratic Front replaced Kamuzu Banda and the Malawi Congress Party in government (see Kaspin 1995; van Donge 1995). As already mentioned, Joaquim Chissano and Frelimo remained in government in Mozambique despite Renamo's success in many provinces.

2. For Dedza–Angónia borderland villagers, the use of dung in agriculture is a sign of poverty when compared to the use of chemical fertiliser. Because few villagers own cattle, however, the giving or selling of dung indicates relative prosperity.

3. For more discussion on land in these families, see Hawadi's case in Chapter 5. Hawadi himself had followed his temporarily estranged wife Maluwa to Kasungu District, where they had apparently re-established their life together and where Hawadi had again found work on a tobacco estate. His absence in the Dedza–Angónia borderland had become as complete as ever, and his relatives had not heard of him for over two years in 1997. He did not even come to Sofiya's funeral in February 1997.

4. The concept of a civil society, despite its prominence in the African debates of the early 1990s, is not a prerogative of liberalism (see Seligman 1992). Nor are all current theorists of African civil society advocates of liberalism. But when Chabal imagines a pre-colonial social order which was organised 'according to principles of social existence which favoured the community over the individual and conceived of the world as an interconnected whole rather than as the sum total of discrete components' (1994: 87), he provides a neat contrast to current liberalism. In his scheme, 'a notion of the individual distinct from that of the community' (1994: 87) is essential for the emergence of civil society. It should be clear that the relational notion of personhood in this book makes the individual–community dichotomy redundant.

BIBLIOGRAPHY

ARCHIVAL SOURCES

The National Archives of Malawi, Zomba

NCD 1/3/1   Dedza District Book 1907
NCD 2/1/4   Dedza District Annual Reports 1936–39
NCD 2/1/6   Dedza District Annual Reports 1946–50
NCN 1/12/2   Gardens in the Portuguese Territory (Ncheu)
NS 1/4/1   Southern Province Anglo-Portuguese Boundary
PCC 1/6/1   Territorial and Provincial Boundaries
S1/2767/23   The Secretariat Records
8.11.5R 14155   Mlanje: Migration
19.3–3F 14966   Nsanje: Migration
17/2 3/10/9R   Correspondence on the International Boundaries

BOOKS, BOOK PARTS, ARTICLES, THESES,
DRAFT PAPERS, ETC.

Abrahamsson, Hans and Anders Nilsson. 1995. *Mozambique: the troubled transition. From socialism to free market capitalism.* London: Zed Books.

Africa Watch. 1990. *Where Silence Rules: the suppression of dissent in Malawi.* New York: Human Rights Watch.

Africa Watch. 1992. *Conspicuous Destruction: war, famine and the reform process in Mozambique.* New York: Human Rights Watch.

Agência de informação de Moçambique. 1994a. *AIM Reports 45,* 8 November.

Agência de informação de Moçambique. 1994b. *AIM Reports 46,* 24 November .

Agência de informação de Moçambique. 1996a. 'War threat dismissed', *Mozambiquefile 237,* 22–3.

Agência de informação de Moçambique. 1996b. 'Statistics on the economy', *Mozambiquefile 243,* 14–16.

Alden, Chris and Mark Simpson. 1993. 'Mozambique: a delicate peace', *Journal of Modern African Studies 31,* 109–30.

Alexander, Jocelyn. 1994. 'Land and Political Authority in Post-war Mozambique: a view from Manica Province', unpublished manuscript, University of Oxford.

Alexander, Jocelyn. 1995. 'Political Change in Manica Province, Mozambique: implications for the decentralization of power', unpublished manuscript, University of Oxford.

Alexander, Jocelyn. 1997. 'The local state in post-war Mozambique: political practice and ideas about authority', *Africa 67,* 1–26.

Allen, Tim (ed.). 1996. *In Search of Cool Ground: war, flight and home-coming in northeast Africa.* London: James Currey.

Allen, Tim and Hubert Morsink (eds). 1994. *When Refugees Go Home*. London: James Currey.

Alpers, Edward A. 1975. *Ivory and Slaves in East Central Africa: changing patterns of international trade to the late nineteenth century*. London: Heinemann.

Alvarez, Robert R. Jr. 1995. 'The Mexican–US border: the making of an anthropology of borderlands', *Annual Review of Anthropology* 24, 447–70.

Anderson, Hilary. 1992. *Mozambique: a war against the people*. London: Macmillan.

Armstrong, Aurelia. 1997. 'Some reflections on Deleuze's Spinoza: composition and agency', in K. A. Pearson (ed.), *Deleuze and Philosophy: the difference engineer*, pp. 44–57. London: Routledge.

Asad, Talal. 1972. 'Market model, class structure and consent: a reconsideration of Swat political organisation', *Man* (n.s.) 7, 74–94.

Asiwaju, A. I. (ed.). 1985. *Partitioned Africans: ethnic relations across Africa's international boundaries 1884–1984*. London: Christopher Hurst.

Austin, Kathi. 1994. *Invisible Crimes: US private intervention in the war in Mozambique*. Washington, DC: Africa Policy Information Center.

Axelson, Eric. 1960. *Portuguese in South-East Africa 1600–1700*. Johannesburg: Witwatersrand University Press.

Banda, Ellias Ngalande, Flora Nankhuni and Ephraim Chirwa. 1998. 'Economy and democracy: background, current situation and future prospects', in K. M. Phiri and K. R. Ross (eds), *Democratization in Malawi: a stocktaking*, pp. 70–86. Blantyre: Claim.

Barnes, J. A. 1951. *Marriage in a Changing Society*. London: Oxford University Press.

Barnes, J. A. 1954. *Politics in a Changing Society: a political history of the Fort Jameson Ngoni*. London: Oxford University Press.

Barnes, J. A. 1959 (1951). 'The Fort Jameson Ngoni', in E. Colson and M. Gluckman (eds), *Seven Tribes of British Central Africa*, pp. 194–252. London: Oxford University Press.

Barnes, J. A. 1962. 'African models in the New Guinea Highlands', *Man* 62, 5–9.

Barnes, Sandra T. 1986. *Patrons and Power: creating a political community in metropolitan Lagos*. Manchester: Manchester University Press for the International African Institute.

Barth, Fredrik. 1966. 'Models of social organization', *Royal Anthropological Institute Occasional Paper* 23.

Basch, Linda, Nina Glick Schiller and Christina Szanton-Blanc. 1994. *Nations Unbound: transnational projects, postcolonial predicaments, and deterritorialized nation-states*. Longhorne, PA: Gordon & Breach.

Bayart, Jean-François. 1993. *The State in Africa: the politics of the belly*. London: Longman.

Bayart, Jean-François. 1999. 'The "social capital" of the felonious state: or the ruses of political intelligence', in J. F. Bayart, S. Ellis and B. Hibou (eds), *The Criminalization of the State in Africa*, pp. 32–48. Oxford: James Currey for the International African Institute.

Beach, D. N. 1984. *Zimbabwe Before 1900*. Harare: Mambo Press.

Besteman, Catherine. 1999. *Unraveling Somalia: race, violence, and the legacy of slavery*. Philadelphia: University of Pennsylvania Press.

Bhabha, Homi K. 1994. *The Location of Culture*. London: Routledge.

Bhaskar, Roy 1993. *Dialectic: the pulse of freedom*. London: Verso.

Bhebe, Ngwabi and Terence Ranger (eds). 1995. *Society in Zimbabwe's Liberation War*. Oxford: James Currey.

Birch de Aguilar, Laurel. 1995. 'Masks, society, and hierarchy among the Chewa of central Malawi', *Anthropos* 90, 407–21.

Birmingham, David. 1992. *Frontline Nationalism in Angola and Mozambique*. London: James Currey.

Black, Richard and Khalid Koser (eds). 1999. *The End of the Refugee Cycle?: refugee repatriation and reconstruction*. Oxford: Berghahn.

Blau, Peter M. 1964. *Exchange and Power in Social Life*. New York: John Wiley and Sons.

Boeder, Robert Benson. 1974. 'Malawians Abroad: the history of labor emigration from Malawi to its neighbours, 1890 to the present', PhD thesis, Michigan State University.

Boeder, Robert Benson. 1984. *The Silent Majority: a history of the Lomwe in Malawi*. Pretoria: African Institute of South Africa.

Bonga, Violet and Ken Wilson. 1993. 'Repatriation of Mozambicans from Malawi: the current situation', *Report for the Refugee Studies Programme, University of Oxford*.

Boothby, Neil, Abubacar Sultan and Peter Upton. 1991. *Children of Mozambique*. Washington, DC: US Committee for Refugees.

Borges Coelho, João Paolo Constantino. 1993. 'Protected Villages and Communal Villages in the Mozambican Province of Tete (1968–1982): a history of state resettlement policies, development and war', PhD thesis, University of Bradford.

Borges Coelho, João Paolo Constantino. 1998. 'State resettlement policies in post-colonial rural Mozambique: the impact of the communal village programme on Tete Province, 1977–1982', *Journal of Southern African Studies* 24, 61–91.

Borges Coelho, João Paulo and Alex Vines. 1995. *Demobilization and Re-integration of Ex-combatants in Mozambique*. Oxford: Refugee Studies Programme.

Bourdieu, Pierre. 1977. *Outline of a Theory of Practice*. Cambridge: Cambridge University Press.

Brantley, Cynthia. 1997. 'Through Ngoni eyes: Margaret Read's matrilineal interpretations from Nyasaland', *Critique of Anthropology* 17, 147–69.

Brito, Luis de. 1988. 'Une Relecture nécessaire: la gènese du parti-état FRELIMO', *Politique Africaine 29*, 15–27.

Brito, Luis de. 1994. 'Des Élections pour la paix au Mozambique', *Politique Africaine* 56, 144–6.

Bulcha, Mekuria. 1988. *Flight and Integration: causes of mass exodus from Ethiopia and problems of integration in the Sudan*. Uppsala: Scandinavian Institute of African Studies.

Burawoy, Michael. 1998. 'The extended-case method', *Sociological Theory 16*, 4–33.

Cahen, Michel. 1993. 'Check on socialism in Mozambique – what check? What socialism?', *Review of African Political Economy 57*, 46–59.

Callamard, Agnès. 1994a. 'Refugees and local hosts: a study of the trading inter-actions between Mozambican refugees and Malawian villagers in the district of Mwanza', *Journal of Refugee Studies 7*, 39–62.

Callamard, Agnès. 1994b. 'Malawian refugee policy, international politics and the one-party regime', *Journal of International Affairs 47*, 525–56.

Cammack, Diana. 1988. 'The "human face" of destabilization: the war in Mozambique', *Review of African Political Economy 40*, 65–75.

Chabal, Patrick. 1994 (1992). *Power in Africa: an essay in political interpretation*. London: Macmillan.

Chabal, Patrick and Jean-Pascal Daloz. 1999. *Africa Works: disorder as political instrument*. Oxford: James Currey for the International African Institute.

Chakanza, J. Chaphadzika. 1980. 'An annotated list of independent churches in Malawi', *Sources for the Study of Religion in Malawi* 3. University of Malawi.

Chanock, Martin. 1985. *Law, Custom and Social Order: the colonial experience in Malawi and Zambia*. Cambridge: Cambridge University Press.

Cheater, A. P. 1998. 'Transcending the state?: gender and borderline constructions of citizenship in Zimbabwe', in T. M. Wilson and H. Donnan (eds), *Border Identities: nation and state at international frontiers*, pp. 191–214. Cambridge: Cambridge University Press.

Chingono, Mark. 1996. *The State, Violence and Development: the political economy of war in Mozambique, 1975–1992*. Aldershot: Avebury.

Chirwa, Wiseman Chijere. 1996. 'The Malawi government and the South African labour recruiters, 1974–1992', *Journal of Modern African Studies 34*, 623–42.

Chirwa, Wiseman Chijere. 1998. 'Aliens and AIDS in Southern Africa: the Malawi–South Africa debate', *African Affairs 97*, 53–79.

Chitsamba, L. S. 1971. 'The international boundaries of Malawi', *History Seminar Paper, 1971–72*. University of Malawi.

Chiume, M. W. Kanyama. 1975. *Kwacha: an autobiography*. Nairobi: East African Publishing House.

Christiansen, Robert and Jonathan Kydd. 1983. 'The return of Malawian labour from South Africa and Zimbabwe', *Journal of Modern African Studies 21*, 311–26.

Clapham, Christopher. 1985. *Third World Politics: an introduction*. London: Croom Helm.

Clarence-Smith, Gervase. 1989. 'The roots of Mozambican counter-revolution', *Southern African Review of Books 4*, 7–10.

Cobbing, Julian. 1988. 'The Mfecane as alibi: thoughts on Dithakong and Mbolompo', *Journal of African History 29*, 487–519.

Cohen, Anthony P. 1994. *Self Consciousness: an alternative anthropology of identity*. London: Routledge.

Coleman, James S. 1988. 'Social capital in the creation of human capital', *American Journal of Sociology 94*, Suppl. S95–S120.

Coleman, James S. 1990. *Foundations of Social Theory*. Cambridge, MA: Harvard University Press.

Colson, Elizabeth. 1962. *The Plateau Tonga of Northern Rhodesia: social and religious studies*. Manchester: Manchester University Press.

Colson, Elizabeth. 1971. *The Social Consequences of Resettlement: the impact of the Kariba resettlement upon the Gwembe Tonga*. Manchester: Manchester University Press.

Colson, Elizabeth. 1999. 'Gendering those uprooted by "Development"', in D. Indra (ed.), *Engendering Forced Migration*, pp. 23–39. Oxford: Berghahn.

Cramer, Christopher and Nicola Pontara. 1998. 'Rural poverty and poverty alleviation in Mozambique: what's missing from the debate?', *Journal of Modern African Studies 36*, 101–38.

Crisp, Jeff. 1986. 'Ugandan refugees in Sudan and Zaire: the problem of repatriation', *African Affairs 86*, 163–80.

Crush, Jonathan, Alan Jeeves and David Yudelman. 1991. *South Africa's Labour Empire: a history of black migrancy to the gold mines*. Boulder, CO: Westview Press.

Cruz e Silva, Teresa. 1992. *Projecto de Angonia*. Maputo: APDC.

Cruz e Silva, Teresa. 1998. 'Identity and political consciousness in Southern Mozambique, 1930–1974: two Presbyterian biographies contextualised', *Journal of Southern African Studies 24*, 223–36.

Daniel, E. Valentine. 1996. *Charred Lullabies: chapters in an anthropography of violence*. Princeton, NJ: Princeton University Press.

Daniel, E. Valentine and John Chr. Knudsen. 1995. 'Introduction', in E. V. Daniel and J. C. Knudsen (eds), *Mistrusting Refugees*, pp. 1–12. Berkeley: University of California Press.

Davenport, T. R. H. 1996. 'The Mfecane debate: a case for deconstruction?', *South African Historical Journal 35*, 193–201.

Davison, Jean. 1993. 'Tenacious women: clinging to Banja household production in the face of changing gender relations in Malawi', *Journal of Southern African Studies 19*, 405–21.

Dinerman, Alice. 1994. 'In search of Mozambique: the imaginings of Christian Geffray in *La Cause des armes au Mozambique*', *Journal of Southern African Studies 20*, 569–86.

Dolan, Chris. 1999. 'Repatriation from South Africa to Mozambique – undermining durable solutions?', in R. Black and K. Khoser (eds), *The End of the Refugee Cycle?: refugee repatriation and reconstruction*, pp. 85–108. Oxford: Berghahn.

Donnan, Hastings and Thomas M. Wilson (eds). 1994. *Border Approaches: anthropological perspectives on frontiers*. Lanham, MD: University Press of America.

Douglas, Mary. 1969. 'Is matriliny doomed in Africa?', in M. Douglas and P. M. Kaberry (eds), *Man in Africa*, pp. 121–35. London: Tavistock.

Egero, Bertil. 1987. *Mozambique: a dream undone. The political economy of democracy, 1975–84*. Uppsala: Scandinavian Institute of African Studies.

Eisenberg, Andrew. 1998. 'Weberian patrimonialism and imperial Chinese history', *Theory and Society 27*, 83–102.

Eldredge, Elizabeth A. 1992. 'Sources of conflict in Southern Africa, ca. 1800–30: the "Mfecane" reconsidered', *Journal of African History 33*, 1–35.

Emirbayer, Mustafa. 1997. 'Manifesto for a relational sociology', *American Journal of Sociology 103*, 281–317.

Englund, Harri. 1996a. 'Between God and Kamuzu: the transition to multi-party politics in central Malawi', in R. Werbner and T. Ranger (eds), *Postcolonial Identities in Africa*, pp. 107–35. London: Zed Books.

Englund, Harri. 1996b. 'Witchcraft, modernity and the person: the morality of accumulation in central Malawi', *Critique of Anthropology 16*, 257–79.

Englund, Harri. 1996c. 'Waiting for the Portuguese: nostalgia, exploitation and the meaning of land in the Malawi–Mozambique borderland', *Journal of Contemporary African Studies 14*, 157–72.

Englund, Harri. 1998. 'Death, trauma and ritual: Mozambican refugees in Malawi', *Social Science and Medicine 46*, 1165–74.

Englund, Harri. 1999. 'The self in self-interest: land, labour and temporalities in Malawi's agrarian change', *Africa 69*, 139–59.

Epstein, A. L. 1958. *Politics in an Urban African Community*. Manchester: Manchester University Press.

Eve, Raymond A., Sara Horsfall and Mary E. Lee (eds). 1997. *Chaos, Complexity and Sociology: myths, models and theories*. London: Sage.

Fauvet, Paul. 1984. 'Roots of counter-revolution: the Mozambique National Resistance', *Review of African Political Economy 29*, 108–21.

Ferguson, Brian. 1990. 'Explaining War', in J. Haas (ed.), *The Anthropology of War*, pp. 26–55. Cambridge: Cambridge University Press.

Ferguson, James. 1995. 'From African socialism to scientific capitalism: reflections on the legitimation crisis in IMF-ruled Africa', in D. B. Moore and G. J. Schmitz (eds), *Debating Development Discourse: institutional and popular perspectives*, pp. 129–48. New York: St Martin's Press.

Ferguson, James. 1999. *Expectations of Modernity: myths and meanings of urban life on the Zambian copperbelt*. Berkeley: University of California Press.

Ferris, Elizabeth G. 1993. *Beyond Borders: refugees, migrants and human rights in the post-Cold War era*. Geneva: World Council of Churches.

Fine, Ben. 1999. 'The developmental state is dead – long live social capital?', *Development and Change 30*, 1–19.

Finnegan, William. 1992. *A Complicated War: the harrowing of Mozambique*. Berkeley: University of California Press.

First, Ruth. 1983. *Black Gold: the Mozambican miner, proletarian and peasant*. Brighton: Harvester Press.

Flower, Ken. 1987. *Serving Secretly: an intelligence chief on record*. London: John Murray.

Flynn, Donna K. 1997a. '"We are the border": identity, exchange, and the state along the Bénin–Nigeria Border', *American Ethnologist 24*, 311–30.

Flynn, Donna K. 1997b. 'Trading traitors: cultural negotiations of female mobility in a West African borderland', *Identities 4*, 245–80.

Fortes, Meyer. 1970. *Time and Social Structure and Other Essays*. London: Athlone Press.

Foucault, Michel. 1972. *The Archaeology of Knowledge*. London: Tavistock.

Fox, Jonathan. 1997. 'The World Bank and social capital: contesting the concept in practice', *Journal of International Development 9*, 936–71.

Gambetta, Diego (ed.). 1988. *Trust: making and breaking co-operative relations*. Oxford: Blackwell.

Geertz, Clifford. 1988. *Works and Lives: anthropologist as an author*. Chicago: University of Chicago Press.

Geffray, Christian. 1990. *La Cause des armes au Mozambique: anthropologie d'une guerre civile*. Paris: Karthala.

Geffray, Christian and Mogen Pedersen. 1988. 'Nampula en guerre', *Politique Africaine 29*, 28–40.

Gersony, Robert. 1988. *Summary of Mozambican Refugee Accounts of Principally Conflict-related Experience in Mozambique*. Washington, DC: Bureau for Refugee Programs.

Giddens, Anthony. 1990. *The Consequences of Modernity*. Stanford: Stanford University Press.

Gledhill, John. 1994. *Power and its Disguises: anthropological perspectives on politics*. London: Pluto.

Gluckman, Max. 1940. 'Analysis of a social situation in modern Zululand', *Bantu Studies 14*, 1–30 and 147–74.

Gluckman, Max. 1950. 'Kinship and marriage among the Lozi of northern Rhodesia and the Zulu of Natal', in A. R. Radcliffe-Brown and D. Forde (eds), *African Systems of Kinship and Marriage*, pp. 168–206. London: Oxford University Press for the International African Institute.

Gluckman, Max. 1960. 'The rise of the Zulu empire', *Scientific American April*, 157–68.

Gluckman, Max. 1968. 'Inter-hierarchical roles: professional and party ethics in tribal areas in South and Central Africa', in M. J. Swartz (ed.), *Local-level Politics: social and cultural perspectives*, pp. 69–93. London: University of London Press.

Gough, Kathleen. 1961. 'The modern disintegration of matrilineal descent groups', in D. M. Schneider and K. Gough (eds), *Matrilineal Kinship*, pp. 631–52. Berkeley: University of California Press.

Gould, Jeremy. 1997. *Localizing Modernity: action, interests and association in rural Zambia*. Helsinki: Finnish Anthropological Society.

Griffiths, Ieuan. 1996. 'Permeable boundaries in Africa', in P. Nugent and A. I. Asiwaju (eds), *African Boundaries: barriers, conduits and opportunities*, pp. 68–83. London: Pinter.

Gulbrandsen, Ornulf. 1995. 'The king is king by the grace of the people: the exercise and control of power in subject-ruler relations', *Comparative Studies in Society and History 37*, 415–44.

Gupta, Akhil. 1992. 'The song of the nonaligned world: transnational identities and the reinscription of space in late capitalism', *Cultural Anthropology 7*, 63–79.

Gupta, Akhil and James Ferguson (eds). 1997. *Anthropological Locations: boundaries and grounds of a field science*. Berkeley: University of California Press.

Guy, Jeff. 1980. 'Ecological factors in the rise of Shaka and the Zulu kingdom', in S. Marks and A. Atmore (eds), *Economy and Society in Pre-industrial South Africa*, pp. 102–19. London: Longman.

Guyer, Jane I. 1993. 'Wealth in people and self-realization in equatorial Africa', *Man* (n.s.) *28*, 243–65.

Guyer, Jane I. and Samuel M. Eno Belinga. 1995. 'Wealth in people as wealth in knowledge: accumulation and composition in equatorial Africa', *Journal of African History 36*, 91–120.

Hall, Margaret. 1990. 'The Mozambican National Resistance Movement (RENAMO): a study in the destruction of an African country', *Africa 60*, 39–45.

Hall, Margaret and Tom Young. 1997. *Confronting Leviathan: Mozambique since independence*. London: Hurst .

Hamilton, Carolyn Anne (ed.). 1995. *The Mfecane Aftermath: reconstructive debates in Southern African history*. Johannesburg: Witwatersrand University Press.

Hamilton, Carolyn Anne. 1998. *Terrific Majesty: the powers of Shaka Zulu and the limits of historical invention*. Cambridge, MA: Harvard University Press.

Hammond, Laura. 1999. 'Examining the discourse of repatriation: towards a more proactive theory of return migrants', in R. Black and K. Koser (eds), *The End of the Refugee Cycle?: refugee repatriation and reconstruction*, pp. 227–44. Oxford: Berghahn.

Hanlon, Joseph. 1984. *Mozambique: the revolution under fire*. London: Zed Books.

Hanlon, Joseph. 1991. *Mozambique: who calls the shots?* London: James Currey.

Hanlon, Joseph. 1996. *Peace without Profit: how the IMF blocks rebuilding in Mozambique*. Oxford: James Currey for the International African Institute.

Hansen, Art. 1979. 'Once the running stops: assimilation of Angolan refugees into Zambian border villages', *Disasters 3*, 369–74.

Hansen, Art. 1982. 'Self-settled rural refugees in Africa: the case of Angolans in Zambian villages', in A. Hansen and A. Oliver-Smith (eds), *Involuntary Migration and Resettlement*, pp. 13–35. Boulder, CO: Westview Press.

Harrell-Bond, B. E. 1986. *Imposing Aid: emergency assistance to refugees*. Oxford: Oxford University Press.

Harrell-Bond, B. E. 1989. 'Repatriation: under what conditions is it the most desirable solution for refugees?', *African Studies Review 32*, 41–69.

Harris, Grace Gredys. 1989. 'Concepts of individual, self, and person in description and analysis', *American Anthropologist 91*, 599–612.

Harrison, Graham. 1996. 'Democracy in Mozambique: the significance of multi-party elections', *Review of African Political Economy 67*, 19–35.

Harrison, Graham. 1998. 'Marketing legitimacy in rural Mozambique: the case of Mecúfi District, northern Mozambique', *Journal of Modern African Studies 36*, 569–91.

Harriss, John and Paolo de Renzio. 1997. '"Missing link" or analytically missing?: the concept of social capital – an introductory bibliographic essay', *Journal of International Development 9*, 919–37.

Harriss, John, Janet Hunter and Colin Lewis (eds). 1995. *The New Institutional Economics and Third World Development*. London: Routledge.

Hatchell, G. W. 1935. 'The Angoni of Tanganyika Territory', *Man 35*, 69–71.

Hedges, David. 1989. 'Notes on Malawi–Mozambique relations 1961–1987', *Journal of Southern African Studies 15*, 617–44.

Henriksen, Thomas H. 1983. *Revolution and Counter-Revolution: Mozambique's war of independence, 1964–1974*. Westport, CT: Greenwood.

Hermele, Kenneth. 1988. *Land Struggles and Social Differentiation in Southern Mozambique: a case study of Chokwe, Limpopo 1950–1987*. Uppsala: Scandinavian Institute of African Studies.

Hill, Polly. 1986. *Development Economics on Trial: the anthropological case for a prosecution*. Cambridge: Cambridge University Press.

Hirschmann, David and Megan Vaughan. 1983. 'Food production and income generation in a matrilineal society: rural women in Zomba, Malawi', *Journal of Southern African Studies 10*, 86–99.

Hoile, David. 1994. *Mozambique, Resistance and Freedom: a case for reassessment*. London: Mozambique Institute.

Hutchinson, Sharon E. 1996. *Nuer Dilemmas: coping with money, war, and the state*. Berkeley: University of California Press.

Hyden, Goran and Donald C. Williams. 1994. 'A community model of African politics: illustrations from Nigeria and Tanzania', *Comparative Studies in Society and History 36*, 68–96.

Indra, Doreen (ed.). 1999. *Engendering Forced Migration: theory and practice*. Oxford: Berghahn.

Isaacman, Allen F. 1972. *Mozambique: the Africanization of a European institution. The Zambezi Prazos 1750–1902*. Madison: University of Wisconsin Press.

Isaacman, Allen F. 1976. *The Tradition of Resistance in Mozambique: the Zambezi Valley 1850–1921*. Berkeley: University of California Press.

Isaacman, Allen F. 1985. 'Chiefs, rural differentiations and peasant protest: the Mozambican forced cotton regime, 1938–1961', *American Economic History 14*, 15–56.

Isaacman, Allen F. 1988. 'Historical introduction', in L. Magaia, *Dumba Nengue: run for your life. Peasant tales of tragedy in Mozambique*, pp. 1–14. Trenton, NJ: Africa World Press.

Isaacman, Allen F. 1996. *Cotton is the Mother of Poverty: peasants, work, and rural struggle in colonial Mozambique, 1938–1961*. Oxford: James Currey.

Isaacman, Allen F. and Barbara Isaacman. 1983. *Mozambique: from colonialism to revolution, 1900–1982*. Boulder, CO: Westview Press.

Ishay, Micheline. 1995. *Internationalism and its Betrayal*. Minneapolis: University of Minnesota Press.

Ishemo, Shubi Lugemalila. 1995. *The Lower Zambezi Basin in Mozambique*. Aldershot: Avebury.

Johnson, William Percival. 1922. *Nyasa the Great Water: being a description of the lake and the life of the people*. Oxford: Oxford University Press.

Juergensen, Olaf Tataryn. 1994. 'Angonia: why Renamo?', *Southern Africa Report 2*, 13–16.

Kandawire, J. A. Kamchitete. 1979. *Thangata: forced labour or reciprocal assistance?*. Zomba: University of Malawi.

Kapferer, Bruce. 1972. *Strategy and Transaction in an African Factory: African workers and Indian management in a Zambian town*. Manchester: Manchester University Press.

Kapferer, Bruce. 1976. 'Introduction: transactional models reconsidered', in B. Kapferer (ed.), *Transaction and Meaning: directions in the anthropology of exchange and symbolic behaviour*. pp. 1–24. Philadelphia: Institute for the Study of Human Issues.

Kaspin, Deborah. 1993. 'Chewa visions and revisions of power: transformations of the Nyau dance in central Malawi', in J. Comaroff and J. Comaroff (eds), *Modernity and its Malcontents: ritual and power in postcolonial Africa*, pp. 34–57. Chicago: University of Chicago Press.

Kaspin, Deborah. 1995. 'The politics of ethnicity in Malawi's democratic transition', *Journal of Modern African Studies 33*, 595–620.

Kearney, Michael. 1996. *Reconceptualizing the Peasantry: anthropology in global perspective*. Boulder, CO: Westview Press.

Kibreab, Gaim. 1989. 'Local settlements in Africa: a misconceived option?', *Journal of Refugee Studies 2*, 467–90.

Kopytoff, Igor. 1987. 'The internal African frontier: the making of African political culture', in I. Kopytoff (ed.), *The African Frontier: the reproduction of traditional African societies*, pp. 3–84. Bloomington: Indiana University Press.

Koser, Khalid. 1997. 'Information and repatriation: the case of Mozambican refugees in Malawi', *Journal of Refugee Studies 10*, 1–18.

Kriger, Norma J. 1992. *Zimbabwe's Guerrilla War: peasant voices*. Cambridge: Cambridge University Press.

Kriger, Norma J. 1995. 'The politics of creating national heroes: the search for political legitimacy and national identity', in N. Bhebe and T. Ranger (eds), *Soldiers in Zimbabwe's Liberation War*, pp. 139–62. London: James Currey.

Kruks, Sonia and Ben Wisner. 1984. 'The state, the party and the female peasantry in Mozambique', *Journal of Southern African Studies 11*, 106–27.

Kuper, Adam. 1970. *Kalahari Village Politics: an African democracy*. Cambridge: Cambridge University Press.

Kuper, Adam. 1993. 'The "house" and Zulu political structure in the nineteenth century', *Journal of African History 34*, 469–87.

Kydd, Jonathan and Robert Christiansen. 1982. 'Structural change in Malawi since independence: consequences of a development strategy based on large-scale agriculture', *World Development 10*, 355–75.

Kymlicka, Will. 1995. *Multicultural Citizenship: a liberal theory of minority rights*. Oxford: Oxford University Press.

Lan, David. 1985. *Guns and Rain: guerrillas and spirit mediums in Zimbabwe*. London: James Currey.

Langworthy, Harry W. 1975. 'Central Malawi in the 19th century', in R. J. Macdonald (ed.), *From Nyasaland to Malawi: studies in colonial history*, pp. 1–43. Nairobi: East African Publishing House.

Legrand, Jean-Claude. 1993. 'Logique de guerre et dynamique de la violence en Zambézia, 1976–1991', *Politique Africaine 50*, 88–104.

Lemarchand, René. 1989. 'African peasantries, reciprocity and the market: the economy of affection reconsidered', *Cahiers d'études africaines 29*, 33–67.

Levi, Margaret. 1996. 'Social and unsocial capital: a review essay of Robert Putnam's *Making Democracy Work*', *Politics and Society 24*, 45–55.

Linden, Ian. 1972. 'The Maseko Ngoni at Domwe: 1870–1900', in B. Pachai (ed.), *The Early History of Malawi*, pp. 237–51. London: Longman.

Linden, Ian with Jane Linden. 1974. *Catholics, Peasants, and Chewa Resistance in Nyasaland 1889–1939*. London: Heinemann.

Loescher, Gil. 1993. *Beyond Charity: international cooperation and the global refugee crisis*. Oxford: Oxford University Press.

Long, Andrew. 1992. 'Goods, knowledge and beer: the methodological significance of situational analysis and discourse', in N. Long and A. Long (eds), *Battlefields of Knowledge: the interlocking of theory and practice in social research and development*, pp. 147–70. London: Routledge.

Long, Norman. 1968. *Social Change and the Individual: a study of the social and religious responses to innovation in a Zambian rural community*. Manchester: Manchester University Press.

Lukes, Steven. 1974. *Power: a radical view*. London: Macmillan.

Macmillan, Hugh. 1995. 'Return to the Malungwana Drift – Max Gluckman, the Zulu nation and the common society. *African Affairs 94*, 39–65.

Magaia, Lina. 1988. *Dumba Nengue: run for your life. Peasant tales of tragedy in Mozambique*. Trenton, NJ: Africa World Press.

Mair, Lucy P. 1951. 'Marriage and family in the Dedza district of Nyasaland', *Journal of the Royal Anthropological Institute 81*, 103–19.

Malawi Government. 1993. *Malawi Population and Housing Census 1987. Volume II: population characteristics*. Zomba: Malawi Government.

Malkki, Liisa H. 1992. 'National geographic: rooting of peoples and the territorialization of national identity among scholars and refugees', *Cultural Anthropology 7*, 24–44.

Malkki, Liisa H. 1995a. 'Refugees and exile: from "refugee studies" to the national order of things', *Annual Review of Anthropology 24*, 495–523.

Malkki, Liisa H. 1995b. *Purity and Exile: violence, memory, and national cosmology among Hutu refugees in Tanzania*. Chicago: University of Chicago Press.

Malkki, Liisa H. 1997. 'Speechless emissaries: refugees, humanitarianism, and dehistoricization', in K. F. Olwig and K. Hastrup (eds), *Siting Culture: the shifting anthropological object*, pp. 223–54. London: Routledge.

Mamdani, Mahmood. 1996. *Citizen and Subject: contemporary Africa and the legacy of late colonialism*. Princeton, NJ: Princeton University Press.

Mandala, Elias C. 1990. *Work and Control in a Peasant Economy: a history of the lower Tchiri Valley in Malawi, 1859–1960*. Madison: University of Wisconsin Press.

Manning, Carrie. 1998. 'Constructing opposition in Mozambique: Renamo as political party', *Journal of Southern African Studies 24*, 161–89.

Marcum, John. 1969. *The Angolan Revolution, Vol. 1: the anatomy of an explosion, 1950–1962*. Cambridge, MA: MIT Press.

Marcus, George E. 1998. *Ethnography through Thick and Thin*. Princeton, NJ: Princeton University Press.

Marwick, Max G. 1965. *Sorcery in its Social Setting: a study of northern Rhodesian Cewa*. Manchester: Manchester University Press.

Marx, Emanuel. 1990. 'The social world of refugees: a conceptual framework', *Journal of Refugee Studies 3*, 189–203.

Matlou, Patrick. 1999. 'Upsetting the cart: forced migration and gender issues, the African experience', in D. Indra (ed.), *Engendering Forced Migration: theory and practice* , pp. 128–45. Oxford: Berghahn.

Maxwell, David J. 1999. *Christians and Chiefs in Zimbabwe: a social history of the Hwesa people, c. 1870s–1990s*. Edinburgh: Edinburgh University Press for the International African Institute.

McCracken, John. 1977. *Politics and Christianity in Malawi 1875–1940: the impact of the Livingstonia mission in the Northern Province*. Cambridge: Cambridge University Press.

McGregor, JoAnn. 1994. 'People without fathers: Mozambicans in Swaziland 1888–1993', *Journal of Southern African Studies 20*, 545–67.

McGregor, JoAnn. 1998. 'Violence and social change in a border economy: war in the Maputo hinterland, 1984–1992', *Journal of Southern African Studies 24*, 37–60.

Metz, Steven. 1986. 'The Mozambique National Resistance and South African foreign policy', *African Affairs 85*, 491–507.

Mhone, Guy. 1992. 'The political economy of Malawi: an overview', in G. C. Z. Mhone (ed.), *Malawi at the Crossroads: the post-colonial political economy*, pp. 1–33. Harare: Sapes.

Miles, William F. S. 1994. *Hausaland Divided: colonialism and independence in Nigeria and Niger*. Ithaca, NY: Cornell University Press.

Minter, William. 1989. 'The Mozambican National Resistance (Renamo) as described by ex-participants', *Research Report Submitted to Ford Foundation and Swedish International Development Agency*.

Minter, William. 1994. *Apartheid's Contras: an inquiry into the roots of war in Angola and Mozambique*. London: Zed Books.

Mitchell, J. Clyde. 1956. *The Yao Village: a study in the social structure of a Nyasaland tribe*. Manchester: Manchester University Press.

Mitchell, J. Clyde. 1969 (ed.). *Social Networks in Urban Situations*. Manchester: Manchester University Press.

Mkandawire, Richard. 1992. 'The land question and agrarian change in Malawi', in G. C. Z. Mhone (ed.), *Malawi at the Crossroads: the post-colonial political economy*, pp. 171–87. Harare: Sapes.

Moore, David B. 1995. 'Democracy, violence, and identity in the Zimbabwean war of national liberation: reflections from the realms of dissent', *Canadian Journal of African Studies* 29, 375–402.

Moore, Henrietta L. and Megan Vaughan. 1994. *Cutting Down Trees: gender, nutrition, and agricultural change in the Northern Province of Zambia, 1890–1990*. London: James Currey.

Moore, Sally Falk. 1978. *Law as Process: an anthropological approach*. London: Routledge and Kegan Paul [reprinted 2000 Hamburg: LIT and Oxford: James Currey for the International African Institute].

Morgan, Glenda. 1990. 'Violence in Mozambique: towards an understanding of Renamo', *Journal of Modern African Studies* 28, 603–19.

Mtukulo, Angels. 1995. 'Malawi: the migrant labour legacy', *SAPEM 3–4*, 26–7.

Munslow, Barry. 1983. *Mozambique: the revolution and its origins*. London: Longman.

Myers, Gregory. 1994. 'Competitive rights, competitive claims: land access in post-war Mozambique', *Journal of Southern African Studies* 20, 603–32.

Nabli, M. and J. Nugent. 1989. 'The new institutional economics and economic development', *World Development* 17, 1333–47.

Newitt, Malyn. 1973. *Portuguese Settlement on the Zambesi: exploration, land tenure and colonial rule in East Africa*. London: Longman.

Newitt, Malyn. 1988. 'Drought in Mozambique 1823–1831', *Journal of Southern African Studies* 15, 15–35.

Newitt, Malyn. 1995. *A History of Mozambique*. London: Hurst.

Nordstrom, Carolyn. 1992. 'The backyard front', in C. Nordstrom and J. Martin (eds), *The Paths to Domination, Resistance and Terror*, pp. 260–74. Berkeley: University of California Press.

Nordstrom, Carolyn. 1997. *A Different Kind of War Story*. Philadelphia: University of Pennsylvania Press.

Nugent, Paul and A. I. Asiwaju (eds). 1996. *African Boundaries: barriers, conduits and opportunities*. London: Pinter.

O'Laughlin, Bridget. 1992. 'Interpretations matter: evaluating the war in Mozambique', *Southern African Report* 3, 23–33.

O'Laughlin, Bridget. 1996. 'Through a divided glass: dualism, class and the agrarian question in Mozambique', *Journal of Peasant Studies* 23, 1–39.

O'Laughlin, Bridget. 2000. 'Class and the customary: the ambiguous legacy of the Indigenato in Mozambique', *African Affairs* 99, 5–42.

Olwig, Karen Fog and Kirsten Hastrup (eds). 1997. *Siting Culture: the shifting anthropological object*. London: Routledge.

Omer-Cooper, J. D. 1966. *The Zulu Aftermath: a nineteenth-century revolution in Bantu Africa*. London: Longman.

Omer-Cooper, J. D. 1993. 'Has the Mfecane a future? A response to the Cobbing critique', *Journal of Southern African Studies* 19, 273–94.

Ortner, Sherry B. 1998. 'Identities: the hidden life of class', *Journal of Anthropological Research* 54, 1–17.

Ottaway, Marina. 1988. 'Mozambique: from symbolic socialism to symbolic reform', *Journal of Modern African Studies* 26, 211–26.

Paine, Robert. 1974. 'Second thoughts about Barth's models', *Royal Anthropological Institute Occasional Paper* 32.

Parry, Jonathan and Maurice Bloch (eds). 1989. *Money and the Morality of Exchange*. Cambridge: Cambridge University Press.

Peires, J. B. 1993. 'Paradigm deleted: the materialist interpretation of the Mfecane', *Journal of Southern African Studies* 19, 295–313.

Pélissier, René. 1984. *Naissance du Mozambique: résistance et révoltes anticoloniales (1854–1918). Tome II*. Orgeval: Editions Pélissier.

Peters, Pauline E. 1997a. 'Revisiting the puzzle of matriliny in South–Central Africa: introduction', *Critique of Anthropology* 17, 125–46.

Peters, Pauline E. 1997b. 'Against the odds: matriliny, land and gender in the Shire Highlands of Malawi', *Critique of Anthropology* 17, 189–210.

Philip, K. D. 1975 (1955). *Onani Angoni*. Blantyre: Dzuka.

Phiri, D. D. 1982. *From Nguni to Ngoni*. Blantyre: Popular Publications.

Phiri, Kings M. 1983. 'Some changes in the matrilineal family system among the Chewa of Malawi since the nineteenth century', *Journal of African History* 24, 257–74.

Phiri, S. H. 1985. 'Integration, rural development and frontier communities: the case of the Chewa and the Ngoni astride Zambian boundaries with Malawi and Mozambique', in A. I. Asiwaju (ed.), *Partitioned Africans: ethnic relations across Africa's international boundaries, 1884–1984*, pp. 105–25. London: Hurst.

Pitcher, M. Anne. 1993. *Politics in the Portuguese Empire: the state, industry and cotton, 1926–1974*. Oxford: Oxford University Press.

Pitcher, M. Anne. 1996. 'Recreating colonialism or reconstructing the state?: privatisation and politics in Mozambique', *Journal of Southern African Studies* 29, 49–74.

Plank, David N. 1993. 'Aid, debt, and the end of sovereignty: Mozambique and its donors', *Journal of Modern African Studies* 31, 407–30.

Platteau, Jean-Philippe. 1995. 'A framework for the analysis of evolving patron–client ties in agrarian economies', *World Development* 23, 767–86.

Poewe, Karla O. 1981. *Matrilineal Ideology: male–female dynamics in Luapula, Zambia*. London: Academic Press.

Preis, Ann-Belinda Steen. 1997. 'Seeking place: capsized identities and contracted belonging among Sri Lankan Tamil refugees', in K. F. Olwig and K. Hastrup (eds), *Siting Culture: the shifting anthropological object*, pp. 86–100. London: Routledge.

Preston, Rosemary. 1999. 'Researching repatriation and reconstruction: who is researching what and why?', in R. Black and K. Khoser (eds), *The End of the Refugee Cycle?: refugee repatriation and reconstruction*, pp. 18–36. Oxford: Berghahn.

Pryor, F. 1991. *The Political Economy of Poverty, Equity and Growth: a World Bank comparative study of Malawi and Madagascar*. Oxford: Oxford University Press.

Putnam, Robert. 1993. *Making Democracy Work: civic traditions in modern Italy.* Princeton, NJ: Princeton University Press.

Putzel, James. 1997. 'Accounting for the "dark side" of social capital: reading Robert Putnam on democracy', *Journal of International Development 9*, 939–49.

Radcliffe-Brown, A. R. 1952. *Structure and Function in Primitive Society.* London: Cohen and West.

Ranger, Terence. 1985. *Peasant Consciousness and Guerrilla War in Zimbabwe: a comparative study.* London: James Currey.

Ranger, Terence. 1986. 'Bandits and guerrillas: the case of Zimbabwe', in D. Crummey (ed.), *Banditry, Rebellion and Social Protest in Africa*, pp. 373–96. London: James Currey.

Ranger, Terence. 1992. 'War, violence and healing in Zimbabwe', *Journal of Southern African Studies 18*, 698–707.

Rapport, Nigel. 1997. *Transcendent Individual: towards a literary and liberal anthropology.* London: Routledge.

Read, Margaret. 1936. 'Tradition and prestige among the Ngoni', *Africa 9*, 453–84.

Read, Margaret. 1938. 'The moral code of the Ngoni and their former military state', *Africa 11*, 1–24.

Read, Margaret. 1956. *The Ngoni of Nyasaland.* London: Oxford University Press.

Reynolds, Pamela. 1990. 'Children of Tribulation: the need to heal and the means to heal war trauma', *Africa 60*, 1–38.

Richards, Audrey I. 1939. *Land, Labour and Diet in Northern Rhodesia: an economic study of the Bemba tribe.* London: Oxford University Press for the International African Institute.

Richards, Paul. 1996. *Fighting for the Rain Forest: war, youth and resources in Sierra Leone.* Oxford: James Currey for the International African Institute.

Riesman, Paul. 1986. 'The person and the life cycle in African social life and thought', *African Studies Review 29*, 71–137.

Rimmington, Gerald T. 1963. 'Agricultural development in the Dedza district of Nyasaland', *Nyasaland Journal 16*, 28–48.

Roesch, Otto. 1988. 'Rural Mozambique since the Frelimo Fourth Party Congress: the situation in the Baixo Limpopo', *Review of African Political Economy 41*, 73–91.

Roesch, Otto. 1992a. 'Renamo and the peasantry in southern Mozambique: a view from Gaza Province', *Canadian Journal of African Studies 26*, 462–84.

Roesch, Otto. 1992b. 'Mozambique unravels?: the retreat to tradition', *Southern Africa Report 5*, 27–30.

Rogge, John R. 1994. 'Repatriation of refugees: a not so simple "optimum" solution', in T. Allen and H. Morsink (eds), *When Refugees Go Home*, pp. 14–49. London: James Currey.

Rosaldo, Renato. 1989. *Culture and Truth: the remaking of social analysis.* Boston: Beacon Press.

Saad-Filho, Alfredo. 1997. 'The political economy of agrarian transition in Mozambique', *Journal of Contemporary African Studies 15*, 191–218.

Sahlins, Marshall. 1976. *Culture and Practical Reason.* Chicago: University of Chicago Press.

Scheffler, H. W. 1985. 'Filiation and affiliation', *Man* (n.s.) *20*, 1–21.

Schmidt, Heike, 1997. 'Healing the wounds of war: memories, violence and the making of history in Zimbabwe's most recent past', *Journal of Southern African Studies 23*, 301–10.

Schoffeleers, J. Matthew. 1968. 'Symbolic and Social Aspects of Spirit Worship among the Mang'anja', DPhil thesis, University of Oxford.

Schoffeleers, J. Matthew. 1972. 'The meaning and use of the name Malawi in oral traditions and precolonial documents', in B. Pachai (ed.), *The Early History of Malawi*, pp. 91–103. London: Longman.

Schoffeleers, J. Matthew. 1992. *River of Blood: the genesis of a martyr cult in southern Malawi, c. A.D. 1600.* Madison: University of Wisconsin Press.

Scott, Catherine V. 1988. 'Socialism and the "soft state" in Africa: an analysis of Angola and Mozambique', *Journal of Modern African Studies 26*, 23–36.

Scott, James C. 1976. *The Moral Economy of the Peasant: rebellion and subsistence in Southeast Asia.* New Haven: Yale University Press.

Scott, James C. 1985. *Weapons of the Weak: everyday forms of peasant resistance.* New Haven, CT: Yale University Press.

Seligman, Adam B. 1992. *The Idea of Civil Society.* Princeton, NJ: Princeton University Press.

Simpson, Mark. 1993. 'Foreign and domestic factors in the transformation of Frelimo', *Journal of Modern African Studies 31*, 309–37.

Smith, Alan K. 1975. 'The Anglo-Portuguese conflict over the Shire Highlands, 1875–91', in R. J. Macdonald (ed.), *From Nyasaland to Malawi: studies in colonial history*, pp. 44–64. Nairobi: East African Publishing House.

Sorensen, Birgitte Refslund. 1997. 'The experience of displacement: reconstructing places and identities in Sri Lanka', in K. F. Olwig and K. Hastrup (eds), *Siting Culture: the shifting anthropological object*, pp. 142–64. London: Routledge.

Strathern, Marilyn. 1988. *The Gender of the Gift: problems with women and problems with society in Melanesia.* Berkeley: University of California Press.

Strathern, Marilyn. 1992. 'Parts and wholes: refiguring relationships in a post-plural world', in A. Kuper (ed.), *Conceptualizing Society*, pp. 75–104. London: Routledge.

Taussig, Michael. 1987. *Shamanism, Colonialism, and the Wild Man: a study in terror and healing.* Chicago: University of Chicago Press.

Taylor, Charles. 1994. 'The politics of recognition', in A. Gutmann (ed.), *Multiculturalism: examining the politics of recognition*, pp. 25–73. Princeton, NJ: Princeton University Press.

Tew, Mary. 1950. *Peoples of the Lake Nyasa Region.* London: Oxford University Press.

Thompson, Richard H. 1997. 'Ethnic minorities and the case for collective rights', *American Anthropologist 99*, 786–98.

Thornton, Robert. 1988. 'The rhetoric of ethnographic holism', *Cultural Anthropology 3*, 285–303.

Tilly, Charles. 1985. 'War-making and state-making as organized crime', in P. Evans, D. Rueschemeyer and T. Skocpol (eds), *Bringing the State Back*, pp. 169–91. Cambridge: Cambridge University Press.

Timpunza-Mvula, Enoch S. 1987. 'Women's Oral Poetry as a Social Strategy in Malawi', PhD thesis, Indiana University.

Turner, Victor W. 1957. *Schism and Continuity in an African Society: a study of Ndembu village life.* Manchester: Manchester University Press.

UNHCR. 1993. *Northern Mozambique Repatriation Operation.* Tete: UNHCR s.o.

UNHCR. 1995. *Mozambique 1993/1995 Review.* Johannesburg: UNHCR Public Information Unit.

Vail, H. Leroy. 1972. 'Suggestions towards a reinterpreted Tumbuka history', in B. Pachai (ed.), *The Early History of Malawi*, pp. 148–67. London: Longman.

Vail, H. Leroy. 1978. 'Religion, language and the tribal myth: the Tumbuka and Chewa of Malawi', in J. M. Schoffeleers (ed.), *Guardians of the Land: essays on Central African territorial cults*, pp. 209–34. Gwelo: Mambo Press.

Vail, H. Leroy. 1981. 'The making of the "Dead North": a study of the Ngoni rule in northern Malawi, c. 1855–1907', in J. B. Peires (ed.), *Before and After*

Shaka: papers in Nguni history, pp. 230–67. Grahamstown: Institute of Social and Economic Research.

Vail, Leroy and Landeg White. 1980. *Capitalism and Colonialism in Mozambique: a study of Quelimane District*. London: Heinemann.

van Donge, Jan Kees. 1985. 'Understanding rural Zambia today: the relevance of the Rhodes–Livingstone Institute', *Africa 55*, 60–76.

van Donge, Jan Kees. 1995. 'Kamuzu's legacy: the democratization of Malawi', *African Affairs 94*, 227–57.

van Velsen, J. 1964. *The Politics of Kinship: a study in social manipulation among the lakeside Tonga of Malawi*. Manchester: Manchester University Press.

van Velsen, J. 1966. 'Some early pressure groups in Malawi', in E. Stokes and R. Brown (eds), *The Zambesian Past*, pp. 376–412. Manchester: Manchester University Press.

van Velsen, J. 1967. 'The extended-case method and situational analysis', in A. L. Epstein (ed.), *The Craft of Social Anthropology*, pp. 129–49. London: Tavistock.

Vaughan, Megan. 1983. 'Which family?: problems in the reconstruction of the family as an economic and cultural unit', *Journal of African History 24*, 275–83.

Vezeau, Roland. 1982. 'The Church in Malawi: a history of Bembeke Parish', unpublished manuscript, Malawi National Archives.

Vines, Alex. 1991. *Renamo: terrorism in Mozambique*. London: James Currey.

Voutira, Eftihia and Barbara E. Harrell-Bond. 1995. 'In search of the locus of trust: the social world of the refugee camp', in E. V. Daniel and J. C. Knudsen (eds), *Mistrusting Refugees*, pp. 207–24. Berkeley: University of California Press.

Walker, Eric A. 1935 (1928). *A History of South Africa*. London: Longman.

Watson-Franke, M.-B. 1992. 'Masculinity and the "Matrilineal Puzzle"', *Anthropos 87*, 475–88.

Werbner, Richard P. 1984. 'The Manchester School in South–Central Africa', *Annual Review of Anthropology 13*, 157–85.

Werbner, Richard P. 1991. *Tears of the Dead: the social biography of an African family*. Edinburgh: Edinburgh University Press for the International African Institute.

Werbner, Richard P. 1998. 'Smoke from the barrel of a gun: postwars of the dead, memory and reinscription in Zimbabwe', in R. Werbner (ed.), *Memory and the Postcolony: African anthropology and the critique of power*, pp. 71–102. London: Zed Books.

West, Harry G. 1997. 'Creative destruction and sorcery of construction: power, hope and suspicion in post-war Mozambique', *Cahiers d'études africaines 147*, 675–98.

West, Harry G. 1998. '"This Neighbour is not my uncle!": changing relations of power and authority on the Mueda plateau', *Journal of Southern African Studies 24*, 141–60.

West, Harry G. and Scott Kloeck-Jenson. 1999. 'Betwixt and between: "traditional authority" and democratic decentralization in post-war Mozambique', *African Affairs 98*, 455–84.

West, Harry G. and Gregory W. Myers. 1996. 'A piece of land in a land of peace?: state farm divestiture in Mozambique', *Journal of Modern African Studies 34*, 27–51.

White, Landeg. 1985. 'Review article: the revolutions ten years on', *Journal of Southern African Studies 11*, 320–32.

White, Landeg. 1987. *Magomero: portrait of an African village*. Cambridge: Cambridge University Press.

Widner, Jennifer with Alexander Mundt. 1998. 'Researching social capital in Africa', *Africa 68*, 1–24.

Williams, David. 1993. 'Liberalism and "development discourse"', *Africa 63*, 419–29.

Williams, Gavin. 1987. 'Primitive accumulation: the way to progress?', *Development and Change 18*, 637–59.

Williams, Holly Ann. 1993. 'Self-settled refugees in north-western Zambia', in M. Hopkins and N. D. Donnelly (eds), *Selected Papers on Refugee Issues II*. Arlington, VA: American Anthropological Association.

Wilson, K. B. 1992a. 'Cults of violence and counter-violence in Mozambique', *Journal of Southern African Studies 18*, 527–82.

Wilson, K. B. 1992b. 'The Socio-economic Impact of War and Flight in Posto Derre, Morrumbala District, Zambezia', unpublished manuscript, University of Oxford.

Wilson, K. B. 1994a. 'Refugees and returnees as social agents: the case of the Jehovah's Witnesses from Milange', in T. Allen and H. Morsink (eds), *When Refugees Go Home*, pp. 237–50. London: James Currey.

Wilson, K. B. 1994b. 'The people's peace in Mozambique', *Southern African Report March*, 22–4.

Wilson, K. B. with J. Nunes. 1994. 'Repatriation to Mozambique: refugee initiative and agency planning in Milange district 1988–1991', in T. Allen and H. Morsink (eds), *When Refugees Go Home*, pp. 167–36. London: James Currey.

Wilson, K. B., D. Cammack, E. Droben and F. Shumba. 1989. *Food Provisioning amongst Mozambican Refugees in Malawi: a study of aid, livelihood and development*. Report for the World Food Programme. Refugee Studies Programme, University of Oxford.

Wilson, Thomas M. and Hastings Donnan (eds). 1998. *Border Identities: nation and state at international frontiers*. Cambridge: Cambridge University Press.

Winterbottom, J. M. 1950. 'Outline histories of two northern Rhodesian tribes', *Human Problems in British Central Africa 9*, 14–25.

Wolf, Eric R. 1998. *Envisioning Power: ideologies of domination and crisis*. Berkeley: University of California Press.

Woolcock, Michael. 1998. 'Social capital and economic development: toward a theoretical synthesis and policy framework', *Theory and Society 27*, 151–208.

World Bank. 1997. *World Development Report 1997*. Oxford: Oxford University Press.

Wright, John. 1986. 'Politics, ideology and the invention of the "Nguni"', in T. Lodge (ed.), *Resistance and Ideology in Settler Societies*, pp. 96–118. Johannesburg: Ravan Press.

Wright, John. 1989. 'Political mythology and the making of Natal's Mfecane', *Canadian Journal of African Studies 23*, 272–91.

Wright, John. 1995. 'Mfecane debates', *Southern African Review of Books 39 and 40*, 18–19.

Yoshida, Kenji, 1992. 'Masks and transformation among the Chewa of eastern Zambia', *Senri Ethnological Studies 31*, 203–72.

Young, Crawford. 1994. 'Zaire: the shattered illusion of the integral state', *Journal of Modern African Studies 32*, 247–63.

Young, Tom. 1988. 'The politics of development in Angola and Mozambique', *African Affairs 87*, 165–84.

Young, Tom. 1990. 'The MNR/Renamo: external and internal dynamics', *African Affairs 89*, 491–509.

Zetter, Roger. 1991. 'Labelling refugees: forming and transforming a bureaucratic identity', *Journal of Refugee Studies 4*, 39–62.

Zolberg, Aristide R., Astri Suhrke and Sergio Aguayo. 1989. *Escape from Violence: conflict and the refugee crisis in the developing world*. Oxford: Oxford University Press.

Zur, Judith N. 1998. *Violent Memories: Mayan war widows in Guatemala*. Boulder, CO: Westview Press.

INDEX

Entries in *italics* refer to figures.